W9-BXM-847

# A SECOND RECKONING

# A SECOND RECKONING

## RACE, INJUSTICE, AND THE LAST HANGING IN ANNAPOLIS

SCOTT D. SELIGMAN

**Potomac Books**  An imprint of the University of Nebraska Press

All rights reserved. Potomac Books is an imprint
of the University of Nebraska Press.
Manufactured in the United States of America.

♾

Library of Congress Cataloging-in-Publication Data
Names: Seligman, Scott D., author.
Title: A second reckoning: race, injustice, and the
last hanging in Annapolis / Scott D. Seligman.
Description: Lincoln: Potomac Books, an imprint
of the University of Nebraska Press, 2021. |
Includes bibliographical references and index.
Identifiers: LCCN 2021000457
ISBN 9781640124653 (hardback)
ISBN 9781640124868 (epub)
ISBN 9781640124875 (pdf)
Subjects: LCSH: Snowden, John, 1890–1919—Trials,
litigation, etc. | Trials (Murder)—Maryland—Baltimore
County—20th century. | Hanging—Maryland—Baltimore
County—20th century. | Discrimination in criminal
justice administration—United States—History. | African
Americans—Civil rights—History. | United States—Race
relations—History. | Pardon—United States. | Evidence,
Circumstantial—United States. | BISAC: SOCIAL SCIENCE /
Discrimination | HISTORY / United States / 20th Century
Classification: LCC KF224.S595 S45 2021 |
DDC 364.152/3092 [B]—dc23
LC record available at https://lccn.loc.gov/2021000457

Set in Adobe Caslon Pro by Mikala R. Kolander.
Designed by L. Auten.

The search for justice has no statute of limitations.

—PARRIS N. GLENDENING, governor of
Maryland (1995–2003), May 31, 2001

# Contents

# Illustrations

# Preface

One hundred years—almost exactly to the day—after the brutal murder of Lottie May Brandon in Annapolis, Maryland, for which John Snowden was hanged, white supremacists marched on Charlottesville, Virginia, to protest the threatened removal from a city park of a statue of Confederate general Robert E. Lee. The "Unite the Right" protest of August 2017 turned violent when armored, torch-bearing hate mongers clashed with counterprotesters, dozens of whom were injured and one of whom was maliciously mown down and slain by the driver of a car.

If ever an event demonstrated the ability of a figure long dead to remain very much alive in people's minds and to motivate passionate behavior in the present, this was it. Robert E. Lee died in 1870, but he and others have remained potent symbols, whether of the shame and tragedy of slavery and segregation or of the "lost cause" of the Confederacy.

The events in Charlottesville, and the videotaped murder of George Floyd by a Minneapolis policeman three years later, have turbocharged the national debate over how to address our country's "original sin" and its aftereffects. Americans today find ourselves more preoccupied than usual with one of our familiar national pastimes: wrestling with our past times.

Reevaluating our collective history, reinterpreting it, and making new judgments about it has always been part of the American experience, and if we are fortunate, always will be. This openness to learning from the past and willingness to make amends and changes where possible and desirable, which has ebbed and flowed throughout our history, is one of the more admirable characteristics of the American people when it prevails. I have serious doubts as to whether there is such a thing as "American exceptionalism," but if there is, this surely must be one of its components.

In these polarized times, the urge to look backward has become especially urgent with regard to our racial history. What is the country to do about the remaining statues erected to honor Confederate generals who fought to preserve human bondage? How should we explain to our children why their high school bears the name of a racist, slave-owning president? How ought we to deal with the legacy of past eras that were less just and less fair than we like to think we are today?

Most importantly, what can we, as a society, do to right the wrongs?

In recent years, civil rights advocates have become more aggressive about lobbying to remove monuments to America's racist past, and those arrayed on the other side have risen up in opposition, their passion fanned by dog whistles from on high. Talk has turned to action, sometimes violent. Nevertheless, new judgments about history continue to be made. Between the debacle in Charlottesville and the killing of Floyd, well over a hundred Confederate monuments and symbols were removed from public spaces, including a statue of Supreme Court chief justice Roger B. Taney, author of the infamous 1857 *Dred Scott* decision that denied citizenship to Blacks, which was moved into storage from the State House grounds in Annapolis in 2017 under cover of darkness. More than a hundred more have been taken down in the aftermath of the Floyd murder, some by administrative or legislative action, others by passionate demonstrators.[1]

Struggling with the detritus of past eras and attempting to right the most egregious wrongs, however, is a challenge that goes far beyond the fate of a few hundred bronze statues and stone markers. Over the years, Americans have eliminated many egregious discriminatory policies imposed by the executive branches of their national, state, and local governments and repealed many of their racist laws. Those are two legs of the stool. But a moral nation must also reckon with its *judicial* past, especially those cases in which prejudice is thought to have tainted procedures, denied rights, or perverted verdicts. Should not historic miscarriages of justice also be subject to a second look?

Reexamining such cases is not merely desirable; it is *necessary* in a self-conscious society willing to make amends for past errors. Many grave, race-based injustices have been committed in the name of what once passed for justice, and rectifying them can be deeply important and healing to people alive today. Addressing them may possess tremendous symbolic value for people a hundred years after the fact and even for others not yet born. Correcting injustices can also create a marker that makes it far more difficult for such errors ever to be repeated.

The story of John Snowden, set in Maryland during the Jim Crow era, is a case in point. Many view him as a falsely accused, innocent victim of a "legal lynching." Of course, depending on one's point of view, he might instead have been a brutal murderer who got exactly what he deserved, or perhaps something in between: a guilty person who was denied due process of law. A century ago, his home town of Annapolis was very much divided as to his guilt. Fast-forward to 2001, when his case was placed for a second time before a governor of Maryland for consideration of a pardon, and people still differed on their view of the appeal.

Posthumous pardons do no demonstrable good to the dead. They are clearly all about the living: principally relatives and friends of the deceased but also their spiritual or political heirs, or those simply interested in—or moved by—their cases. Put another way, just as the debate over Confederate statues is less about those depicted in them than about the values of those who walk past them every day, pardons are about the present, not the past. They are most valuable when they redeem the living, of course, and living prisoners must always go to the front of the line. But applied to the dead, they can also be extremely worthwhile when they heal, or when they send an affirmative message that the discredited values of the past are no longer the values of the present, and must not be those of the future.

John Snowden was just as dead in 2001 as he was on the day of his hanging in 1919. His pardon was important to his family, which believed stalwartly in his innocence and, more broadly, to the Annapolis Black community, which, in the main, viewed his execution as a miscarriage of justice. It was also meaningful as a statement to the entire country that—as Governor Parris Glendening put it so eloquently at the time—"the search for justice has no statute of limitations."

A moral society must never cease to pursue it.

I HAPPENED ON the story of John Snowden soon after I wrote a book about another case that bears some resemblance to it. *The Third Degree: The Triple Murder That Shook Washington and Changed American Criminal Justice*, published by Potomac Books in 2018, tells of Ziang Sung Wan, a young Chinese man accused of the murder of three of his compatriots in Washington DC in 1919 and abused by local police during his interrogation. Unlike Snowden, Wan confessed, though he recanted at trial, and the issue of whether his confession should have been thrown out of court eventually landed the case in the Supreme Court. In its ruling, penned by no less a light than Justice Louis Brandeis, the court set America on the road to what, several decades later, would become the decision that conferred Miranda rights on all those arrested.

The two cases occurred at about the same time. Both involved minority defendants subjected to abusive treatment, and both men were initially convicted. But Wan was eventually released, whereas Snowden was hanged.

My work on *The Third Degree* got me interested in how minorities have historically been treated, and often mistreated, by the legal system, and the Snowden case beckoned as a potentially compelling case in point. I learned that the view of many Annapolitans—Black *and* white—that he had been wrongly convicted was strong, not only in the immediate aftermath of his execution but pretty much throughout the twentieth century. It was a presumption with tremendous staying power. But after sifting through the evidence several times, I realized that Snowden's guilt or innocence could simply not be established conclusively a century after his trial. That is, I would never be able to tie up all the loose ends of the case in a neat bow and declare him innocent of the charge against him with certainty.

So I decided to work on a different project.

Something about the case beckoned me back, however, and when I took a second look at it, it dawned on me that perhaps its importance did not rest on his guilt or innocence after all. Of equal consequence was the question of whether he had been treated fairly by the judicial system. And I concluded that he had not.

Maryland was not the Deep South, and John Snowden's treatment in court was certainly better than that accorded the "Scottsboro Boys," the nine Black Alabama teenagers infamously accused of raping two white women in 1931, who were never told they had a right to counsel, were given no advance access to attorneys, and were sentenced to death in rushed trials that lasted just a day. None of that happened to Snowden, but his case demonstrates that there are many ways justice can be denied that are far more subtle but just as nefarious as railroading hapless defendants through racist kangaroo courts. It also shows the value of justice, even when it is delayed by decades. And these struck me as compelling reasons to recount Snowden's story and try to make some sense of it.

Here, then, as accurately as I can reconstruct it, is the cautionary tale of John Snowden and his long journey—eight decades plus—through the Maryland legal system, and what I believe it means for us today.

# Dramatis Personae

**Joseph H. Bellis** (1867–1920): Sheriff of Anne Arundel County who oversaw the execution of John Snowden in 1919

**Georgianna Brice Boston** (1869–1932): Spiritual advisor to John Snowden who recorded and distributed his final statement

**Albert Theodore Brady** (1869–1935): Annapolis attorney who defended John Snowden at trial and on appeal

**Lottie May Haislup Brandon** (1893–1917): Young wife of Valentine Brandon, found murdered in her Annapolis home on August 8, 1917

**Valentine Noland Brandon** (1896–1968): Stenographer at the U.S. Naval Engineering Experiment Station in Annapolis and husband of Lottie May Brandon

**James A. Briscoe** (1878–after 1930): Pastor of Mt. Moriah A.M.E. Church and spiritual advisor to John Snowden

**Robert Dudley Carter Sr.** (1852–1936): Baltimore police marshal who oversaw the interrogation of John Snowden

**Edith H. Creditt** (1876–1953): Second Street neighbor of the Brandons and one of the principal witnesses against John Snowden

**Joseph F. Dougherty** (1873–1938): Police lieutenant who headed the Baltimore Detective Bureau and investigated the Brandon murder

**Frank Irwin Duncan** (1858–1946): Baltimore County circuit court judge who tried John Snowden and sentenced him to death

**Parris Nelson Glendening** (1942–): Governor of Maryland from 1995 to 2003, who issued a posthumous pardon for John Snowden

**Carlton Gus Grason** (1881–1953): Towson attorney who defended John Snowden at trial and helped file a motion for his appeal

**Nicholas Harwood Green** (1871–1935): Anne Arundel County state's attorney who argued the case against John Snowden at trial and on appeal

**Emerson Columbus Harrington** (1864–1945): Governor of Maryland from 1916 to 1920, who refused to pardon or commute the sentence of John Snowden

**George Hartman** (1880–1929): Baltimore County state's attorney who assisted in the prosecution of John Snowden

**Mary Grace Winterton Quackenbos Humiston** (1869–1948): New York detective hired by the *Washington Times* to solve the Brandon murder and later by Ella Rush Murray to exonerate John Snowden

**Linda Miriam Isel King** (1893–1950): Next-door neighbor of the Brandons who was, for a time, suspected of Lottie May Brandon's murder

**John H. Kratz** (1861–1948): Baltimore detective seconded to Annapolis to investigate the murder of Lottie May Brandon

**Judith Kay Johnson Kulawiak** (1947–2019): Great-niece of Lottie May Brandon, who opposed the granting of a posthumous pardon to John Snowden

**Robert Moss** (1863–1940): Anne Arundel County circuit court judge who presided over John Snowden's aborted Annapolis trial

**Ella Day Rush Murray** (1876–1943): Civil rights activist and suffragist who brought the two principal witnesses against John Snowden to the authorities and later worked for his exoneration

**George Luther Pendleton** (1866–1943): Baltimore attorney who spearheaded John Snowden's appeal to the U.S. Supreme Court

**Mary Perkins** (1885–?): Second Street neighbor of the Brandons and one of the principal witnesses against John Snowden

**Herman Pohler** (1858–1924): Baltimore detective seconded to Annapolis to investigate the murder of Lottie May Brandon

**Margaret Queen** (1856–1929): Employee of Ella Rush Murray, whose daughters came forward to accuse and testify against John Snowden

**William Donald Schaefer** (1921–2011): Governor of Maryland from 1987 to 1995, who declined to issue a posthumous pardon for John Snowden

**Thomas W. Simmons** (1867–1951): Maryland secretary of state from 1916 to 1919, who initially refused to sign John Snowden's death warrant

**Leroy Sisco** (1907–67): Eleven-year-old delivery boy who testified to having seen evidence of a struggle at the Brandon home on the day of the murder

**Jerry L. Smith** (1874–1929): Attorney who tried to obtain Snowden's release and later became legal advisor to Sheriff Joseph H. Bellis

**Carl O. Snowden** (1953–): Civil rights activist and government official who lobbied two Maryland governors to pardon John Snowden

**Hazel Geneva Snowden** (1957–): Niece of John Snowden, who petitioned Governor Parris Glendening for his pardon

**John Snowden** (1890–1919): Annapolis ice man accused, convicted, executed, and pardoned posthumously for the murder of Lottie May Brandon

**James French Strange** (1872–1926): Mayor of Annapolis from 1909 to 1919

**John R. Sullivan** (1860–1920): Sheriff of Anne Arundel County from 1916 to 1917

**Edna Wallace** (1893–?): Partner of John Snowden and sometime laundress to Lottie May Brandon

**Edward Douglass White** (1845–1921): Chief justice of the United States from 1910 to 1921, who refused to consider John Snowden's appeal

**Charles S. Williams** (1876–1943): Washington DC attorney who served on Snowden's defense team

**Ernest Sumner Williams** (1874–1929): Pastor of Asbury United Methodist Church who lived in the parsonage next door to the Brandons

# A Note on Language

At the turn of the twentieth century, words like "colored," "negro," "nigger," and other terms not generally acceptable today were commonly used to refer to African Americans, sometimes by Blacks as well as whites. Blacks were also sometimes described by whites in juvenile terms, such as when "boy" or "girl" was used to refer to an adult, and the word "black," when used in its racial sense, was not capitalized. In the interest of historical accuracy, such expressions and spelling do appear in this work but only in direct quotations from historical materials.

As with my previous works, every bit of dialogue and anything else that appears between quotation marks or as a block quote was written or recorded at the time. I have, however, occasionally condensed material to make for smoother reading and added italics for emphasis.

# A SECOND RECKONING

# Prologue

Even though the two men shared a surname and a home town, Carl O. Snowden had never heard of John Snowden until 1984, when he was thirty years old. Not that the two could ever have met; they were not related, and John had died more than three decades before Carl was born. But Black people in Annapolis still recounted John's story to their children.

A politician and civil rights activist, Carl Snowden had a well-deserved reputation as a firebrand. Deeply influenced by *The Autobiography of Malcolm X* as a teenager, he had managed to get himself expelled from Annapolis High School for "inciting a rebellion" when he helped organize a boycott to protest the lack of Black teachers and courses in African American studies. At twenty-two he had sued the FBI for illegally keeping him under surveillance—and secured a $10,000 settlement from the agency. And more recently he had helped lead a group of Annapolis residents in a rent strike against the Department of Housing and Urban Development.[1]

Carl was a man-about-town and a fighter. "Everybody knows him," Mayor John C. Apostol once told the *Baltimore Sun*. "They may not know who the *mayor* is, but they've heard of Carl Snowden."[2]

In 1984 Carl had set his sights on a seat on the Annapolis City Council, and it was while he was out campaigning that the name of John Snowden first came up. While knocking on doors in College Creek Terrace, one of the oldest public-housing complexes in the city, he ran into Louis Snowden, John's younger brother, then in his mid-eighties.

"What are you going to do about my brother?" Louis had demanded of the candidate.

Although his brother John had been dead for more than six decades, the case against him that had resulted in his execution had remained very much alive for Louis Snowden. In 1917 John had been accused of the murder of Lottie May Brandon, a pregnant white woman who lived near him, and convicted of the crime on circumstantial evidence early the following year by an all-white jury. His appeal had been unsuccessful and the governor at the time had refused to intervene in his case, so he had been hanged in 1919. Many Black Annapolitans—and a goodly number of whites as well—believed he had been the victim of a "legal lynching."

Several years earlier, Louis Snowden had spoken to a reporter from the *Evening Capital*, the local newspaper, who was writing a retrospective about his brother's case. Louis said he believed the principal witnesses who had testified against John had been paid off, because otherwise the authorities wouldn't have had enough evidence to convict him. "Me and my sister got to see him the week before they hung him," he said. "He couldn't tell where he was that day," he recalled, speaking of the day of the murder. "He was drunk. It was just because he didn't know where he was at."[3]

Louis Snowden gave Carl a fresh account of his view of his brother's arrest and trial. "For him, it was as if it happened yesterday," Carl recalled. "He said it was common knowledge that John Snowden had been executed for a crime he didn't commit. There was such passion and bitterness. He convinced me that something terrible had happened."[4]

As a practical matter, Carl didn't need much convincing. A student of history, he was well aware of the indignities and atrocities Black people had suffered in Jim Crow Maryland. It was no stretch to believe that justice had been denied John Snowden. His trial had taken place at a time when cases against Black defendants were routinely heard by all-white juries concerned more with convicting the accused than with facts. Just a few years before the Snowden trial, a Black man accused of the rape of a white woman hadn't even *made* it to trial in Annapolis; he had been forcibly taken from the jailhouse and lynched by an angry mob.[5]

Carl Snowden won his election, and the story stayed with him. In 1919 the governor of Maryland had refused to intercede in the case, but why did that have to end the story, especially if the man had been wrongfully convicted? John Snowden was long gone, but that didn't have to mean it was too late to try to secure a measure of justice for him.

So in 1990, Alderman Snowden decided to petition Governor William Donald Schaefer for posthumous clemency for John Snowden. In an exchange of letters, the governor agreed to look into the case, and he turned it over to the Maryland Parole Commission for review.

And there it sat. The file stayed with the Parole Commission for the remainder of the governor's term; no recommendation was ever forwarded to him. A Democrat, Schaefer was also a proponent of capital punishment, and he did not commute a single death sentence during his eight years in the governor's mansion between 1987 and 1995. In 1992, in response to public outrage over violent crime, he was persuaded to create a commission to study the death penalty, but it was not charged with debating its efficacy or the future of capital punishment in the state, only with considering how to expedite the process. The body ended up suggesting ways Maryland could kill more efficiently, such as speeding up the appeals process and switching the method of execution from the gas chamber to lethal injection.[6]

Carl was eventually forced to conclude that the Schaefer administration was just going through the motions on the John Snowden case. The time was not ripe, and this governor was not the right man. It would seem that Schaefer, who had little interest in commuting the sentences of living prisoners, had even less in pardoning one long dead.[7]

In 1997 Carl Snowden ran for mayor of Annapolis. He lost the Democratic primary by fifty-five votes, but his campaign caught the attention of Parris Glendening, another Democrat, who had taken over the governor's mansion from Schaefer two years earlier. Glendening offered Snowden a position in his administration. The following year, Snowden joined the campaign of Janet S. Owens, who was running for Anne Arundel county executive. After she won, she appointed Snowden her special assistant for legislative matters.

On the very first day he reported for work at the county executive's office, which was located at 44 Calvert Street in Annapolis, Carl

Snowden noticed an elderly Black man lingering outside. The man looked perturbed. Snowden assumed he was there to pay a bill but had gotten lost.

"How can I help you?" he asked the man.

"I don't need your help," was the reply.

"But you look confused," Snowden said.

"I'm *not* confused," the man muttered before he walked away. "I know what this building is. This is where they murdered that Snowden guy."[8]

It was, indeed. The Anne Arundel Center had been built in the 1960s on the site of the former county jail, the very spot on which John Snowden had met his end in what became the last hanging ever to take place in the county. For the newly minted special assistant for legislative affairs, it was a reminder of some unfinished business.

There was now a new governor in the executive mansion, and Snowden knew him. Why not raise the issue of a pardon for John Snowden with him? There wasn't a great deal of reason for optimism; a liberal on many social issues, Glendening had run on a law-and-order platform and, like Schaefer before him, he favored the death penalty.

But it was worth a try.

PART I    1917

# 1

## "A Love Match, Pure and Simple"

Valentine Brandon had just over an hour to get up, get dressed, go shopping, and scarf down his breakfast in time to catch the ferry across the Severn River to get to work. It was Wednesday, August 8, 1917, and the weather in Annapolis the previous week had been even hotter and muggier than usual. In fact, the night before, he and his wife had been forced to sleep in the front room of their flat on a sanitary cot—an ancestor of the foldout sofa-bed—because the air in the middle room, which they normally used for a bedroom, was so stifling.[1]

The couple had risen just before seven o'clock, and Valentine had to be out the door shortly after eight if he was to reach the Maryland Avenue ferry launch in time for the 8:35 boat. From the Naval Academy it was a short, ten-minute ride across the river to the northeast bank, where he worked as a stenographer at the U.S. Naval Engineering Experiment Station, a research facility that tested guns and shells for the navy—hence its location away from the population center.

This was Valentine and Lottie's first summer in Annapolis. Both had grown up in the District of Columbia, she the daughter of a bricklayer, he the son of a printer. They had kept company for two years. Valentine had been employed as a messenger at the Government Printing Office where his father worked as a foreman and subsequently at the Commerce Department's Weather Bureau in Washington. When he received notice of his transfer to the Department of the Navy, the couple had decided to elope. They were married by a Presbyterian minister in Baltimore on October 16, 1916, and they arrived in Annapolis the very next day.

As Washingtonians, the newlyweds were used to hot, sticky weather. What they were likely *not* accustomed to was racially mixed neighborhoods. Both Lottie and Valentine had grown up on lily-white streets and gone to whites-only schools. Most housing in the District of Columbia was strictly segregated, sometimes by means of restrictive covenants that barred certain ethnic groups from certain neighborhoods. Not until 1948 were such contracts held by the Supreme Court to be unenforceable.

Things in Annapolis, far smaller than the nation's capital, were somewhat more relaxed. Not that the community didn't have oppressive Jim Crow laws, its all-Black and all-white neighborhoods, and its share of racial tensions and covenants. But in Annapolis there were also areas where the races lived cheek by jowl, and in relative harmony, though not equality.

The Brandons' neighbors immediately to the north of their townhouse at no. 29 Second Street—now Lafayette Avenue—were the Kings: Thomas, an instructor at the Naval Academy, and his wife, Miriam, married the previous December. Thomas had lived at no. 27 for only a few weeks; Miriam had moved in just three days earlier. North of them, at no. 25, were John Burch, a machinist, and his wife, Ida; after them, at no. 23, were Benjamin Sarles, also a machinist, and his wife, Grace. All were white.

To the south, however, the Rev. Ernest S. Williams, pastor of the nearby African American Asbury United Methodist Church, lived next door across a narrow alleyway with his wife at no. 31. And there were several Black families across the street, including Mrs. Ella Carroll at no. 34 and two sisters, Mrs. Mary Perkins and Mrs. Edith Creditt, who had moved into no. 30, directly across from the Brandons, at the end of May.

These people would play key roles in the tragic drama that would begin to unfold on Second Street later that day.

If the Brandons objected to living on an integrated block, there is no indication of it. Indeed, like other white Annapolitans, they enjoyed their privileges—at least those available to them on the salary of a government stenographer—and employed local Blacks to help with domestic chores. Twenty-four-year-old Edna Wallace, who lived almost directly behind their back fence in a ramshackle house on all-Black Acton Lane (now City Gate Lane), for example, did their washing.

Nearly twenty-four herself, the former Lottie May Haislup, a handsome, pale, and diminutive brunette, was two years older than her husband. The third of nine siblings, Lottie had gone right to work after graduating from grammar school. She had held jobs at a department store and two candy stores before she married. Valentine, for his part, was fair-haired, blue-eyed, of medium height, and slender—he weighed only about 128 pounds. He had graduated from Business High School and then entered the civil service.

Although he had welcomed the transfer, Valentine hoped eventually to return to Washington, and he was toying with leaving government service entirely. But looming on the horizon also was the possibility he would be sent overseas. Shortly after arriving in Annapolis, he had registered for the draft, as was required by law of all men between the ages of twenty-one and thirty-one; at twenty-one and three months, he was just barely eligible. Nearly three million American men would be conscripted before World War I was over.

Because it was wartime, Annapolis, a naval hub, was experiencing a steep influx in new residents. Even well-to-do arrivals had to settle for any sort of dwelling they could find, and the Brandons were of decidedly modest means. For several months after their arrival, they had lived at temporary addresses, and had finally been fortunate to secure the Second Street apartment. Located in the west end of town, it occupied the ground floor of the last of six freshly painted row houses that made up what was known as Freimel's Row, named for Charles A. Freimel, the local harness maker who owned them. A string of modest, two-story "double-decker" clapboard structures, they were built on twelve-and-a-half-foot lots on the east side of the street. The thin, shared walls didn't afford much privacy, as goings on in one house were easily overheard in the next.

Lottie May was just over seven months pregnant and was no longer working, so the couple had to make do on Valentine's salary. Fortunately, it was sufficient to pay the rent on the three-room flat and to furnish it. They had moved in on January 1.[2]

1. The arrow shows the location of 29 Second Street, Annapolis, at the end of Freimel's Row, ca. 1917. No. 31, the parsonage of the nearby Asbury United Methodist Church, is partially visible at right, across a narrow alleyway. *True Detective Mysteries*, March 1930.

The apartment was a railroad flat. It consisted of a parlor in the front, a bedroom in the middle and a kitchen and bathroom at the rear. The couple had filled the front room, about twelve by sixteen feet in size, with the cot, several chairs, a large table, a rug and a Grafonola—an early twentieth-century wind-up phonograph that was a proper piece of furniture in its own right. That room opened to a somewhat smaller bedroom, a bit larger than its nine-by-twelve rug and overcrowded with a brass double bed, a couple of chairs, a dresser, and a chiffonier—a chest of drawers topped with a mirror.

One door in the bedroom, normally kept locked, led to the cellar; another, which had originally concealed a now-blocked stairway to the vacant apartment on the second floor, led to a closet. Two others opened to the kitchen in the rear, which contained an ice box, a gas range, a dining table, and some cabinets. The kitchen, in turn, led to a bathroom with a toilet, tub, and a sewing machine, and a rear porch whose steps descended into a small, fenced-in yard.

Lottie May was in charge of the money. Valentine made a point of handing over his salary envelope each payday, and it was her job to spend what was needed for daily necessities and put the remainder in a savings account they had opened in her name. That Wednesday morning, August 8, however, she was out of change, so she gave her husband a dollar bill and sent him off to the bakery—there was one at the end of their block—for a loaf of bread and a quart of milk. But the baker couldn't change the bill so early in the morning. Promising that Lottie would be back later to settle accounts, Valentine took the items home and sat down with his wife to breakfast.

By this time Lottie had dressed. She had put on a blouse, a sailor jumper, and a white skirt. She fixed Valentine a couple of ham sandwiches for his lunch pail, tossed in a pear, and then joined him for a quick meal.

Valentine Brandon and Lottie Haislup were, her father recalled later, "a love match pure and simple." After they met, neither had had eyes for anyone else, and they were a happy couple. Comfortably settled in their new home, they were expecting their first child in about six weeks. As they ate their morning meal, they discussed possible names for the baby, settling tentatively on Valentine if it was a boy, and Martha—his mother's name—if a girl. Then, at a little after eight a.m., Valentine rose to leave. He grabbed his lunch and kissed his wife goodbye as he went out the door.[3]

It was the last time he would ever see her alive.

# 2

## "Aren't You Going to Come and Kiss Me?"

Valentine arrived at the Naval Experiment Station at 8:45 a.m. and was at his desk by nine. He was an assistant to Rear Admiral Thomas W. Kinkaid, the head of the entire operation. He worked steadily until the noon whistle sounded, at which point he took a quick swim in the Severn and then ate the lunch Lottie May had packed for him. After an uneventful afternoon, he caught the 4:32 p.m. ferry back to the Naval Academy and walked directly home from the dock.[1]

Lottie usually met him at the door, but today there was no sign of her. Valentine whistled for her but got no response. So he called out, "Baby, baby, aren't you going to come and kiss me?"

Still nothing.

He passed through the front parlor to the door to the bedroom and saw her lying motionless on their bed. The blinds in the room were drawn, so in the dim light he didn't get a good look at her. He approached her and touched her shoulder, but there was no response. He knew she had suffered from a few fainting spells during her pregnancy, but he had always been able to rouse her, and when he could not this time, he became alarmed. Without wasting any time, he turned on his heels and ran outside to seek help.

First he knocked on Ida Burch's and Grace Sarles's doors and asked them to look in on Lottie while he ran for a doctor. He didn't actually know where to look, though; even though Lottie was pregnant and near term, she had been seeing a midwife and had not had occasion to consult a physician in the time they had been in Annapolis. So he hurried to the bakery where he had bought bread that morning and asked someone there to telephone for a doctor. Then the young man called his mother in Washington to summon her.

Meanwhile, Ida and Grace entered the Brandons' apartment, together with Ella Carroll, a Black neighbor from across the street whom Ida invited to join them. They passed quickly through the front room, and in the middle room they found Lottie lying on her left side, her head at the foot of the unmade bed. One arm was extended, her legs were crossed and her dress was halfway up her thighs; they could see that she was naked underneath it. One stocking was up; the other was hanging from her toe. There was a nasty gash on her forehead. And there was froth coming out of her mouth.

Ida felt her left arm; it was cold. Ella felt to see if she had any pulse but detected none. It was clear that Lottie May was dead. Together they covered her body with a sheet, and then one of them went to summon the sheriff. When Valentine returned—he had been gone only about ten minutes—he asked whether Lottie had come to yet. Not wishing to shock him, they told him only that she had not, but that she was very ill and that he mustn't enter the bedroom.

In a few minutes, thirty-three-year-old Dr. Joseph C. Joyce arrived and ordered everyone out of the bedroom. A University of Maryland graduate, he had been practicing medicine for seven years. When he lifted the sheet, the first thing he noticed was the wound on Lottie's forehead. He moved the hair away from her neck, revealing that blood from that gash had seeped into the bedclothes below, leaving a bright red stain on the white sheets and saturating an area of the seven-inch thick mattress below. He called for water and bathed her forehead and then her throat, revealing lacerations on her neck. There were also scratches and bruises on her cheek, hands, knees, and ankles. He did not investigate further; there was no need. He estimated she had been dead for at least five hours.

While he waited for John R. Sullivan, the portly, white-haired sheriff of Anne Arundel County, and State's Attorney Nicholas H. Green to arrive, Joyce made a cursory search of the premises to see if he could locate a blunt instrument that might have caused the wound on Lottie May's forehead, but he found nothing.

As he left, he told the officers he did not believe she had died a natural death.

**2.** Lottie May Brandon. *Washington Times*, August 13, 1917.

Sullivan had been in the job for only two years, but he had been in public service since 1872. He had served in both branches of the state legislature and had been clerk of the Maryland senate for two terms. He naturally suspected Lottie's husband of the crime, as any experienced police detective might have. After he, too, had examined the body and taken stock of the premises, he ordered Valentine into the middle room. He wanted to gauge the young man's reaction to the death scene.

"Come with me," he said to Valentine, who obediently followed him into the darkened room as Sullivan switched on the lights. "Look at *that!*" the sheriff ordered, as he dramatically lifted the sheet that covered Lottie's bruised, lifeless body and the blood-stained bedding below her.

Valentine recoiled at the sight. He clenched his fists and nearly lost his balance as he drew back. "Oh, my God! Oh, my *God!*" he exclaimed. "This is the first dead person I ever saw in my life. In the name of God, how could anybody have committed such a crime? Baby, baby, *my baby!*"[2]

Sullivan then led him away. With few clues to go on and no obvious suspects other than Valentine, he and State's Attorney Green, who had held his present office for twelve years and prosecuted an average of four murders in each of them, realized that the local police would need reinforcements if they were to solve a murder of this kind.[3]

3. Anne Arundel County sheriff John R. Sullivan. *Washington Times*, August 13, 1917.

Fortunately, there was a protocol for getting help in such situations. Annapolis had its own police force but no detective bureau, so anything beyond local capability usually involved summoning help from nearby Baltimore, the largest city in the state. A call was placed to Marshal Robert D. Carter, chief of the Baltimore police department and himself a noted criminologist. He obliged with a posse of his ace detectives. Herman Pohler and John Kratz, regarded as "two of the best third degree men in the country," took off at once for Annapolis in Carter's car, together with Lieutenant Joseph F. Dougherty, the head of the detective bureau and Baltimore's "star homicide investigator."[4]

The two detectives had often worked together in the past. Pohler, short and stocky and regarded as industrious and indefatigable, was celebrated for staying the course of an investigation "until he has run down his quarry, secured his conviction and sees him sentenced in court." Kratz, tall and angular, was known for the art of "sweating" a prisoner to elicit a confession. Both were methodical men with a

4. Baltimore police lieutenant Joseph F. Dougherty and detectives Herman Pohler and John Kratz. Clinton McCabe, *History of the Baltimore City Police Department, 1774–1907*.

proven track record of breaking down recalcitrant suspects; between the two of them they had sent a couple of dozen men to the gallows and scores more to the penitentiary.

Dougherty, "quiet, cool and deliberate" and known familiarly as "Gentleman Joe," was brought in on all major murder investigations in the state. The Baltimore men went directly to Sheriff Sullivan's office, and there they met with State's Attorney Green, who briefed them on the case.[5]

A careful search of the premises had revealed some anomalies. The breakfast dishes had been only partially washed; this was taken as an indication that Mrs. Brandon had been attacked before she had finished her morning chores. The back door was locked, and a block of ice left on the rear porch had almost completely melted. The ice box door was hanging from one hinge, suggesting a struggle in the kitchen before the action shifted to the middle room. In fact, one of Lottie's shoes was found in the kitchen, while the other was in the bedroom. Her clothes were scattered about the room. There was no blood anywhere in the apartment but the bed on which she was found.

The kitchen blinds were drawn, which was unusual. It was also odd that the door that opened onto the stairway to the cellar was unlocked. But no weapon that could have inflicted a wound such as the one Lottie had sustained on her head could be found. Nor was there any sign of robbery; Lottie's diamond ring remained on her finger, and both Valentine's

**Diagram of Annapolis' Shocking Crime and Picture of Lottie May Brandon of Washington, the Victim**

All women and men are intensely interested in the solution of this shocking crime—which at this time especially arouses anxiety, so many homes being now left without a defender.

5. Diagram of the crime scene at 29 Second Street. *Washington Times,* August 9, 1917.

watch and a pendant had been left untouched. In other words, there were clues, but none seemed to point toward a motive or a murderer. The hope was that the fingerprints on Lottie's neck, though apparently indistinct, might do just that, and an expert was called in to take impressions.

Valentine remained in the front parlor with the detectives for most of the evening, even as curious neighbors gathered on the street outside. The police did their best to keep them at bay on the narrow street. At about eleven p.m., Valentine was taken to the sheriff's office in back of the courthouse for a third degree of his own: endless, probing questions from the Baltimore detectives about his history, his marriage, his whereabouts that day, and about whether he had any enemies, or Lottie had had any previous suitors, who might have been motivated to do her harm. Absent any other leads, he was, for the moment, the principal suspect.

In the meantime, as was the custom at the time, Coroner William S. Welch convened a Coroner's Jury to conduct an inquest. The all-white, twelve-man panel was charged with ruling on the cause of death and deciding whether a crime had been committed. The panel held a brief session that evening and heard from a few witnesses but then adjourned to await the outcome of the police investigation.[6]

At the same time, Coroner Welch tapped both Dr. Joyce and thirty-five-year-old county health officer Dr. Walton H. Hopkins, a University of Maryland graduate in practice for about a dozen years, to perform an autopsy. Dr. Joyce had returned to the Brandon home with Hopkins at about ten p.m., at which point Lottie May's body was transported a couple of blocks away to the Annapolis Emergency Hospital and the two physicians labored into the night to determine what had killed her.

They found bruises on the back of her left hand, on both arms, on her knees, elbows, and neck, and scratches on the side of her neck that appeared to have been inflicted by fingernails, probably from someone grabbing her from behind. But most importantly, they examined the large depression in Lottie's forehead that Joyce had noticed immediately when he had examined her hours earlier. The wound had nearly reached the bone. When they opened Lottie's skull and removed her brain, they discovered a significant dural hemorrhage—bleeding of the brain—in the area that had been hit. The doctors concluded that death had resulted from the blow that had caused that injury, as well as strangulation and shock. In other words, Lottie May had not only been struck, and struck hard; she had also been choked.

They also noted the condition of her genitals, which suggested that someone may have had, or have attempted, intercourse with her. They took samples of a mucus-like discharge in her genital area that Dr. Hopkins suspected, from its odor, was semen. These would be analyzed later at the University Hospital in Baltimore, and until then, the autopsy would not be finalized nor would its results be released. Dr. Joyce did speak with the press and detail Lottie's wounds, but the possibility of "criminal assault," by which was meant rape, was withheld from the public. As far as the newspapers were concerned, nothing of the kind was suspected.

Saddest of all, they determined that Lottie had been close to term with a male child who had also died. When they had finished, they gently returned the fetus to the womb and sewed up the mother. Then the remains of Lottie May Brandon were released to the custody of John M. Taylor, a local undertaker, for cleansing, embalming, preparation for burial and transport back to her native Washington.[7]

# 3

## "Altogether Separate and Different Lives"

Annapolis was a prosperous seaport in the waning years of the second decade of the twentieth century and a pleasant place to live—if you happened to be among the nearly three-quarters of the population who were white. Blacks accounted for just over 26 percent of the 11,214 people counted in the 1920 federal census, a percentage substantially lower than that of ten years earlier, when the number had been 37 percent. But their population had not shrunk; it was the white population that had grown, largely because of the war. The number of African American residents had remained steady during this period at about three thousand.[1]

The city's commercial backbone had always been its seafood industry, which thrived off the bounty of the Chesapeake Bay. But government, too, provided a huge boon to the local economy. Annapolis was both the seat of Anne Arundel County and the state capital. And the federal government rounded out the government footprint when it established the U.S. Naval Academy on the banks of the Severn in 1845. It soon became the city's largest employer.

Although Blacks and whites led separate lives—they did not, as a rule, worship, study, or fraternize together—in a city as compact as Annapolis the two communities were mutually dependent and couldn't have lived without each other. In general, Blacks there fared better than they did in many other places because there were more employment opportunities. The Naval Academy hired whites *and* Blacks, and had done so almost since its establishment. It was, in fact, the single largest employer of Blacks in town. Although it did not graduate its first African American midshipman until 1949, it retained a substantial number of Blacks far earlier than that in support roles—groundskeepers, cooks, dishwashers, waiters, maintenance workers, janitors—as did St. John's College, a quasi-military school located nearby.[2]

The seafood industry needed fishermen, dredgers, oyster shuckers, ice men, fishmongers, and canners. And the large number of government employees depended on porters, waiters, busboys, bartenders, and maids who served in the hotels and restaurants. They also engaged the personal services of barbers, cooks, laundresses, nannies, dressmakers, domestics, and housekeepers, among others.

A substantial number of European immigrants arrived in Annapolis in the years following the Civil War, and the Naval Academy brought in whites from other places in America as well. They joined the old-stock Marylanders who more or less made up the power establishment, many of whom were descended from colonial-era settlers who had been slaveholders. And among local Blacks were myriad descendants of their slaves; Annapolis had, after all, been a major center for the Atlantic slave trade.

The city had for years also been home to a large complement of free Blacks. Just about half of the African Americans in the state were free by the onset of the Civil War. Although much of Annapolis's Black community lived in poverty in the early twentieth century, not a few were prosperous small businessmen who made a comfortable living and were by any objective measure members of the middle class.[3]

Maryland had been a slave state, but despite the fact that the Confederacy had enjoyed a good deal of popular support in the Chesapeake Bay watershed and other areas, the state had not seceded from the Union. Because it had remained, it had been unaffected by President Lincoln's 1863 Emancipation Proclamation, which applied only to the Confederate states. The following year a state constitutional convention was held and a new constitution that outlawed slavery was approved and narrowly ratified by popular vote. But it was not until 1870, with the passage of the Fifteenth Amendment, that African Americans were allowed to vote in the state.

This initial push toward racial equality was not sustained, however. Because it had not rebelled, Maryland was also not subject to the federal military rule imposed on the Southern states during Reconstruction, and it did not take long for Democrats to regain political control and use it to keep African Americans from amassing any real power. Beginning in 1870 and extending well into the twentieth century, Jim Crow laws were passed to legalize racial discrimination and, in essence, codify American-style apartheid.

This effort picked up steam after the Supreme Court ruled in 1896 in *Plessy v. Ferguson* that segregated public facilities were constitutional. The white powers-that-be took that as a signal to do all they could to roll back the gains made by the African American community. Jim Crow laws passed in Maryland during the first decades of the twentieth century extended segregation to virtually all aspects of life—political, economic, and social. Theaters, schools, restaurants, drinking fountains, and public toilets were segregated. Although the court had ruled in *Plessy* that facilities had to be "separate but equal," the second half of that equation was routinely ignored.

There was little mixing of whites and Blacks in public events. When Billy Sunday, a nationally celebrated evangelist, made an appearance in Annapolis in 1916, the Rev. Ernest S. Williams of the Asbury United Methodist Church and another Black minister were denied entry to the event. An usher barred them from the premises, promising a separate service at a local Black church at another time.[4]

Even Republicans, who were somewhat more sympathetic to Blacks than their Democratic counterparts during this period, weren't immune to Jim Crow values. Those Blacks who attended a Republican Party gathering at the Colonia Theatre in October 1915 were shunted off to the balcony, the main floor having been reserved for whites. When many expressed their indignation, the organizers blamed the theater owner, but he retorted that he had attached no conditions when he rented the facility to the Republican committee, and that the decision had been their own.[5]

Nor was there anything approaching equality in education in Jim Crow Maryland. Early efforts to provide elementary education to African American children were all private schools funded by churches and benevolent associations. Although the state constitution mandated that a portion of taxes paid by Black property owners be used to establish schools for Black children, that didn't amount to much money. Before 1900 there was not a single public school for Black children in Annapolis. The Stanton School, an eight-room building with an unfinished attic built that year, received students up to the sixth grade. But it didn't offer a full year of classes. As late as 1915, Black public schools in Anne Arundel County were open for only four months a year.

Until 1917, secondary education was available only to those Black children whose parents could afford to send them to Washington or Baltimore or to a boarding school elsewhere. It took until that year for the city to get around to providing a high school education for African Americans, and even then it did it on the cheap, fitting out the Stanton School's attic into four classrooms.[6]

But Blacks in Annapolis and elsewhere strove in myriad ways to enlarge their spheres of activity and gain political rights, even if they succeeded only incrementally. They built institutions—churches, social and welfare organizations, fraternal societies and clubs—to take care of their needs and represent their interests, and raised money for their own schools.

Sometimes they resorted to boycotts or demonstrations. At other times the courts offered them recourse. In 1904, for example, the state legislature passed a bill requiring all railroads and steamboats to provide separate accommodations for white and Black passengers. Customers who resisted the new measure and conductors who failed to enforce it could be fined. The law was challenged by African American groups, some of whom organized a boycott against the trains and boats that lasted several months. And the bill's sponsor, Delegate William G. Kerbin of Worcester County, who earned the sobriquet "Jim Crow Kerbin" for his advocacy of it, also felt Black backlash of a sort. When he returned to his home in Snow Hill, where he boarded at a local hotel, the cook, an African American, refused to prepare meals for him, and no Black washerwoman in town would do his laundry, nor would any bootblack shine his boots.[7] Although that law was ruled unconstitutional by the Maryland Court of Appeals in 1905 as it applied to interstate, but not intrastate, transportation, only the former being under federal jurisdiction, in 1908, new state laws went further and mandated separate toilets and sleepers on steamships.

Also in that year, Marylanders saw an effort by the Democratic-controlled state legislature to disenfranchise Black voters. The General Assembly had passed a measure in 1904 to amend the state constitution with a grandfather clause that would limit the vote to men who had been eligible to vote on January 1, 1869, and their direct male descendants. This excluded African Americans by definition, since prior to 1870 only whites had been permitted to register. That amendment failed, as did a second effort only slightly less draconian: it would have preserved the grandfather clause but offered an exception to men who owned assessed property in the city worth $500 or more.[8]

But what couldn't be accomplished on the state level could still be forced on the city, and in March 1908 a Democratic delegate from Anne Arundel County named A. Theodore Brady introduced a bill to amend Annapolis's charter that passed the legislature and was signed into law the following month. The new law had the effect of denying the vote to all but a handful of Black men. Although Annapolis had been the first jurisdiction in Maryland to elect Black politicians after the Civil War, this law caused the one Black alderman on the City Council to lose his seat to a white Democrat until it was declared unconstitutional by the Supreme Court in 1915, after which he was reelected to his old office.[9]

"There was just one Annapolis," the late Philip L. Brown recalled in his 1994 book, *The Other Annapolis*, "but, because of customs, practices and laws calling for the separation of the colored and white races, there were two groups of people living in one geographic area, but living altogether separate and different lives."[10]

Because of the relatively small size of that geographic area, the city had always had integrated neighborhoods. Even if they didn't socialize with them, employers found it convenient for their servants to live nearby. Although the trend in the early twentieth century was toward separation, and realtors began to decline to sell Blacks property in white neighborhoods, Annapolis was ultimately too compact for total segregation, nor was it ever mandated by law. There were always streets where working class Blacks and whites lived side by side. Second Street, where the Brandons lived among many Black neighbors, was a good example.

African Americans met the most dangerous of the city's exclusionary practices when they came up against law enforcement and the judicial—and often the *extrajudicial*—system. There were no Blacks on the Annapolis police force—the first was not hired until 1960—and despite their percentage in the population, Blacks were very rarely called to serve on juries. Those charged with selecting potential jurors from among male pillars of the community saw to that. There were no Black judges, no Black prosecutors, and only a handful of Black attorneys. And lacking political power, Blacks were in no position even to lobby effectively for gubernatorial clemency when it might have been deserved. Between 1905 and 1919 alone, six Black men were hanged in Annapolis after trial and conviction.[11]

In fact, such men were not the only Black men hanged; they were just the ones hanged *legally* after they had had their day in court. Sometimes the judicial system wasn't even permitted to finish, or even to begin, its job. When passions and resentments boiled over, white men in Anne Arundel County sometimes took matters into their own hands.

John Simms, accused in 1875 of the rape of a young white woman near Odenton, was one victim. His lynching was predicted even before it happened. "It would be no surprise if the brute were taken forcibly from jail, by the indignant citizens, and summarily hung," the *Aegis and Intelligencer* (a Bel Air, Maryland, newspaper) noted after he was captured and jailed. And sure enough, four days after that item appeared, upward of thirty masked men descended on the county jail in Annapolis, pistols drawn, and forced the jailer to give up the keys to Simms's cell. Once they freed him from his chains, they dragged him out of the building and took him to a secluded spot a mile and a half from town. As he begged for his life, they slipped a noose around his neck and hanged him.[12]

George Briscoe, accused not of murder or rape but merely of robbery, also never made it to court. Arrested in Baltimore, he was on his way to Annapolis in response to a warrant when a party of eighteen armed, masked men seized him and hanged him on the spot. The *Evening Capital*, the local afternoon daily and no friend to Blacks, came close to endorsing the act. "While we do not approve of the lynch law," it opined about Briscoe's lynching, "yet there are some instances where it is justifiable."[13]

Wright Smith was arrested in Baltimore and jailed in Annapolis in 1898 for the assault with intent to rape of a married white woman. Here, too, his fate was essentially predicted when the *Baltimore Sun* noted that "several men from the scene of the outrage were lurking around the jail today, anxious to know in what cell the prisoner was confined." The paper was confident the sheriff would take the necessary precautions to protect his prisoner, but it ought not to have been. Whatever he did was not sufficient to foil a party of several dozen men who arrived at the jailhouse, pointed guns at the night watchman, and seized Smith. He was taken to a lot near the city cemetery and shot repeatedly.[14]

It had become painfully apparent by the turn of the century that the Anne Arundel county jail did not provide sufficient protection from mob justice. In 1903 local Black residents had to take matters into their own hands to protect a fellow Black man incarcerated there. Lloyd Boyd had been charged with the shooting death of a white sailor, and all signs pointed to a possible lynching by the man's fellow mariners one night. Local African American men mobilized and patrolled the area around the jailhouse, determined to meet force with force if necessary. Trouble was averted, and the prisoner was transferred to safety in Baltimore the next day.[15]

But the most recent lynching in Annapolis, the one whose memory was still fresh in the second decade of the twentieth century, had taken place in 1906. Like Wright Smith before him, Henry Davis was suspected of the attempted rape of a married white woman. The maximum penalty for this crime was ten years in prison, but Davis paid with his life. In view of local law enforcement's poor record of protecting controversial prisoners, many people urged the then-sheriff of Anne Arundel County to arrange his transfer to Baltimore, but he refused, convinced he could protect Davis from summary justice.

Although he initially feigned innocence, Davis eventually confessed, and State's Attorney Nicholas H. Green anticipated a speedy trial and conviction. Neither Green nor the sheriff reckoned with a vigilante party that assembled one night. Concerned that the evidence against Davis might be insufficient to convict, they determined to end his life then and there. When they stormed the jailhouse, they encountered little resistance from the guards. They dragged Davis through the town to a vacant lot about a half mile away, strung him up to a tree and fired a half dozen bullets into him as one member of the mob cried out, "Another white woman is avenged."[16]

In 1917, when Lottie May Brandon's body was found, there had not been a murder in Annapolis for five years. If Dr. Joyce was right that she had been the victim of foul play, it would be big news in town. There was no particular reason to believe her assailant had been of one race or another, but if it turned out that he or she had been Black, memories of the Davis lynching were fresh enough that there would be ample reason to worry that *her* death might be avenged in the same way.

# 4

## "All Annapolis Is Shocked"

Annapolitans of all stripes found the news of the murder of Lottie May Brandon alarming when they read about it the next day, and in the absence of facts, wild rumors and theories of the crime began circulating. Had Brandon himself killed his pregnant wife? Had it been an enemy of his? A jilted lover of Lottie's? A disappointed rival for her hand? A crazed degenerate who had hopped the back fence and hidden out in the cellar, waiting to make his move? Could the attack have been part and parcel of a rape?

The newspapers were quick to judge this the worst such incident in memory. The *Evening Capital* was among the first out of the box. "The tragedy is the most baffling that has ever occurred in the criminal annals of the city, and besides is a horrifying one in the extreme," it declared on its front page.[1]

In an editorial likely penned by Emma Abbott Gage, the *Evening Capital*'s editor and daughter of its publisher, the paper suggested that "if our women are not safe in their own homes in broad daylight, then we should at once begin to organize a Home Guard. All Annapolis is shocked, is horrified at this cruel murder and it will be some time before we fully recover from the shock."[2]

Gage did not speculate in the editorial about the identity of the murderer, but she didn't hesitate to spin her own unfounded theory of the crime to the *Washington Times*. "There is no proof of a 'discarded lover,' and it is cruel to suggest such a thing when this woman, who evidently loved her husband and expected a baby, lies dead and cannot speak," she told the paper. "The case seems to have narrowed down to a negro assailant," she concluded, without citing a shred of evidence to support the allegation.

"Our women are not properly protected," she complained to the *Times*, "especially in these days when the draft is taking so many white men away to war. The population of Annapolis is 43 per cent colored," she said, overstating the number substantially, "and some of the colored are not law abiding. There are rumors of ugly remarks about whites by the lower class negroes."[3]

In other words, it was sacrilege to impugn the character of a dead white woman with the suggestion that she might have had a lover but perfectly acceptable to cast aspersions on the entire Black population of the town.

Nor was it only to the *Evening Capital* that the possibility of a Black assailant occurred. Washington's *Evening Star* reported rumors that the police were on the lookout for "colored men engaged in delivery work on wagons driving about the neighborhood" where the murder took place. And noting that there was a "negro settlement" separated from the back fence of the Brandon home only by a field of tall weeds and a narrow street—that is, Acton Lane, which was indeed an all-Black neighborhood—the *Washington Times* speculated that "a passing negro might have seen Mrs. Brandon alone in the kitchen and entered the house for the purpose of assault."[4]

The *Times* did, however, plow in right behind the Annapolis police in suggesting that the investigation should begin with Valentine Brandon. It quoted local DC detectives as saying that if they were in charge, their first step would be to get an accounting from the husband as to his whereabouts and his movements on the day of the murder.[5]

And that is exactly what the two Baltimore detectives did with Valentine Brandon. They "sweated" him until three a.m. on Thursday, August 9, before they released him. He insisted he had been at the office all day, and that others could vouch for his presence there and on the ferries he took across the Severn to and from work. He was persuasive, and the detectives judged his grief genuine. Besides, his hands did not appear to them large enough, or strong enough, to have choked his wife and left the bruises that had been found on her neck.

But what clinched it for him was an interview with Miriam King, who lived next door. Mrs. King told police she had talked with Lottie between ten and eleven o'clock that morning, which was two or three hours *after* Valentine had left for work. That is, his wife had been seen alive well after his departure, and was judged by a physician late that afternoon to have been dead for only about five hours. This narrowed considerably the window in which Lottie had likely been killed. Since Valentine's whereabouts during the entire workday could be substantiated, his alibi was airtight.

One potentially useful item the detectives did pry out of him was the name of a man in Washington he said bore ill will toward Lottie and himself. The detectives withheld the man's name from the press, but they did ask the Washington police department for help tracking his movements over the past couple of days.

Since there was no call to hold him any longer, the grieving husband was released. He joined his mother, who had arrived in town at 8:45 p.m., a few hours after he had called her. The pair departed for Washington the following afternoon to make arrangements for Lottie's funeral. Just before seven p.m. they arrived with her body, which was taken to 408 H Street, N.E., the establishment of an undertaker named William H. Sardo. Her funeral was planned for the following day.

"After I bury my wife," Valentine vowed to the *Washington Times*, "I shall return to Annapolis, sell my household effects and leave there for all time. I never want to see the town again." And indeed, the paper reported that Captain Kinkaid, his boss, had already written the secretary of the navy asking that Valentine be reassigned to duty in Washington.[6]

Even though he was exonerated, Valentine had been shaken up by the treatment he received from the authorities and was mortified that anyone might suspect him of harming his wife. As he told the *Times*, "From the number of times the detectives have questioned me and the nature of their questions, I am convinced that they suspect me of killing my wife. This is a monstrous idea. It is horrifying to think of. I was devoted to my wife and she was the most loving helpmate to me. I would not have harmed a hair of her head, and would gladly have laid down my life to protect her from harm or injury."

"I want to see the brutal murderer of my beloved wife, who was soon to become the mother of my child, brought to justice, and I do not think any penalty would be too severe," he continued. "The only theory I have is that she was attacked by a brutal assailant while washing the dishes in the kitchen and was dragged to the bedroom, where she was choked into insensibility and beaten over the head with some blunt instrument like a hammer, hatchet, piece of pipe or a stick of wood."[7]

Together with his brother, Valentine then went back to Annapolis to assist the detectives in their search for the perpetrator. They did not go near the Second Street house but rather spent the night at the Maryland Hotel. Their plan was to return to Washington the following morning.[8]

In the meantime, a member of the Maryland National Guard told the detectives he had passed the Brandon home a day or two before the murder and seen a man in a pink shirt in the window. He insisted that the man, whom he had noticed in the neighborhood a few times before, was not a local. Noting that Valentine owned no such shirt, the police wondered if perhaps this was the man they had asked the Washington police to find.

Absent hard evidence, they were grasping at straws.

The *Washington Times* was all over the story. A reporter sought out Lottie May's family for a reaction to another rumor, that she had told her neighbors of a liaison with a man other than Valentine, and had kept a picture of her paramour hidden at home. Her mother, on the verge of collapse, refused to speak with the reporter, but two of her siblings did their best to put that idea to rest.

"She was a jolly girl," her elder brother Emmett told the paper, "but when it came to talking about her personal affairs she had nothing to say, and I don't believe she ever met any old sweetheart after her marriage, or that she ever told any of her neighbors that she had such a meeting. I was living at home when my sister was going with Brandon, and she wasn't receiving attentions from anybody else."

Her sister Mabel added, "I am sure she was never engaged to anybody except the man she married, and I don't believe she was concealing any man's picture from her husband." Nor did the police find any such photo when they searched the premises.[9]

Randall J. Haislup, Lottie's father, who had just returned from Annapolis himself, was not content with the apparent lack of success of the Baltimore detectives and wanted the Washington police involved. Accompanied by the Rev. Robert Talbot of St. Paul's Episcopal Church, he called on Major Raymond W. Pullman, the chief of police, who explained that he could not send men to Annapolis willy-nilly, absent a request from the Maryland authorities. But now that Lottie's body was within his jurisdiction, he did agree to dispatch a fingerprint expert to the undertaker's to examine it.[10]

Haislup also spoke up in support of his son-in-law. "Next to finding out who killed my daughter," he wrote in a *Washington Times* column, "I believe the most important thing I should do is to clear the name of my son-in-law, Valentine N. Brandon, from any shred of suspicion that may cling to him. Val was never anything but a model husband, and no better son-in-law ever lived. He loved Lottie, his wife, better than he loved his life."[11]

The *Times* glommed onto the murder far more aggressively than any other local paper. It took a deep interest in the crime and ran multiple articles about it, sometimes more than half a dozen in a day. The paper had recently been bought by Arthur Brisbane, a well-known associate of William Randolph Hearst in New York City. Brisbane had cut his teeth as a reporter for Joseph Pulitzer's *New York World*—the paper that had given the world "yellow journalism"—before Hearst had hired him away.

A seasoned newsman who knew a blockbuster, sensational story when he saw one, Brisbane pulled out all the stops in his coverage of the murder of Lottie May Brandon. He offered a $500 reward for information leading to the apprehension and conviction of the killer. He consulted a noted criminologist about the investigation. And he engaged *two* private detectives to solve the crime.[12]

Brisbane used the Brandon murder to burnish his paper's reputation. On August 10, for example, he devoted several column inches to expressions of gratitude he had received for retaining the detectives and offering the reward. Those praising the *Times*' largesse included Lottie's father, Major Pullman, Annapolis Mayor James French Strange, the president of the Anne Arundel County Board of Commissioners,

*Evening Capital* editor Emma Abbott Gage, State's Attorney Green, Sheriff Sullivan, and the two Baltimore detectives working on the case. It was announced soon afterward that Sheriff Sullivan would offer out of his own pocket a similar reward—$500—for information leading to the arrest of the killer.[13]

Although Valentine was no longer a suspect, Sullivan did accompany him back to Washington to retrieve the shirt he had worn on the day of the murder, which his mother had taken home with her. There was a red spot on it, but a close examination revealed that it was not a bloodstain but rather red ink he had spilled on himself at work. Sullivan also generously advanced Valentine some cash, since the young man was unable to withdraw funds from Lottie's bank account and the $118 insurance policy on her life, for which the couple had paid ten cents a week, had yet to pay out.[14]

Lottie's death remained a mystery, and as Friday, August 10, drew to a close, the detectives were exhausted. They had been on the case for two full days with little rest, and they wanted to return to Baltimore to consult with Marshal Carter, their boss, and to get some sleep.

In their time in Annapolis, they had more or less concluded that a struggle in the kitchen had led to death in the bedroom. They were convinced from the size and depth of Lottie's bruises that a man had been involved; they gave no serious consideration to the possibility of a female killer. And whoever had slain her had done so quietly; Mrs. King, to the immediate north, insisted she had heard no noise from the Brandons' flat after her conversation with Lottie. Nor had any other neighbors with whom the police spoke, including Reverend Williams to the south, who had been home the entire morning and most of the afternoon.[15]

The detectives were actively considering two principal theories, neither of which had much in the way of evidence to support it. The first was that a jealous, rejected suitor, or else an enemy of Valentine, had extracted revenge on poor Lottie. That person might have been the man in the pink shirt. And the second was that "a colored man who was delivering goods in the neighborhood," and who had perhaps entered the apartment through the cellar, had killed her during an attempted rape as she fought desperately for her honor and her life.[16]

In support of this second hypothesis, the *Evening Star* echoed the *Evening Capital* in asserting that "responsible residents of the city declare that colored members of the community, who are not of the highest standing, and who have recently been disturbed by race troubles at East St. Louis and other places, have made various threats as to how they will handle themselves when the white men who have been taken from Annapolis by the selective draft and the National Guard of Maryland stationed here go into the training camps."[17]

There wasn't much of a case for either possibility, but at least *someone* claimed to have seen a man in a pink shirt. As far as a Black assailant was concerned, there was not a scintilla of evidence to suggest it.

# 5

## "Not the Faintest Clue,
## Theory, or Speculation"

On Saturday, August 11, the police still had no weapon, no motive, and no suspect. Lacking these, they had little choice but to pursue a multitude of fanciful theories and unproductive leads.

The *Baltimore Sun* reported that they had their sights on a Black man who worked at a local hotel and who lived on a street just behind the Brandons—probably Acton Lane. He came under suspicion simply because he had tried to borrow ten dollars from a white man to travel to Washington, because he had seemed nervous at the time, and because he had not been seen in town since the previous Tuesday night, which would have been the night before the murder took place.[1]

That description was enough for the District of Columbia Police, who by now had been asked formally for help by Annapolis mayor James French Strange, to question a "suspicious-looking colored man" with scratches on his face and bloodstains on his clothing. The man, James Davis, had recently come to Washington and was conveniently already in custody; he had been picked up for intoxication the previous night and discovered to be in possession of stolen goods. Plus he had a criminal record and had spent time in an insane asylum. When they strip-searched him, they found $39 in his pockets and an additional $139 bound to his legs. But he insisted he had come to town from Philadelphia and Baltimore, not Annapolis. Lacking any evidence to link him to Lottie Brandon's murder, they eventually released him.[2]

Washington police had also detained Francis Rucker, a tinner's helper, who had married Lottie May's sister Mabel less than two weeks earlier. He was the man Valentine had told the Baltimore detectives had been on unfriendly terms with Lottie and himself, and who the detectives had asked their counterparts in Washington to investigate. Rucker had not been at work on the day of the murder, a fact that his wife, who was also questioned, initially denied. This discrepancy gave the police reason to be suspicious of him. But he was able to account for his whereabouts on that day, so he was also let go.[3]

The Baltimore detectives were looking for a "colored huckster," according to Washington's *Evening Star*. The man in question, whose name was not given, was described as a "well-known character" who lived on a farm outside the town and usually made three visits a week to Annapolis, announcing his wares in a singsong voice. The police had no evidence against him apart from the fact that he had supposedly been seen in the vicinity of the Brandon home on the day of the murder, but lacking any other suspects, they were eager to find him to see if he bore any scratches on his body.

Detectives Kratz and Pohler also brought Miriam King in for another round of questioning, together with her husband, Thomas, and interrogated the couple separately. They had received a tip that Tom King, a husky, athletic man, had been "paying undue attention" to Lottie while Valentine was away. The "jealous lover" theory remained an attractive avenue of pursuit, even in the face of flat denials from Lottie's family. It seemed worth investigating if only because none of their other ideas appeared to be leading anywhere.

But even in the face of withering third-degree interrogation tactics, Tom insisted he knew the Brandons only slightly. More importantly, he maintained he not been at home on the day of Lottie's murder, and he easily accounted for his activities on that day. Miriam, who by now had been quizzed by several newspapermen and was reportedly on the verge of a nervous breakdown, repeated that she had spoken with Lottie after Valentine had left for work on the morning of her death, and that she had heard no noises coming from the Brandons' flat after that. She also insisted to the police that her husband did not own a pink shirt. After six hours of questioning, the two were released.[4]

Nor had the detectives given up entirely on an idea the doctors had already dismissed: that Lottie had not been murdered at all but had died accidentally as a result of convulsions related to her pregnancy. In this scenario, she had had a fainting spell in the kitchen, hitting her head on the ice box door as she collapsed, but had somehow managed to reach the bed before she died. In view of the lack of suspects, this would certainly be a convenient, if highly improbable, way to explain her death and close the case.

But it was a preposterous theory, and the physicians who had performed the autopsy on her had soundly rejected it, insisting that if she had sustained such a severe injury in the kitchen she would never have been able to make it as far as the bedroom, and pointing out as well that she had been strangled in addition to having her skull bashed. Nor was there any trail of blood from the kitchen. Sheriff Sullivan and the local police dismissed the idea, too, but the *Evening Star* reported that Detectives Kratz and Pohler, desperate for leads, were consulting other doctors to see if the theory could hold water.[5]

Three full days into their investigation, the authorities were nowhere. "I have not the faintest clue, theory or speculation as to who perpetrated this crime," State's Attorney Nicholas H. Green admitted candidly to the *Washington Times*. A lineal descendant of Col. Richard Harwood, a colonial-era immigrant who fought in the Revolutionary War, and Jonas Green, the official printer of the Province of Maryland in the eighteenth century and the scion of slave owners, the Annapolis-born Green had graduated from St. John's College. He had been a teacher for two years before passing the bar in 1892, and he had been one of the city's leading lawyers before being elected state's attorney in 1905.[6]

Sheriff John R. Sullivan agreed, noting that "the case was a mystery on Wednesday afternoon and still is." Detectives Kratz and Pohler also concurred, the latter admitting that the investigation "has produced absolutely nothing that would shed any light on the mystery."

Both Randall Haislup, Lottie's father, and Valentine himself were impatient at this lack of progress, and felt that more ought to be done to solve the crime. Haislup cabled Emerson C. Harrington, the governor of Maryland, urging him to call in the District of Columbia police:

> TODAY, 72 HOURS AFTER MY CHILD BREATHED HER LAST, THE MAN IN CHARGE OF THE CASE ADMITS THEY ARE NO NEARER A SOLUTION OF THE MYSTERY THAN THEY WERE TWO HOURS AFTER THEY STARTED TO WORK. IF THIS CRIME HAD BEEN COMMITTED IN THE DISTRICT OF COLUMBIA, THIRTY DETECTIVES AND SIX HUNDRED POLICEMEN WOULD BE ON THE TRAIL OF THE MURDERER. . . . I APPEAL TO YOU GENTLEMEN WITH THE SINCERITY AND ANGUISH OF A FATHER BOWED DOWN IN DEEPEST GRIEF TELEGRAPH TO MAJOR PULLMAN YOUR FORMAL REQUEST FOR THE AID OF THE DISTRICT POLICE IN CAPTURING THE MURDERER.[7]

Valentine, too, felt they could benefit from reinforcements. In a telegram of his own, he urged Governor Harrington to send "all detectives in the Baltimore Police Department who can be spared . . . to Annapolis at once" and to ask the superintendent of police of the District of Columbia to send as many as he thought wise. He went on to warn that "if the murderer is not caught, he may find another victim in a Baltimore or Washington home." He sent a similar cable to the mayor of Baltimore.[8]

Valentine was also concerned about a rumor that he had been critical of the Baltimore detectives assigned to the case. The memory of his ten-hour interrogation was still quite fresh, and he may well have felt vulnerable to any additional accusations they might decide to direct his way, especially given the paucity of suspects. In another telegram to Governor Harrington, he took pains to assert that "I wish to state to you that Messrs. Kratz Pohler and Sullivan . . . are doing all in their power to clear up this mystery. I have the greatest confidence in these men."[9]

He contributed a column to the *Washington Times* to make the same point: he did not want to appear to be complaining about the team already assigned to the case. He added his opinion that the culprit "may have been a negro degenerate or it may have been someone actuated by motives of enmity."[10]

RECEIVED AT 7 MARYLAND AVE., ANNAPOLIS, MD.,
TELEPHONE No. 25.

1-B   V   69   N   L

WASHINGTON D C 11 AUG 1917

GOV. HARRINGTON,
     ANNAPOLIS, MD.

HAVING JUST BEEN IN ANNAPOLIS I FIND THAT THE DRIFT OF OPINION IS THAT
I DISSATISFIED WITH THE PROGRESS OF THE MEN ON THE CASE I WISH TO
STATE TO YOU THAT MESSRS KRATZ POHLER AND SULLIVAN HAVE AND ARE DOING
ALL IN THEIR POWER TO CLEAR UP THIS MYSTERY I HAVE THE GREATEST CONFIE
DENCE IN THESE MEN AND FEEL A GREAT INJUSTICE HAS BEEN DONE THEM

             VAL N BRANDON

   9-A.M.

**6.** Telegram from Valentine Brandon to Maryland governor Emerson C. Harrington, August 11, 1917. Collection of the Maryland State Archives (MSA SI046, 2-30-1-4).

He was not alone in this view. According to the *Washington Times*, there was widespread belief in Annapolis that the crime was committed "by some person of inferior mentality, a degenerate, or a negro brute." Apparently the idea that it might have been a *white* brute was dismissed out of hand. But the *Evening Capital*, whose editor had been first out of the gate to raise the prospect of a Black assailant, now spoke up in defense of the local Black community. "We do not for a moment entertain the thought that there is in this community any negro so beastial [*sic*] as to have murdered this woman, and this theory is also cast to the winds by right-thinking people."[11]

Lottie May Brandon's corpse, which had been on view at the undertaker's establishment, was taken to 914 Sixth Street N.W., the home of Leroy and Martha Brandon, on Saturday morning for her funeral. The ceremony began a few minutes after eleven a.m. Dr. Robert Talbot, rector of St. Paul's Episcopal Church, the church Lottie had attended as a child, conducted the service. Only relatives of Lottie and Valentine were invited into the house; an additional three hundred people, some of whom were childhood friends of the couple, waited outside. The heat was stifling and mourners had to cool themselves with fans in the dark parlor and dining room.

There were no references in the service to the manner in which Lottie had died. Nor did anyone mention the revelation in the *Washington Times* that morning by Dr. Walton H. Hopkins, one of the physicians who had performed the autopsy, that had her body been discovered sooner, the life of her unborn son might have been saved.[12]

When the ceremony was over, Lottie's casket was borne by eight of Valentine's high school classmates to a motor-driven hearse waiting outside as local police officers parted the crowd. Her bereft husband had to be helped into a car; he had barely eaten or slept for three days and was near collapse.

"There goes the only witness," one of the officers was heard to remark as the hearse bearing Lottie's body pulled away. It was headed for Glenwood Cemetery in northeast Washington, where it was interred.[13]

But not for long.

# 6

## "The Woman Sherlock Holmes"

When Valentine Brandon and his father-in-law lobbied the governor of Maryland for reinforcements for the investigators, what they had in mind was more police detectives. But in fact, additional A-list talent was already being deployed on the case, and it had nothing to do with the Annapolis, Baltimore, or Washington police departments. It was Arthur Brisbane's *Washington Times* that got into the act by retaining experts to solve the murder.

The first, and least prominent, was a local gumshoe named Morgan Bradford Jr. He had established his Washington-based agency, the Bradford Detective Service, in 1885, and the *Times* brought him in at the request of Lottie May's father, who couldn't afford to hire him himself. Bradford's was a full-service agency; he investigated everything from embezzlement and robbery to divorce and murder.[1]

Bradford made the trek to Annapolis on the *Times'* dime and, based on the day he spent at the Brandon home searching for clues—the police do not seem to have cordoned off the premises—he wrote a column in which he declared flatly that the crime had been perpetrated by someone who had access to the home and who had known Lottie May. He dismissed the old lover theory and the accidental injury theory out of hand and imagined that her assailant had entered through the kitchen door and promptly clutched her by the throat, the immediacy of the act preventing her from making so much as a sound. This would explain why neighbors had heard nothing. Bradford boasted that he had already drawn a conclusion as to *who* the murderer was but that he was "not at liberty" to divulge the man's identity.[2]

The *Times* also consulted Dr. William MacDonald, author of a volume on criminology. MacDonald found nothing mysterious or remarkable about the murder. "The probability is that it was an ordinary attack by a brute driven mad by lust who lost his power when he discovered the condition of the woman," he asserted in a column in the paper. "Brutality stands out as the one striking feature. An expert robber would not have done this," he insisted. But he refused to play the race card, adding that in his opinion, "Mrs. Brandon's assailant may have been a white man or a negro."[3]

The real star of the show, however, was the third figure the *Times* brought in, a nationally known, New York–based lawyer-cum-private-eye destined to play a large role in the investigation. An 1888 graduate of Hunter College, Grace Humiston was a force of nature. Born Mary Grace Winterton to a well-to-do, progressive family, she had married and become a teacher. But when her marriage ended in divorce, she decided to pursue a law degree, opting for New York University, which at the time was home to the only law school in the city willing to admit women. After spending a year with the Legal Aid Society, she had passed the bar and, in 1905, opened her own legal clinic—the "People's Law Firm"—pledging to focus her efforts on helping the poor.

Humiston earned most of her notoriety not as a lawyer, however, but as a detective, and she specialized in locating missing persons. Prompted by the disappearance of the husband of an immigrant client, she famously traveled to Florida in disguise to expose forced labor in the turpentine peonage camps, prompting a federal investigation of the camp operators. This, in turn, secured for her an appointment in the Theodore Roosevelt administration as special assistant U.S. attorney for the Southern District of New York and later as special assistant to the attorney general of the United States, making her the first female to occupy such a high position in the Justice Department. She used that perch to investigate and expose others involved in the exploitation of immigrant labor, often at considerable personal peril.[4]

After she returned to private practice, Humiston was most celebrated for cracking a case that had stymied the New York police department: the disappearance of eighteen-year-old Ruth Cruger on February 17, 1917. The attractive schoolgirl, daughter of a well-to-do family, had left

The Woman Sherlock Holmes Who Has Shaken New York

Remarkable Rise of Mrs. Grace Humiston, Who Traced the Murderer of Ruth Cruger, and Is Now the Busiest Sleuth in the Metropolis.

MRS. GRACE HUMISTON at Her Desk in New York. She Is Now One of the Busiest Persons in the Metropolis with Unlimited Resources and the Co-operation of the Police Behind Her Great Work as a Modern Sherlock Holmes.

7. Grace Humiston, the "Woman Sherlock Holmes." *Boston Herald*, October 14, 1917.

home that morning, taking her ice skates to be sharpened, but when she failed to return home that night, her family feared the worst. The police searched the area in which she had last been seen and questioned Alfred Cocchi, the Italian proprietor of the bicycle shop where she was thought to have taken the skates. He was eventually released, and promptly fled to Italy.

The media coverage of the case was intense, and fears that Ruth had been sold into "white slavery" were raised in the papers. The police chose to believe that the girl had probably eloped. But as time passed with no progress on the case, her father, certain she had *not* run away, sounded off with a withering criticism of the force, accusing the police of negligence. He then posted a substantial reward for information leading to her return and retained Grace Humiston, who by this time had been appointed a special investigator in the New York City police department, to solve the case. Humiston may have set out to serve the poor, but she was never averse to taking on a rich client or two.

Humiston did not buy the elopement theory either, and proceeded on the assumption that Ruth had been a "good girl" who had been taken against her will. She focused her efforts on the bike shop and eventually prevailed on the police to dig in the shop's cellar, where Ruth's decomposed body was discovered. Cocchi was subsequently arrested in Italy and confessed his guilt. The detective had not only solved the case; she had shown up the New York police in the process.[5]

For her efforts, Humiston was celebrated as a master sleuth and dubbed the "Woman Sherlock Holmes" by the papers. And when Lottie May Brandon's body was discovered just shy of two months after Ruth Cruger's had been unearthed, she was still very much in the limelight and seemed to the *Washington Times* the perfect person to crack the case. It's possible editor Brisbane, the *Times* publisher, knew her from his time in New York with William Randolph Hearst, but if not, he certainly knew *of* her, as, indeed, did most of the country. As soon as Humiston got the call from the *Times*, she packed her bags, arriving in Washington just in time for Lottie May's funeral.[6]

After interviewing Randall Haislup and Valentine Brandon, she set out for Annapolis, but before departing, she gave her initial impressions to the *Times*. She felt strongly that the murder had *not* been committed by a Black man, though her reasons for coming to this tentative conclusion were laced with racism.

The crime, she believed, had been premeditated, and possibly planned for quite some time. "Very few crimes start all in a moment," she explained. "Lottie Brandon's murderer was undoubtedly someone Lottie Brandon had known," she insisted. "He was also someone who wasn't unacquainted with the house." This much was in complete agreement with Morgan Bradford's analysis. "It is hardly conceivable that any ruffian, any negro could have invaded that little woman's home and committed the deed without the neighbors having heard something of the scuffle and the struggle that must have followed," she added.

"While it is too early to state definitively yet, I feel almost sure that it is *not* a negro crime. In the first place, it bears none of the earmarks of such a thing. Lottie Brandon's murderer took care to arrange her body in a natural position. I cannot imagine a negro doing this. Also, a negro would almost certainly have committed a theft while in the house," she went on, noting that Lottie's diamond ring had been found on her finger and other jewelry had remained on her dressing table.

The assumption that a Black perpetrator could be ruled out because no Black person would have had the delicacy to position the corpse or would have left the premises without stealing something was as odious as it was unfounded. But Mrs. Humiston wasn't finished. "Also, if a negro committed the crime, he was actuated by lust. The coroner's report almost certainly refutes that theory."[7]

Actually, it didn't. It was silent about it.

# 7

## "The More Delicate Hand of a Woman"

The murder of Lottie May Brandon was the subject of several sermons and much gossip at area churches on Sunday morning. "Singing evangelist" Rev. George Lawrence, speaking at Bradburn M.E. Church in Washington, predicted that "God will send a wireless message to someone, and through that agency, the murderer of Lottie May Brandon will be found." The Rev. Amos Clary exhorted his flock at the Mt. Tabor Baptist Church to contribute to a reward fund for the capture of the murderer. And Annapolis ministers, including Dr. John S. Sowers of the College Avenue Baptist Church and the Rev. John Ridout of St. Anne's Episcopal Church, praised the *Washington Times* for its $500 contribution to such a fund, something the paper was pleased to trumpet that same morning.[1]

But Sunday was no day of rest at the state's attorney's office. No wireless message from the heavens having been received, they continued their investigation, complicated by the arrival the previous afternoon of Grace Humiston, who had waltzed into town with a gaggle of criminologists and fingerprint experts. Although she had no authority over the investigation, her notoriety was such that the police were remarkably deferential to her and compliant with her requests. According to the *Times*, she overshadowed all the local officials and "owned the town."[2]

She accompanied Sheriff Sullivan in his motor car on a trip fifteen miles out of town to track down the "colored huckster" who allegedly visited town three times a week and who, Sullivan now told the press, had been heard to "make disrespectful remarks about white women" shortly before he visited the block on which the Brandons lived. The lead, however, went nowhere. When they finally found the sixty-five-year-old man, they discovered he had not been in Annapolis on the day of the murder and could prove it.

The authorities also readily acceded to Humiston's demand that she and her party be given access to the crime scene. She, in turn, excoriated them because of what she found there. In her Sunday night column in the *Times*, she complained that "already the trail is four days old and the elements involved become hourly more complexing and confusing. The scene of the crime and its immediate surroundings have been gone over and over again by dozens of people until now every clue which might have come from scent, fingerprints, footprints or such things are forever lost, and the task of unearthing the culprit made increasingly difficult."[3]

Still, Humiston remarked on a few clues she found potentially significant. She noted that the murder house had recently been painted, and had learned that Charles Freimel, the landlord, had quarreled with the painters and replaced them with new men who had not been thoroughly vetted. "These extra men were both white and colored," she wrote, and "all had plenty of opportunity to get the lay of the land, to know how easy it was to gain entrance to the Brandon bedroom by a stairway leading from the cellar, and also to know just when the woman was alone and unprotected." She advocated prevailing on Freimel to reveal their names so the men could be questioned, and the police obligingly followed up on the lead, to no ultimate avail.

Because both the outside basement door and the one leading from the cellar to the bedroom had been left unlocked on the morning of the murder, she also hypothesized that the perpetrator had gained entry via the cellar and attacked Lottie stealthily, perhaps while she was at the sink washing dishes. This could account for the fact that no noise was heard from the apartment, and the fact that she appeared to have been strangled from behind.

Most surprisingly, however, Humiston suggested that although Lottie's killer might have been a vicious brute of a man—"white or colored"—the murderer might also have been a woman. "It is well known that a man usually chokes with one hand; a woman with two," she wrote, without citing any evidence for this crackpot theory. "It is evident that Lottie Brandon was choked twice; grabbed once and choked, and then the throat grabbed again in another place and the act repeated. This, too, would indicate a woman, who might have taken hold once, and then, not being as strong as a man, grabbed again to get a better hold."[4]

Morgan Bradford Jr., the DC-based detective also retained by the *Times*, agreed about the gender. He felt sure not only that the perpetrator was female but that she had been a neighbor. "The thickly populated street, the large number of people passing . . . would have made it almost impossible for a stranger to have entered the house, committed the murder and then have gone away, unobserved," he said.[5]

Humiston elaborated on her theory in her column the following day. "There are countless little touches about the thing that indicate the more delicate hand of a woman," she wrote. "For example, I understand that when the body was discovered, the woman's hair was draped about the throat, temporarily concealing the cruel attack which caused death. That in itself strongly indicates a woman. Who but a woman would have the finesse to apply this little touch?"

"Then, too, the careful arrangement of the body on the side, one arm tucked up under the head as the poor woman was known to sleep in life. That care would certainly not be the thought of the vicious brute type. That, too, indicates a more delicate hand." She also rejected the assumption that strangling Lottie from behind would have required the strength of a man. "It does not take a particularly strong person to be successful at choking," she insisted.

Humiston called for a more extensive autopsy. "We cannot have false premises from which to work. I have known cases where a particularly skilled pathologist could almost reconstruct a murder just from his accurate knowledge of the condition of the body." Here, too, her words carried a great deal of weight. That same day, Anne Arundel County officials and the Baltimore detectives began making arrangements for the disinterment of Lottie May's body.[6]

The female assailant theory gained some currency with the police, and not necessarily because of Humiston's questionable reasoning or Bradford's assumptions, but rather because they thought they might have found a woman with a motive. Sheriff Sullivan announced on

Sunday that he intended to question Miriam King yet again. Although he made a point of adding that he did not suspect her, the papers the next day were full of predictions that a female suspect answering her description would be subjected to "a thorough third degree," by the police and that an arrest would likely be made.[7]

The police were coy about the lead that had led them to suspect Miriam; Lieutenant Joseph Dougherty would say only that he had received the information in the neighborhood. The gist of the allegation was that Thomas King had shown Lottie Brandon undue attention, and that a jealous Miriam, realizing this in the short time she had been in town, had slain her in a fit of jealousy and then lied about it, saying she had heard nothing.

The police already learned from Ida Burch that she and several members of her family *had* heard noises of a struggle just after noon on the day of the murder, an observation confirmed by Emily Grant, who lived above them. If this was true, it was hardly plausible that Miriam King, who lived between them and the Brandons, would not have heard the same sounds.[8]

Gertrude Stevenson, a *Washington Times* reporter, did some research on Miriam. Like Lottie and Valentine, she had been a Washingtonian all her life, growing up as the daughter of an electrician. The former Linda Miriam Isel was an accomplished musician and composer. Stevenson visited Miriam's younger sister, who described her as "placid." But she also noted that Miriam was partially deaf, which could have accounted for the fact that she had heard no noises from the Brandon home.

But most importantly, her sister insisted that "there never was the slightest jealousy on Miriam's part about her husband, for she never had any reason for it. He wasn't the susceptible type, and he was devoted to Miriam." Stevenson also quoted Miriam's brother, who had much the same thing to say. "Mrs. King does not come from the stock of which criminals are made," the reporter concluded.[9]

Grace Humiston had already spent several hours questioning Miriam King before the police brought her in once again for several more. She reiterated that she and her husband had not known the Brandons very long. Thomas had lived in the house only since July 16, and been preoccupied with getting it ready for her; she had joined him there only three days prior to the murder. She could recall only a few conversations with Lottie Brandon in that short time, and had no reason to be resentful of her.[10]

Fortunately for Miriam, the police had no concrete evidence against her. And the heat would soon be off of her entirely with the emergence of a new suspect more to their liking.

# 8

## "His Name Is Snowden"

Acton Hall, an eighteenth-century waterfront mansion on Acton Place, had once been a plantation house. Built in the mid-1700s by John Hammond on what was then a 256-acre tract he inherited from his father—a planter, merchant, landowner, and slaveholder—it backed up to Spa Creek, just off the Severn River. The brick, Georgian-style residence had always been home to prominent Annapolitans, and in 1845 it had been purchased by Captain James D. Murray, the U.S. Navy's pay director.

Murray's name was given to Annapolis's tony Murray Hill neighborhood when, in the early 1890s, he subdivided much of the property. Lots were sold off for development and many substantial homes were built on them.[1]

In the early twentieth century, the iconic, four-bedroom brick manor house with its twin pedimented end pavilions, hipped roof, massive chimney stacks, prominent portico, and lush interiors stood at the center of a small farm. By then it had passed into the hands of Murray's grandson, William Spencer Murray, a nationally renowned engineer who had supervised the first high-tension electrification of a steam railroad—the New York, New Haven, and Hartford Line—a pioneering, $25 million project. He and his wife, Ella, whom he had wed in 1905, split their time with their three sons between Annapolis and New England.[2]

Ella Day Rush Murray was descended from American royalty. Through her father she was a scion of Benjamin Rush, a signer of the Declaration of Independence and a surgeon in George Washington's

**8.** Acton Hall, as it appeared in 1936. Library of Congress (HABS MD, 2-ANNA, 20-5).

Continental Army, and of his son Richard Rush, the eighth attorney general and the eighth secretary of the treasury of the United States, who had been John Quincy Adams's running mate in the latter's unsuccessful bid for reelection in 1828. She could also cite Richard Stockton, another signer of the Declaration, as an ancestor.

Five foot five, with grayish-blue eyes, an oval face, and flaming red hair, Ella Murray had never seen a liberal cause she couldn't support. A civil rights activist and a committed suffragist, she was a staunch advocate of Black enfranchisement, among other causes. She sat on the board of directors of the National Association for the Advancement of Colored People, was a charter member of the National Woman's Party, and a member of the Consumers' League and a host of other civic organizations.[3]

Although it was only three blocks away, Acton Hall was worlds apart from the narrow, clapboard structures the Brandons and their working class neighbors called home. And it's fair to say that the Murrays occupied a prominent social position in town commensurate with the opulence of their residence, a far cry from that of those who lived on Second Street. The Murrays lived well, and they employed several servants to maintain their affluent lifestyle.

**9.** Ella Day Rush Murray. Library of Congress, National Woman's Party Records, Group 1, Container 1:155, http://hdl .loc.gov/loc.mss/mnwp .155008.

Why Ella Murray was in Annapolis in August of 1917, and not relaxing in a cooler northern climate, is not clear. William was out of town. But on the afternoon of Monday, August 13, while Ella was in the kitchen talking with her cook and her waitress, fifty-one-year-old Margaret Queen, her longtime laundress, showed up at the house unexpectedly. Mrs. Queen, a Black woman and a widow, was the mother of Edith Creditt and Mary Perkins, the sisters who lived directly across Second Street from the Brandons. She had brought her daughters along with her.

Instantly, the other servants fell silent, and Ella, sensing unease, thought there might have been some trouble among them, so, misreading the situation, she left the kitchen to enable them to sort the problem out themselves. But Mrs. Queen followed her into the pantry. She asked for a word in private.

Ella knew Edith Creditt but didn't remember having met Mary Perkins before. It was Mary, however, who wanted her counsel. Mary had information about a person who might have committed the Brandon murder, Margaret told Ella, but she was fearful of divulging it.

Hearing this, Ella invited Mary into the library and sat down with her.

Mary Perkins told Ella that as she was writing a letter to her husband, a navy man, in the front parlor of no. 30 Second Street at a few minutes after eleven o'clock on the morning of August 8, she had heard a noise coming from the Brandon home across the street. It sounded as if something had slammed against the front door. As she looked up, she had seen in the window of no. 29 a chair go speeding by, and then heard the sound of it, or something else, striking the floor.

She had summoned her sister Edith, a navy widow, from the kitchen. "My goodness!" she had exclaimed. "That man surely *can't* be beating his wife while she is in such a condition!" The racket continued for about fifteen or twenty minutes as Mary peered at the house through the blinds. Shortly after it stopped, she saw a Black man in dark trousers, a light-colored shirt, and a grey sweater with sawed-off sleeves poke his head out of the front door and look up and down the street. Finding the road empty, he emerged from the house, closed the front door behind him, and walked up the block in the direction of West Street, never looking back. When he got in front of the Kings' house, he took what appeared to be a bottle or a flask out of his hip pocket and transferred it to one of his side pockets.

Mary knew the man by sight but didn't know his name. So she called Edith back to the window. By this time only his profile was visible.

"Who is that fellow? Do you know him?" she had asked her sister.

"Yes," Edith responded. "His name is Snowden, and I think he drives an ice wagon."

Mary told Ella she had thought no more about the incident until that afternoon, when she heard the alarming news that Lottie Brandon had been found dead in her bed. By evening, she had become so upset that her mother had called in Dr. Ambrose Garcia, a prominent Black physician, an immigrant from Trinidad who was a Howard University graduate. Upon learning the cause of Mary's anxiety, Garcia gave her a decidedly mixed message about what to do. On the one hand, he counseled her to go to the authorities and tell what she had witnessed.

But on the other, he predicted a race riot if she did. Mary also told several friends about what she had seen, she confided to Ella, all of whom had advised her to keep her mouth shut.

In the morning of the next day, Mary and Edith had taken a walk over to Parlett and Parlett, the ice supplier at the foot of Main Street for which Snowden worked, for a surreptitious viewing of Snowden to make sure he was, indeed, the man Mary had seen on Second Street. Once she got a good look at him, she was sure, she said. He was wearing the same clothing.

Mary could not make up her mind what to do, which is why she sought Ella's counsel. On the one hand, she felt guilty for concealing her knowledge of the identity of the person all Annapolis was searching for. But she was loath to come forward and accuse a Black man for fear of repercussions within the Black community, and because, as she told Ella, she felt she would die if she had to appear in court. She might also have been dissuaded by a common practice in Annapolis whereby the authorities routinely locked up Black witnesses for several months pending trial in important cases, whether to prevent them from fleeing the jurisdiction or to protect them from possible harm.[4]

Ella Murray didn't hesitate. She advised Mary that it was her Christian duty to tell. Mary then suggested that she speak with Grace Humiston, who had actually already paid a call on her home. The two had not met, however, because she had been sick in bed at the time. Ella obligingly telephoned Carvel Hall, the hotel at which Grace was staying, only to be told that she was out for the day.

The hotel clerk suggested she ring the state's attorney's office, which Ella was loath to do, as she hoped to stay out of the entire affair. She decided to consult with the Rev. John Ridout, the rector of St. Anne's Episcopal Church. At the rectory, he listened to the sisters' story, and then escorted Mrs. Murray and the two sisters to the state's attorney's office, where they repeated it to State's Attorney Nicholas H. Green himself.[5]

As soon as Green heard it, he dispatched the Baltimore detectives and a local deputy to Parlett and Parlett. Snowden, who drove a supply wagon that did not itself make deliveries but rather replenished the delivery wagons with three-hundred-pound cakes of ice, was not there

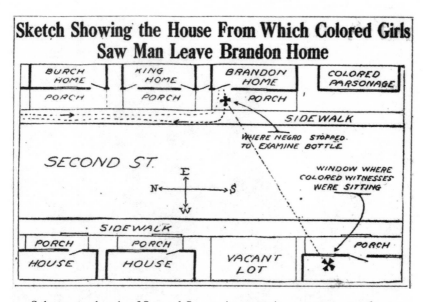

**Sketch Showing the House From Which Colored Girls Saw Man Leave Brandon Home**

BURCH HOME / KING HOME / BRANDON HOME / COLORED PARSONAGE

PORCH / PORCH / PORCH

SIDEWALK

WHERE NEGRO STOPPED TO EXAMINE BOTTLE

SECOND ST.

WINDOW WHERE COLORED WITNESSES WERE SITTING

E / N / S / W

SIDEWALK

PORCH / PORCH / PORCH

HOUSE / HOUSE / VACANT LOT

10. Schematic sketch of Second Street showing the vantage point from which Mary Perkins and Edith Creditt observed a man leaving the Brandon home. Despite the fact that the sisters were aged thirty-two and forty-one years, respectively, and that one was married and the other a widow, they were frequently referred to in the press condescendingly as "girls." *Washington Times*, August 14, 1917.

when they arrived. But he soon appeared, together with another Black man, a coworker named Bernard Chambers.[6]

The twenty-seven-year-old Snowden, who had stopped to water his horses, showed no fear when the detectives identified themselves and did not resist when they took both Chambers and him into custody. He did not even ask what he was wanted for, and obligingly walked the several blocks to the sheriff's office in the courthouse with them. But word had gotten out that an arrest was imminent, and a large crowd had already massed outside the courthouse when they arrived. A loud shout went up when they appeared, and some in the crowd uttered threats. Fearing for the safety of their prisoners, the police rushed the men inside and locked the doors behind them.

John Snowden was not unknown to the local police. He had been arrested and fined for disturbing the peace in 1911, and more recently, in 1916, he had been accused of assaulting and robbing an elderly man

**11.** Acton Lane, where John Snowden lived with Edna Wallace. It was later called Larkin Street and is known today as City Gate Lane. Collection of the Maryland State Archives (MSA SC 2140-1-401).

named Henry Cowman. Snowden had again been arrested, but when Cowman told police he was not certain of his assailant's identity, he had been released.[7]

The detectives plied Snowden with questions for about four hours, pressing him in vain for a confession. The interrogation was intense, and it terrified him. He told them he had not gone to work on the day Lottie Brandon was found dead, that he had overslept, and that just before one p.m. he had gone out drinking at John Martin's saloon at the corner of West and Second—at the end of the block on which the Brandons lived. He admitted to having traversed Second Street but denied entering the Brandon home. And he could not account for his whereabouts for the hour before he arrived at the bar.

When told he had been seen leaving the murder house, he faltered and broke down. According to several accounts the intense questioning caused him to drop to the floor in a heap and beg for the questioning to stop.[8]

The police also determined that Snowden lived on Acton Lane, together with Edna Wallace, a Black woman with whom he was in a romantic relationship. Wallace, they discovered, sometimes did washing for the Brandons. They also noted that he had scratch marks on his face.[9]

When the questioning was finished, officers picked seven Black men from the crowd outside and brought them into the courthouse for a lineup, together with Snowden. The two sisters were then escorted into the room.[10]

"Do you see the man?" Detective Dougherty asked.

"That is the one, next to the door," Edith Creditt responded unhesitatingly, pointing to John Snowden.[11]

Outside, as many Blacks who had gotten word of Snowden's arrest also crowded around the courthouse, so did a contingent of white members of the Annapolis Machine Gun Company of the Maryland National Guard. Many believed this was no coincidence, especially when the guardsmen made it clear that they were prepared, if necessary, to "clear up any misunderstanding" that might arise. But their threatening appearance had not been sanctioned by their superiors, who rebuked them for their improvised show of force.[12]

Although Snowden insisted on his innocence, the police had more than enough evidence to hold him, and a decision was made to take him to Baltimore. It had been agreed several days earlier that if the suspect should turn out to be a Black man they would get him out of town as soon as possible. Although the county had recently spent $50,000 to replace the hundred-year-old jail with a new structure that was heavily fortified, the authorities had decided to take no chances with mob justice. Memories of the Henry Davis lynching were still fresh.[13]

There was no reason to hold Bernard Chambers, who easily persuaded detectives that he had had nothing to do with the murder, and State's Attorney Green came up with a clever ruse to get both men out of the courthouse safely. At eight thirty p.m., he took Chambers out the front door and announced to the crowd, by one estimate now more than a thousand strong, "Gentlemen, this man is innocent. We are satisfied that he had nothing to do with the crime. Please let him pass." The throng parted to let Chambers by, although someone struck him on the knee and another deliberately tripped him as he passed, to the amusement of the whites in the crowd. He quickly disappeared.[14]

At precisely the same time, Sheriff Sullivan, Mayor Strange, and the detectives hustled John Snowden out the back door and into the mayor's waiting automobile, which quickly spirited him off to Baltimore.[15]

# 9

## "We Have Got This Negro Dead Right"

Snowden reached Baltimore's police headquarters at 10:15 that evening and was taken immediately to Marshal Carter's private office, where he was handcuffed. Ordered to stand, he collapsed against a wall but was caught by Detective Pohler before he hit the floor. Carter said nothing to him about the crime, asking only if he had had anything to eat. When Snowden reported that he had not eaten since noon, the Marshal ordered a meal for him.

"Thank you, boss," Snowden replied.

There would be no more questions that night. He was taken to the central police Station, confined in a guarded cell, and permitted no visitors—not that anyone he knew would have known where to find him. He slept fitfully that night.[1]

The following morning, he was photographed and fingerprinted and his measurements were taken. As the *Baltimore Sun* reported, he was five feet ten inches tall, of "powerful build," and "of a dark, ginger-cake color," adding that he "appears to be a rather low grade of intelligence, judging by his looks." After his measurements were recorded, he was brought back to Marshal Carter's office for further grilling.[2]

John Snowden had lived his entire life in Annapolis. He was the son of Charles Snowden, a laborer, and Lizzie Tasker, who had borne at least fifteen children, most of whom had not survived to adulthood. Born in 1890, John had been enumerated in the 1900 federal census with his parents and four siblings at 40 Acton Lane—just a few houses away from where he now lived.

12. Baltimore Courthouse and Police Headquarters, ca. 1907. Clinton McCabe, *History of the Baltimore City Police Department, 1774–1907.*

He had attended the Stanton School on West Washington Street but only for about six months, after which time, at age fifteen or sixteen, he had gone to work driving an ice wagon. By 1910 he was residing with his maternal grandparents on Pleasant Street, together with two brothers and a cousin. And at some point in his late teens he had moved in with his partner, Edna Wallace.[3]

That morning, the papers were full of reports of his arrest and interrogation, and pundits weighed in on his guilt or innocence. In Annapolis, opinion was divided. Although many were certain the police had their man, others were not so sure. "Among the negroes Snowden has a rather peaceable reputation," the *Sun* noted, "but is known to be a hard drinker and a vicious fighter whenever a fight is forced on him. He is strongly built. The negroes declare, however, they do not believe Snowden is guilty."[4]

Morgan Bradford did. The local detective retained by the *Washington Times*, who seems to have reacted to newspaper reports rather than done much additional investigating of his own, declared in print that as far as he was concerned, the mystery was solved. He reminded readers that he had maintained all along that the murderer was a local person familiar with the Brandon home. But he failed to mention the fact that he had *also* predicted that the criminal was a female, and that he had claimed to have figured out the identity of the killer several days earlier, when Snowden's name had not even been mentioned.[5]

Detective Pohler boasted to the *Washington Times* that "we have got this negro dead right. I am sure he is the man who murdered Mrs. Brandon. The evidence against him is positive, uncontradictory and conclusive. I intend keeping after him until he breaks down and confesses." An unnamed deputy sheriff, quoted in the *Evening Star*, agreed. "We have almost got the rope around his neck," he told the paper.[6]

For her part, Grace Humiston wasn't so sure. "I still believe there are clues leading in entirely different directions which have not been followed, but which should be investigated," she wrote in the *Times*. She was bothered by the fact that all of the evidence arrayed against Snowden was circumstantial; there was nothing concrete.

Humiston also asserted in her column that Snowden had been in the Brandon home twice before the murder, once to deliver a load of wood and another when Edna Wallace was doing laundry for the Brandons. She did not name a source for the information, however. Parlett and Parlett, his employer, had found no record of him ever having made an ice delivery to the Brandons.

Humiston also revealed that although Edith Creditt and Mary Perkins had reported seeing Snowden leave the Brandon home between eleven and twelve o'clock, the Rev. Ernest S. Williams, the Black pastor who lived in the parsonage next door, had seen nothing, and was positive no one could have entered or left the home during that period without him noticing, as he was sitting on his front porch with a friend, he claimed, for the entire time.

Reverend Williams had told her he believed his wife had overheard a struggle in the Brandon flat the previous night. She was now out of town, but Grace Humiston had taken the minister to the state's attorney's office to repeat the story.

"I believe the credibility of the negro women should be thoroughly investigated inasmuch as they kept the evidence quiet so many days and disclosed it only at a time when another arrest was expected," Humiston asserted. By this, she probably meant Miriam King, the sisters' neighbor.

And finally Humiston couldn't resist another swipe at the Baltimore detectives. "It is singular, to my mind, that the detectives who have discredited the negro assault theory in this case from the very first, should suddenly give so much credence to it and become confident that they now have the guilty man in custody in Baltimore," she wrote.[7]

The search for new evidence continued. While Snowden sat in jail in Baltimore, Detectives Kratz and Pohler and Lieutenant Dougherty returned to Annapolis to search for more clues. An intense hunt was made for the bottle Mary Perkins claimed he had transferred from one pocket to another, on the theory that it might have been the object used to smash Lottie Brandon's forehead.

Edna Wallace was arrested, and she told a story that conflicted with Snowden's account of his activities on August 8. In what the detectives believed was a misguided effort to protect him, she told them he had not left the house that day. They searched the Acton Lane home she shared with Snowden for bloody clothing but found none.[8]

Then there was the question of missing money. Snowden had told police while still in Annapolis that he had been in possession of three dollars on the day of the crime, but Morgan Parlett, his employer, insisted he had been advanced only *two* dollars the afternoon before. Where had the other dollar come from? The bill Lottie Brandon had given her husband to buy bread and milk, which had been refused by the bakery, was nowhere to be found.

A drugstore clerk told police Lottie had purchased a small quantity of aspirin that morning and received change from a dollar bill, which would have accounted for that. But no money *at all* was found in her purse, nor was any aspirin recovered. The barkeep from the saloon Snowden visited recalled receiving a crumpled dollar bill that day, but he wasn't at all certain it had come from Snowden.[9]

Leroy Sisco, a young Black boy employed by John Strohmeyer, a West Street grocer, furnished the detectives with an additional clue. He claimed that while he was delivering flour in the neighborhood, he had seen Lottie May Brandon struggling with someone in the front

**13.** Marshal Robert Dudley Carter Sr. Clinton McCabe, *History of the Baltimore City Police Department, 1774–1907.*

room of her house on the morning of her death. She seemed to be trying to escape, he said, but was restrained by someone behind the door. He had not gotten a look at her assailant, however.[10]

And another possible lead came from Washington. John H. Redman, the husband of Lottie May's sister Dorothy, visited Marshal Carter in Baltimore that morning. He said that while living in Washington, Lottie May had caused the arrest of several Black men who had been loitering near her home. He wondered if Snowden might have been one of them who had gone to Annapolis to seek revenge.[11]

The detectives knew their work would be done if they could only wear Snowden down and elicit a confession. On the morning of August 14, they served him a large steak, potatoes, bread, and water for breakfast, and then resumed interrogation at nine a.m. It went on all morning. He had pulled himself together by this time and, as the *Sun* described, "began to spar for time and show more cunning in his answers." As far as his whereabouts on the day of the murder was concerned, he admitted that he had been *near* the Brandon home that day but continued steadfastly to deny any connection to the crime. When informed that Edna Wallace had told them he had been home all day, he had dismissed her as a "damn liar."[12]

At 2:15 that afternoon, Marshal Carter emerged and made a statement to the press. "There is not the slightest doubt in our minds we have got the guilty man," he announced. He added that the prisoner would be charged formally with murder that very afternoon, and that an inquest would be held in Annapolis the following evening.[13]

# 10

## "A Maze of Circumstantial Evidence"

The arrest of John Snowden did not obviate the need to exhume the body of Lottie May Brandon for a second autopsy. If anything, the lack of direct evidence against him made it more urgent. No one seems to have disputed Grace Humiston's assertion that there might be more to be learned from Lottie's remains than had been revealed in the hasty postmortem exam conducted in Annapolis on the night of her death. This included her family.

On Monday, August 14, therefore, Valentine Brandon called at District of Columbia police headquarters to give his permission for disinterment, and then, together with W. H. Sardo, the Washington undertaker who had arranged Lottie's burial, went to the city's health department to obtain a permit. The plan was to remove the body from Glenville Cemetery that afternoon and transport it to the Washington Emergency Hospital for a more thorough examination. The state of Maryland was to bear all expenses.[1]

The postmortem was conducted that evening by Drs. Joyce and Hopkins, both of whom had done the initial autopsy, together with Drs. J. R. Nevitt and William B. Carr, coroner and deputy coroner respectively, of the District of Columbia. Also on hand were Lieutenant Dougherty, Sheriff Sullivan, and three local police detectives. But nobody representing the murder suspect participated.

Despite instructions from State's Attorney Green not to reveal the results, they were leaked almost immediately and widely reported in the press. They did not call into dispute any of the earlier conclusions, but they did reveal two new, and very important, findings.

First of all, the postmortem found what Washington's *Evening Star* euphemistically characterized as "certain conditions which led them to believe that Mrs. Brandon had been attacked by a man." Up to now, there had been no public report of the analysis of the samples of mucus discharge found on her body and sent to the University Hospital in Baltimore on the night of the first autopsy. Anne Arundel county health officer Dr. Hopkins had suspected it was semen, and now, without stating so directly, he more or less confirmed it. He told the press that Mrs. Brandon had been "criminally attacked"—that is, an attempt had been made at sexual assault—by a male during her ordeal. He did not assert, however, that her assailant had actually committed rape.[2]

Second, the examination had yielded strong evidence that her assailant was African American. This time the doctors looked more carefully at Lottie's fingers, removing five of her fingernails. They discovered what they believed to be skin underneath some of the nails, suggesting that the dead woman had had not been a passive victim but rather had fought back against her assailant and left some marks on him. And a microscopic examination revealed that that skin had belonged to a Black person. There were also a couple of short black hairs, which could have come from Snowden, who had scratches on his face where his beard was heaviest.[3]

Grace Humiston, never given to modesty, took a victory lap at the news. "It is a matter of very great satisfaction to me that I suggested and as far as possible insisted upon the disinterment of the body," she crowed. "The disinterment has definitely established at least the race and color of the fiend who committed the crime, and has thereby eliminated from consideration and suspicion any white persons who, under blind and conflicting circumstances, might never have been able to outlive the lurking thought that they were connected in some way to the tragedy." She had a right to boast about the new evidence uncovered as a result of the second autopsy, but she made no mention of the fact that she had previously dismissed the possibility that the killer had been Black as highly unlikely, or that she had favored the theory that the murder had been the work of a woman.[4]

Randall Haislup had a different, and predictably emotional, reaction. "I would like to get my hands on the negro who killed my daughter,"

**14.** Central Dispensary and Emergency Hospital, Washington DC, where the second postmortem examination of Lottie May Brandon's remains was conducted. U.S. National Library of Medicine (101403381).

he wrote in the *Times*. "I would save the state a lot of expense." But he didn't go so far as to accuse Snowden. "I hope a confession will be obtained from Snowden, if he committed the crime, right away," he wrote. "If he did not, I hope the real assailant will be captured."[5]

Snowden continued to protest his innocence, but the news from the Washington autopsy was not helpful to his case, especially since he bore what appeared to be newly healing scratch marks on his face that he was unable to explain to the satisfaction of his questioners. One, a half-inch long, was on his right cheek; another, an inch in length, was on his left. And there were scratches on both of his arms. He insisted the marks were left over from a scuffle he had had with Edna Wallace ten days earlier.[6]

But here, too, Edna had not been of much help to him. She had initially contradicted him by telling police he had not left her house on the day of the murder. After the newspapers printed his story, however, she admitted that he had, in fact, gone out that day. Most unfortunately for him, she denied having scratched him, and insisted she had seen the marks for the very first time when he got home that day.

"Did you scratch this man's face?" Detective Dougherty had asked her.

"No," she responded. "I was sitting on the porch with him and noticed his face was scratched. I asked him where he got those scratches and he said he didn't know he had any and would not tell me anything about them."[7]

If Edna Wallace was trying to help him, she wasn't doing an especially good job of it.

As the relentless questioning continued, Snowden filled in a bit more of his story. He had left his home just before eleven a.m. on the morning of the murder, he said, visited a saloon, and then went to the home of his sister Sedonia Isaacs. He had spoken briefly with her daughter—his niece—and then walked up Second Street. While he was passing the Brandon home, he had thought he heard a friend calling him, which caused him to pause in front of the house.[8]

Then he told police for the first time that as he stopped to light a cigarette, he had seen a Black man he knew run from the Brandon house. He identified him as John Henry Green, who, together with his brother Frank, worked on a farm owned by John E. Wagner several miles outside of town. The local police dutifully hauled both John and Frank Green in for questioning. But Wagner, a methodical man who kept time sheets for all of his employees, produced documentation that proved that both brothers had worked for him all day on the day of the murder—from seven a.m. until six p.m.[9]

Coroner William S. Welch had announced that there would be a formal inquest that evening, and the plans for it included bringing Snowden back to Annapolis. His presence was not required under the law, but the Baltimore detectives thought that confronting him with the raft of evidence against him might evoke the confession they continued to believe was probably forthcoming. Arguing against returning him to town was the worry that, as the *Evening Star* put it, "the citizens will take affairs in their own hands and 'wind up this case in short order.'" But Sheriff Sullivan and his men were confident the new jailhouse was well fortified against an invasion and that they could stave off any attempt at a lynching.[10]

State's Attorney Green, however, changed his mind about the inquest. He decided to postpone it until the investigation was over. For one thing, Mary Perkins and Edith Creditt, Snowden's principal accusers, were in a highly nervous state and in no condition to testify. Mary, it was reported, was bordering on a breakdown. According to the *Star*, the sisters had been severely upbraided by an unnamed Black clergyman for their testimony in the investigation. "The negro preacher denounced the two maids in the most vehement language and concluded his denunciation by calling down upon them the vengeance of God for what he called their treachery toward one of their own race."[11]

For his part, Green found the women quite credible. "Usually our trouble is in getting colored people to testify against members of their own race, and when they *volunteer* information the assumption is that they are telling the truth," he told the *Times*.

That afternoon, Snowden was formally charged with the murder of Lottie May Brandon. "We have a very strong case against John Snowden and are bending all our energy to strengthen the chain of circumstantial evidence against him," Green told the press. But although Sheriff Sullivan was convinced they had found their man, Green wanted more evidence, and the lack of a confession disturbed him. The detectives believed an admission of guilt was simply a matter of time, so Green was not yet willing to declare the case closed and Snowden guilty.[12]

Neither was much of Annapolis—Black *or* white.

If racism was behind the belief of those who thought the murder must have been the work of an African American, it was also behind that of many who didn't. "There is a decided belief among many persons about the city that the negro is innocent and that the crime was committed by . . . someone in the immediate neighborhood," the *Evening Capital* wrote. As the paper explained, "It is realized that there are more or less bad characters among the negro population of the city, but many persons have pointed to the fact that a negro would hardly enter the home of a white man in broad daylight, and in a thickly settled section of the city, and commit such a brutal act."

It added that a Black murderer would not have left behind the jewelry on Lottie's bureau or the diamond ring on her finger. And then there was the stubborn fact that Snowden would not confess. "As a general rule," the paper smugly assured its readers, "a negro breaks down when he is submitted to the third degree methods of examination."[13]

The next day, a hearse transported the body of Lottie May Brandon, in its gray casket, from the Emergency Hospital back to Glenwood Cemetery. With only her tearful husband, his brother, and the undertaker present this time, and with no prayers and no flowers except the faded blooms from three days earlier, it was returned unceremoniously to her grave, never to be disturbed again.[14]

# 11

## "I Ain't Scared"

On the morning of Wednesday, August 15, the detectives subjected John Snowden to the full-court press. They wanted a confession and they sensed one might be near. The prisoner was brought back to Marshal Carter's office and they went to work on him.

First they confronted him with the results of the second autopsy. According to press reports, he began trembling violently. The air of defiance seen the previous evening was gone. He cowered in his chair as he was told of the skin found under Lottie Brandon's fingernails and of its pigmentation.[1]

Then they brought in John Green, the man Snowden claimed to have seen emerge from the Brandon home. As Green looked squarely at him, Snowden looked away. Asked why he had implicated Green, he simply stammered. Shortly afterward, the Green brothers were freed.

Next Edna Wallace was ushered in. Carter kept the couple several feet apart. As Snowden tried to meet her eye, Edna repeated that she had not scratched him, and that she had first noticed the marks on his face on the afternoon of the murder. She told the detectives she and John had been sitting on her porch when they first heard about the death of Lottie Brandon but that John had evinced little interest in the topic and had never left the porch. Snowden agreed with her account of how they had learned of the crime. But when Carter asked him why he had said Edna had scratched him, he fell silent.

"We have the man," Marshal Carter told the *Evening Star* later. "There is no question in my mind that Snowden is the guilty negro," he said. Indeed, a *Star* reporter wrote that by this time they had basically given up on pursuing other theories, including the one that envisioned a female murderer, and were focusing their efforts on strengthening their case against John Snowden.[2]

To that end, back in Annapolis and Washington detectives continued chasing down leads. They visited Parlett and Parlett to ask Snowden's fellow ice men if he had said anything to them about the crime. And they probed the reputations of Edith Creditt and Mary Perkins to determine whether they would make credible witnesses. Father Cornelius J. Warren, the rector of St. Mary's Catholic Church, of which the sisters were members, vouched for them and said he felt sure they were telling the truth, though he reminded the detectives that the two women were still very anxious and upset, and in fear for their lives. "They feel that if the authorities do not succeed in pinning the murder on Snowden and he should be released, he will do them whatever injury is in his power, even to killing them," he said.[3]

In order to corroborate the testimony of Reverend Williams, who had told them he had been on the front porch of his home on the morning of the murder and had seen no one enter or leave the Brandons' house, the detectives also interviewed the Rev. William A. C. Hughes. He was a Washington preacher who had been sitting with Williams on the porch that day. He echoed Williams's account.[4]

August 15 also saw the end of any good feeling between the Baltimore detectives conducting the investigation and Grace Humiston, the carpetbagger from New York. Detective Dougherty had resolved to question Reverend Williams's wife, Mary, who Williams believed had heard a scuffle at the Brandon home the night before the murder, but she had taken a trip to West River, several miles outside of town. When Dougherty and Williams got into Dougherty's automobile to drive there to speak with her, Grace Humiston demanded to come along with them.

"You cannot get into this machine, madam," Dougherty recalled telling her.

"Why not?" she asked. As Dougherty recalled it later, she then recited a list of her credentials, asserting that "I represent the State in this case and I am a member of the New York Police Department" and flashing her badge.

"I don't care whom you represent, madam; you cannot go in this machine. I know that you are a newspaper reporter and that you are writing articles for a newspaper about this case under your own name. I am not going to let the Baltimore newspaper men or any other reporters go with me, and you can't go. When Baltimore detectives need the assistance of New York detectives, the chief of the Baltimore Police will ask the aid of the chief of the New York Police."

"You're not giving that negro a fair show and I'll get a lawyer for him," Humiston threatened, as far as Dougherty could recall.

"That's your privilege," he responded coldly as he drove off.[5]

Humiston was not about to give Dougherty the last word, however. And after she read his account of their interchange in the *Washington Herald*, which had referred to her as an "amateur detective," she used her *Times* column to counterattack:

Why Detective Dougherty should make such a deliberately false statement to a newspaper, I cannot imagine, but I never even intimated that I represented the New York Police. I am a lawyer and investigator, and as such I'm trying to solve the mystery of the murder of Mrs. Brandon. As to the "amateur detective," it seems to me that Dougherty and some of his associates of the Baltimore Police have played this part to perfection.

They failed to rope off the premises where the murdered woman was found—a precaution which, it seems to me, any detective would have the judgment to take. As a result, scores of people were allowed to pass through the house and into the room where the crime was committed. Further, they never knew that screams had been heard until I made inquiries. They didn't know that Mrs. King had heard screams, but when I saw her and talked with her, she admitted to me that she had.

Dougherty and his associates have treated me with great discourtesy. . . . I am going over to Baltimore today and shall make it a point to call on the Chief of Police there and tell him of the way I have been treated. I am sure he will be surprised.[6]

She apparently did not get very far with Dougherty's boss, however, because the following day she was denied permission to interview

Snowden in his cell. Thus thwarted, she abruptly returned to New York to take up a new assignment.[7]

Annapolis, however, had not seen the last of her.

Dougherty's annoyance with the press may have been shared by his colleagues. There is evidence that at this point the detectives were getting fed up with the scrutiny and second-guessing they were receiving in the newspapers. For his part, State's Attorney Green adopted a policy of absolute silence.[8]

But the press could also be used to advantage. To persuade the papers that they had done their level best to break Snowden, the detectives decided to permit reporters from Baltimore and Washington to question him themselves. They even thought it possible that the journalists might be more successful than they had been in penetrating the prisoner's defenses.[9]

Snowden seemed nervous to the newsmen; he chewed on matchsticks and shifted his cap from hand to hand as he talked. But he didn't really say anything that had not already been reported. The *Washington Times* printed some of the questions and answers verbatim. And since it was the first time reporters had gotten anywhere near Snowden, they also treated readers to their first detailed description of him:

> Snowden appears to be of almost pure African stock. His head is bullet shaped and closely cropped; the bridge of his nose is slightly prominent, but the nostrils are broad and flat; his lips are thick and prominent and overshadow his chin.
>
> In figure the negro is short and stocky, and of powerful build. He was dressed in a dirty cotton shirt, with short sleeves, and open at the neck, a pair of tattered black trousers and canvas "sneakers" that were once white, but are now very much dilapidated.

Since Grace Humiston and others had asserted that he had been in the Brandon home before, they began the interview by asking if he had ever visited there.

"I never was in Mrs. Brandon's home in my life," he told them. "I only went by her house a week ago yesterday because I wasn't working, and was going a roundabout way to Martin's saloon."

"When was your face scratched?" he was asked.

"That happened a week ago Sunday, when I was fooling with Edna."

"You did not get them Wednesday?"

"No."

"Did you hear Edna say she asked you on Wednesday where you got those scratches?"

"Well, she never asked me such a question."

"Then she lied about it, did she?"

"Well, it ain't so."

"She's a liar then, is she?"

"Yes, she lied."

"But you and she had not quarreled, and yet she is trying to get you in trouble by lying. How is that?"

Snowden had no answer for this.

"Did Edna wash for Mrs. Brandon?"

"Sometimes."

"Did you ever take the washing home for her?"

"I never took any washing there at all."

"Who did you see around Preacher Williams's home, next door to the Brandon home, when you went by there?"

"I saw Preacher Williams on his back porch. He was bending over like he was picking something off the floor."

"Was anyone on the front porch?"

"No, there was nobody there."

"You did not see Preacher Williams sitting out there with another colored preacher from Washington?"

"No, I didn't see anybody else around his house at all."

This, of course, contradicted Reverend Williams's story that he and Reverend Hughes had sat on his front porch all morning on the day of the murder.

"Do you know Mary Perkins?"

"I know her when I see her."

"She is a good girl, isn't she? Does she associate with you?"

"Well, I know who she is."

"Why would she say you came out of the Brandon house if it wasn't so?"

"I don't know."

"Do you know Edith Queen?" This was a reference to Edith Creditt; Queen had been her surname before marriage.

"Yes, she is Mary Perkins' sister, and her husband—he's dead—was a cousin of mine. She is some kin to me."

"Do you think she would lie about her own kin?"

"I don't know why she would."

"What did you have in the bottle you took out of your pocket in front of the Brandon house?"

"I never had any bottle in my pocket, and I never took any out."

"But both of these women say they saw you take a bottle out of your pocket. Why would they say that?"

Snowden made no reply.

"When you bought those three bottles of beer at Martin's saloon on Wednesday, what did you pay him with?"

"A one-dollar bill."

"What did Martin say about it being torn?"

"It wasn't torn. It was just like any other dollar bill."

"Where had you gotten it?"

"Mr. Morgan Parlett give it to me when he paid me off the day before."

Finally, the reporter wanted to know how Snowden thought the case against him would play out. "How do you think you're going to come out on this charge?" he asked.

"I got to come out all right. I ain't done nothin'."

"But the police say they've got a strong case against you."

"They ain't. They can't have. I never done it," he responded. "They'll find it out pretty soon and turn me loose. I ain't scared. I never did it."[10]

# 12

## "Guilty Men and Women Do Not Always Confess"

The *Baltimore Sun* observed that "no negro has been grilled so severely as Snowden," who despite the best efforts of the police department's crackerjack interrogators declined to confess.

Those best efforts, however, may have been quite aggressive and even illegal, as would be asserted later. But despite all of their "third degree" interrogation tactics, nobody broke John Snowden, and after Thursday, August 16, they stopped trying. He did, however, remain under "secret observation" in his cell, where police thought it significant that he was passing sleepless nights, eating little, and mumbling to himself.

To be sure, he had been caught in several lies and inconsistencies, but a confession, which would have closed the case against him, wouldn't come. Absent such a declaration, the authorities were loath to claim publicly that they were certain they had their man. They would not even admit that they had more or less ceased to pursue other possibilities.[1]

As a practical matter, though, they were already convinced of Snowden's guilt, and Lieutenant Dougherty asserted defensively that a confession was not absolutely necessary. "Guilty men and women do not *always* confess," he told the *Washington Times*, "and especially is this true of persons like Snowden who have had previous experience with the police and to whom rigid cross-questioning is no novelty. All these circumstances point to him as the guilty man. We are building up a circumstantial case against him which he cannot successfully combat when brought to trial."[2]

Building that case required the detectives to tie up a lot of loose ends, however, and to that end, they continued to spend their days in Annapolis questioning people. In another setback for Snowden, both his sister and his niece denied that he had stopped at their house on the morning of the murder, insisting they had not seen him at all that day. That part of Snowden's story was now also contradicted.

Snowden had told Detective Pohler that while he was on Second Street, he had paused for a short conversation with Florence Baker, who lived at no. 19, about halfway between the Brandons' house and Martin's saloon. She had asked him why he was not at work, he had reported, and made a comment about how hard he and his fellow ice men had to labor. But when questioned, Mrs. Baker recalled no such conversation, or even seeing Snowden on that day.[3]

To account for his whereabouts the night before the murder, Snowden had told police he had been shooting craps. He even named three other participants in the game. But when these men were interrogated by State's Attorney Green, none confirmed the story.[4]

A final piece of bad news for Snowden was a statement from Coroner William S. Welsh that in his opinion, based on the fingerprints and other wounds found on Lottie Brandon's body, her assailant had been a man of unusual strength rather than a woman. Welsh also opined that the brutality indicated by them "leads him to believe the man was a negro." This little piece of abject racial prejudice was not evidence, of course, but Welsh was a respected figure in town and it would be he who would preside over the inquest into Lottie's death.[5]

Whether all this was enough to keep Snowden behind bars, however, was an open question, and on the afternoon of August 16, two attorneys set about trying to free him. Although it is not clear who engaged or paid them, two attorneys, Jerry L. Smith of Annapolis and Henry H. Dineen of Baltimore, went to court on the prisoner's behalf to obtain his release on a writ of habeas corpus on the grounds of insufficient evidence. To nobody's surprise, the effort failed.

Smith predicted to the *Washington Times* that if and when Snowden came to trial, he would not be tried in Annapolis. "On a charge of this kind, feeling in Annapolis runs too high to ensure an impartial hearing," he asserted. "I think we should have no trouble getting the change of

**15.** Leroy Brandon, 1921. Courtesy of James Ball.

venue to some court outside of Anne Arundel County. Whether the case would be transferred to Baltimore or not, it is too far in advance to say." He added his view that, given the evidence against Snowden, it was by no means certain that a Grand Jury would even indict him.[6]

On Saturday, August 18, Valentine Brandon returned to Annapolis to wind up his business affairs, which included closing his wife's bank account, seeking a payout on her life insurance policy, and drawing some back pay from his employer. He brought along his father. For the first time since the night of his wife's death, he entered the home they had shared. He told a reporter he had no interest in reclaiming the furniture in the house, calling it "naturally repugnant to me."

Leroy Brandon took the opportunity to question Mary Perkins and Edith Creditt across the street and others who were expected to be witnesses against Snowden. He later told the press that from what he had learned, all indications were that Snowden had killed his daughter-in-law, and that he hoped the man would confess.

Valentine told the press at the same time that he was considering enlisting in the military. He had registered for the draft in Annapolis and was in any event likely to be called for service in the not-too-distant future. "If I went to France," he told the *Times*, "it would afford an opportunity for me to get my mind off this tragedy."[7]

Shortly after the discovery of the murder, the police had begun to receive crank letters, several claiming to reveal the name of the killer. More than one accused Valentine of the crime. They were typically handwritten and unsigned, and the authorities never shared them with the public, nor did they take them seriously. One, written from Los Angeles, was typical. It read:

August 19th 1917

Gov Harrington of Maryland
and Mayor Strange of Annapolis

Dear sirs:

Stop all efforts in endeavoring to obtain further information relative to the murder of Mrs. Valentine Brandon.

The <u>murderer</u> is within your reach. Valentine Brandon the husband is the man who committed the horrible crime. Motive—he had grown tired of her in every respect. Murder premeditated several months. The man is feigning grief, interest, knowledge etc. acting well his part . . .

The horrible deed veiled in mystery nerve racking and baffling the best and wisest can be solved in a very short time. "<u>Jail</u>" <u>Valentine Brandon</u>. Let him read this letter from the west. Watch his countenance. Perhaps it will reveal what lies in his heart. "A confession."

Yours Truly
"Justice"
Los Angeles California

A formal inquest into the death of Lottie May Brandon still had not been scheduled, although all signs pointed to reconvening the coroner's jury soon. The inquest had been postponed several times, once to await more concrete evidence against Snowden; a second time

The murderer is within your reach. Valentine Brandon the husband, is the man who committed the horrible crime.

Motive— he had grown tired of her in every respect.

Murder premeditated several months.

The man is feigning grief interest, knowledge etc. acting well his part.

16. One page of a letter from an anonymous correspondent to Maryland governor Emerson Harrington and Annapolis mayor James Strange fingering Valentine Brandon for the crime. Collection of the Maryland State Archives (MSA S1046, 2-30-1-4).

because both State's Attorney Green and Sheriff Sullivan, who sat on the local draft board, were busy compiling the names of the next four hundred men to be sent to war; and a third time to allow police one more round of interviews with Miriam King and her husband, which were concluded on Sunday, August 19. But the inquest was likely to be a formality anyway, as it was already crystal clear who would be accused of the murder. Virtually all of the evidence the police had gathered pointed to the Black man being held in Baltimore.[8]

Whether John Snowden would be brought back to Annapolis for the inquest was an open question. He himself was said to be apprehensive about the possibility of a lynching, though the authorities were confident they could handle any disturbance. Local police had already made tentative arrangements for reinforcements, and Sheriff Sullivan was prepared to swear in temporary deputies to help keep order if necessary. Plus, several Baltimore detectives would escort him back to Annapolis if and when his presence was sought.[9]

On Tuesday, August 21, the detectives announced that they were absolutely confident John Snowden was the murderer and that their investigation was complete. They then turned their work over to State's Attorney Green and returned to Baltimore until they were needed to testify.

But although the authorities had given up on extracting a confession from Snowden, they weren't averse to letting others try. To this end, Governor Emerson Harrington gave permission to the Rev. J. W. Hogue, a member of the Prisoners' Aid Society of Maryland, to visit Snowden. With many years' experience counseling prisoners under his belt, he was confident he could obtain a confession if he appealed to Snowden on religious grounds.[10]

He was quite wrong.

# 13

## "Fairer for the Man, the County, the State"

The coroner's jury everyone assumed would resume its work once the Baltimore detectives submitted their report to State's Attorney Green never actually reconvened. Confident in the evidence he had at hand, Green decided to bypass an inquest. He never recalled the coroner's jury and decided to present the case against John Snowden to a grand jury once the Circuit Court for Anne Arundel County began its October session.

If the body indicted Snowden, as Green felt sure it would, he would likely proceed immediately to trial, and the lack of a public record of an inquest would place the defense at a decided disadvantage. Without one, Snowden's attorneys would be unsure of the fact pattern the state intended to use to portray the cause of Lottie May Brandon's death.

This meant that Snowden remained in custody in Baltimore for the entire month of September 1917, although he was no longer subjected to daily interrogation or heightened scrutiny. On Tuesday afternoon, October 2, he was smuggled back to Annapolis, where he was incarcerated in the county jail on Calvert Street. A handsome brick building built in 1913, the new jail, with its thirty-eight cells, had cost $50,000.[1]

The police denied that Snowden had been transferred, however, and his presence in Annapolis was not confirmed by the press until the following Friday. The reason for the secrecy was the same as it had been when he was rushed out of town in August; the authorities wanted to avoid any public demonstration against him and any possible violence. They might have overestimated the danger, though, because many of

**17.** Anne Arundel County Jail on Calvert Street. Collection of the Maryland State Archives (MSA SC 2140-1-667).

the newspapers insisted that a substantial number of Annapolitans—Black *and* white—simply did not believe he was guilty.[2]

The investigation of Lottie Brandon's murder had already cost Anne Arundel County $1,000, which included a $415 bill for the services of the sheriff, $275 for those of the Baltimore detectives, $100 for Dr. Joyce's services in performing the autopsies and $13 for exhuming Lottie's body in Washington.[3]

Snowden's case, if it went to trial, was expected to cost $1,000 more, and it would have been heard by Judge James R. Brashears, who had been on the bench since 1908, if the judge had not died suddenly on August 19. State's Attorney Green expected to be named to the job, but it went instead to state senator Robert Moss. Under the law, however, Moss would serve only until the next general election in November. Green, disappointed, announced almost immediately that he would run for the bench at that time. For the moment, however, he had to bide his time.[4]

Moss, who had also served as secretary of the Maryland senate, had been admitted to the bar in 1886. A staunch Democrat, he was a descendant of some of the original settlers of Anne Arundel County, who had arrived in 1649. He lost no time in assuming his new responsibilities.[5]

**18.** Judge Robert Moss. Courtesy of the Circuit Court for Anne Arundel County.

The way the Fifth Judicial Circuit Court operated was to draw a panel of forty-eight prominent male citizens—women were not permitted to serve on juries in Maryland until 1947—whose service would begin the day court convened and continue for the duration of the session. Of these, twenty-three would be chosen to sit on the grand jury, which was concerned only with indictments, and the remainder would be relegated to service on petit juries, which sat in actual trials. During this particular session, the most prominent cases on the docket would be those of the murders of Lottie May Brandon and of Abraham Edelstein, a cattle dealer to whose slaying a man had already confessed. And of those two, the Brandon case, because of its racial implications, was clearly the more radioactive.

Potential jurors for this session were called in three panels: forty-eight on September 21 and more on October 1 and 10 to replenish the pool after many in the first group were excused for one reason or another. All their names were published in the *Evening Capital*. Of those called, a review of the 1920 census records reveals that the vast majority, and very likely *all*, were white. Since Blacks accounted for more than 25 percent of the residents of Anne Arundel County at the time, a systematic effort to keep them off of juries seems very likely.[6]

All-white juries were not a rare phenomenon. Although it had been unconstitutional since 1880 for Blacks to be *categorically* excluded from jury pools, this was nonetheless often done in turn-of-the-century Annapolis. Those who assembled venire panels were white men charged with selecting men of means and standing in the community, and they almost always chose other white men. There were, in fact, only two Black businessmen in town who were routinely included in the mix for jury service in the early years of the century.[7]

In his very first charge to a grand jury, Judge Moss tried to impress the potential jurors with the seriousness of the cases they would be asked to consider. In addition to the Brandon and Edelstein cases, there would be four other murder cases, two of assault with intent to rape, fourteen larceny cases, two pickpocketing, and five assault cases. When Moss got to the specifics of the Brandon case, he urged the jurors to "spare neither time, labor nor expense in order that the guilty party or parties may be brought to justice," noting that in his opinion, the crime was "the most horrible in the annals of Anne Arundel County."[8]

Moss designated former orphan's court judge Benjamin Watkins Sr. foreman of the grand jury; he and the others selected were all white. The body began its inquiry into the Brandon murder on October 15, with State's Attorney Nicholas H. Green leading the prosecution. The entire process took only a couple of days. Valentine Brandon is known to have testified, as did detectives Kratz, Pohler, and Dougherty, and, presumably, Mary Perkins and Edith Creditt. And on October 18, to nobody's surprise, the body returned an indictment against John Snowden. It consisted of two counts: one for first-degree and the other for second-degree murder.[9]

Snowden, of course, pleaded not guilty, and his trial was set for Monday, October 29, though there was widespread expectation that the defense would ask for a change in venue, which was Snowden's right under the Maryland constitution. Many believed that Annapolis jurors might be prejudiced against him or have already made up their minds that he was guilty.

On the Sunday before the trial was to begin, however, the papers carried the news that Snowden did *not* intend to ask for a venue change. What remained unclear was whether he would ask for a jury trial at all or allow the case to be decided by Judge Moss and his associate, Judge William H. Forsythe, a Carroll County jurist who was assisting because two judges were the rule in capital cases.[10]

Long before ten a.m. on the morning of Monday, October 29, when court was scheduled to convene, the streets outside the courthouse were jammed with people, Black and white. Snowden was brought to the venue by motor car and was led into the building in handcuffs. Those assembled got their first look at the man, whom the *Evening Capital* described as "short of stature, stockily built, brown-skinned with heavy, thick lips and a pudgy face."[11]

He entered the courtroom betraying no emotion, seemingly oblivious to the presence of spectators. There were more women in court that morning than was usual, many craning their necks for a good look at him. He paused long enough to talk with a Baltimore reporter, telling him that "I'm innocent and I know no twelve men on a jury will convict an innocent man."[12]

The prisoner had engaged forty-eight-year-old A. Theodore Brady, an Annapolis attorney and Anne Arundel County Democratic boss, as his chief counsel. He had been a member of the state house and senate from 1898 to 1912 and was a descendant of early Maryland settlers. The choice of Brady was quite surprising, because he had been no friend of the Black man. He was the very man who had spearheaded the successful effort in the legislature in 1908 to deprive most of the city's African American men—no women of any race were yet eligible—of the right to vote. By one estimate, the amendment robbed some seven hundred of Annapolis's eight hundred Black voters, who generally chose Republicans during this period, of the franchise until it was invalidated by the Supreme Court in 1915.[13]

Brady would be assisted by Charles S. Williams, a Black lawyer from Washington DC who was granted a special order by the court to permit him to appear. But when the trial began, a third attorney showed up, ostensibly also on Snowden's behalf. He was W. Ashbie Hawkins, a prominent Black attorney from Baltimore. The Virginia-born Hawkins had received his initial legal training at the University of Maryland, which had admitted Black students beginning in 1887, but had been expelled in 1891 when the school resegregated in response to complaints from white students. One of Baltimore's first Black lawyers, he had completed his legal education at Howard University Law School and been in practice since 1897.

But Hawkins had not been appointed by Snowden to represent him. He had been retained by an African American congregation in Baltimore on the defendant's behalf. When he showed up in court, both the prosecution *and* the defense objected to his appearance, and he was not permitted to sit at the defense table.[14]

Actually, nobody sat at the defense *or* the prosecutor's tables for very long that morning, because Anne Arundel County was in the process of sending its first quota of 100 young Black men into the army. Since State's Attorney Green chaired the local draft board and Sheriff Sullivan sat on that body as well, both men were expected to see the men off and march in their honor parade. Moss, too, wished to participate, so he was forced to postpone the proceedings until 12:45 p.m. that day.[15]

When court reconvened, Judge Moss announced his determination to exclude all minors and "wall flowers" from the proceedings, by which he meant curiosity-seekers. He also instructed the bailiffs to permit no one entry once all of the seats in the room were filled.[16]

After attorney Brady announced that Snowden's preference was for a jury trial, the first order of business was to pick a jury from the pool of twenty-five talesmen who remained after the grand jury had been chosen. Attorney Brady was more than prepared; he had compiled a type-written list of questions to ask each potential juror, something to which the prosecution objected. After discussion, Judge Moss commented that if Brady were permitted to interrogate each candidate with all of the questions on his list, a jury of twelve men would never be achieved. As hard as it is to believe, Moss ruled the whole list out of order.[17]

In cases of this kind, the law permitted the prosecution only ten challenges to specific candidates for the jury, but those of the defense were unlimited. And by the time all twenty-five men had been exam-

**19.** Anne Arundel County Courthouse, ca. 1907. Raphael Tuck and Sons.

ined, most had been excused, either because they had already formed an opinion about Snowden's guilt or innocence, because they objected to capital punishment, or for some other reason.[18] By the end of the day, only six men had been empaneled, all white, all middle-aged and all farmers. And there were no more left to interview.

So Moss instructed Sheriff Sullivan to summon a panel of twenty-four more "of the most representative men" to appear the following morning at nine thirty, making clear he was to draft only mature men, and none from among the throngs who had gathered outside the courthouse. The assignment surely forced the sheriff and his men to work overtime, but by the next morning there were twenty-four new talesmen in court. Probably due to the rush, their names were never printed in the *Evening Capital*.[19]

The process of voir dire continued. By ten thirty a.m., eleven jurors had been empaneled, but the prosecution had used up its allotment of ten challenges. What this meant was that the defense could have its choice from all the remaining talesmen to fill the last spot on the jury.[20]

**20.** State's Attorney Nicholas H. Green. *Evening Capital*, November 8, 1911.

Then something quite unexpected happened. "Like a thunderbolt from a clear sky," the *Evening Capital* declared dramatically, just as Brady was in the process of examining a potential twelfth juror, State's Attorney Green moved for a change in venue.[21]

There had been persistent rumors that the *defense* might make such a motion on the grounds that Snowden could not count on a fair trial in the city in which the murder had occurred. But no one had expected it to come from the prosecution. Attorney Brady was taken by surprise by the request, which was unprecedented in the history of the local circuit court.

As a practical matter, Judge Moss had no choice but to grant the motion; the state's attorney, like the defense, was entitled to a venue switch as a matter of right. But exactly where Snowden would be tried was then the subject of spirited consultation between the attorneys. Green suggested Carroll County, but Brady objected, as did Judge Moss, who thought the expense of transporting witnesses to Westminster, the county seat, would cause hardship to the defense. Moss then suggested the city of Baltimore, which was unacceptable to Green. Finally, the two sides and the judge agreed on Towson, Baltimore County's county seat.

Green made no effort to clarify his reasons. He simply stated that transferring the trial would be "fairer for the man, the county, the state and all parties concerned." Brady, for his part, took the move as a sign that the state lacked sufficient evidence to convict, though if that were the cause, it is hard to see how a change of venue would have made any difference.[22]

One likely reason, however, was not discussed at the time. Because names of the additional talesmen recruited overnight were never published, it is impossible today to determine the group's racial makeup, but it is possible that the group included at least one Black man. Had that been so, it could easily explain the sudden change of heart by State's Attorney Green, who up until that point had seen nothing unfair to Snowden, the county, *or* the state about an Annapolis-based trial.

Having exhausted all of his challenges, Green would have been powerless to keep a Black man off of the jury, and given the overwhelming sentiment in the local Black community that Snowden was innocent of the charges against him, this may simply have been a risk he was unwilling to take. Such a consideration could explain why he was also opposed to moving the trial to downtown Baltimore, where the chance of getting a Black talesman on the venire panel was surely much higher than in other locations. Also possible is that Green was concerned about empaneling even a white juror who might be sympathetic to the defendant; there were many such people in town.

If Green *had* been trying to ensure a lily-white jury, he would not have been breaking the law as it was then understood. Race-based use of peremptory challenges was not ruled unconstitutional until 1986. It was, in fact, standard practice for many prosecutors in Maryland, even as late as the 1970s, to keep Blacks off juries in cases in which a defendant was Black.[23] On the other hand, if the exhortation by the judge to recruit only the "most representative men" had been a dog whistle to the sheriff to confine his choices to white men, or if Sheriff Sullivan had, on his own initiative, pointedly excluded Blacks from the new panel he recruited overnight, that *would* have been a violation of federal law. As previously noted, the Supreme Court had ruled in 1880 that *categorical* exclusion of Blacks from jury pools simply because of their race ran counter to the Equal Protection Clause of the Fourteenth Amendment.[24]

Whatever Green's or Sullivan's motives, the trial of John Snowden would be moved to the Baltimore County Circuit Court at Towson, whose docket was already quite full. It now looked as if Snowden would have to languish in jail at least until January before he could have his day in court.[25]

# PART 2　　1918

# 14

## "Most Heinous and Diabolical"

A special train took John Snowden, in the custody of Sheriff Sullivan and several policemen, from Annapolis's West Street Station to Towson in time for the opening of the trial for his life on the morning of Wednesday, January 23, 1918. Anne Arundel County state's attorney Nicholas H. Green had been in Towson since the day before, consulting with George Hartman, his Baltimore County counterpart, who would assist in the prosecution. Hartman assured him Snowden would get fair and impartial treatment there.[1]

The trial, expected to take two to three days, had landed on the docket of Judge Frank I. Duncan. The Maryland-born Duncan had been a traveling candy salesman before enrolling in the University of Maryland Law School. In 1885 he had purchased a Republican newspaper, changed its political affiliation, and renamed it the *Baltimore County Democrat*. He went on to a career in politics before his appointment to the bench, where he had sat for more than two dozen years. He was a seasoned jurist with a lot of experience conducting trials.

In Jim Crow Maryland, however, this meant that all of the Black witnesses were seated separately from the white ones, relegated to a far corner of the courtroom. The room was crowded with relatives and friends of the Brandons, the large number of witnesses, and delegations of prominent African Americans who had made the journey from Annapolis and Baltimore.[2]

But the scene was far more placid than it had been in Annapolis, where crowds had lined the hallways. Snowden seemed calm as he was escorted into the courtroom. Although he fidgeted a bit in his chair, there was little drama as the proceedings began.

Of the first panel of twenty-five jurors, only four were selected; a second panel was brought in at eleven thirty a.m. and these proved sufficient to fill the jury box. Of the forty-four talesmen questioned, five were challenged by the prosecution, sixteen by the defense, and eleven were excused by the court for cause. Among those excused were at least one who claimed to have formed an opinion about the case, more than one who declared himself opposed to capital punishment, and one who admitted to prejudice against Black people.[3]

By one p.m., all the jurors were seated and sworn. All twelve were white. But "contrary to the usual order of things, the jury will not be made up of tobacco-chewing farmers with corn-tassel beards," the *Washington Times* assured its readers. That being said, however, one of the potential jurors, a farmer, had been excused from service because a barrel of pork waiting for him at the railroad station was in danger of spoiling.

After the lunch recess, court reconvened. There were fifty-eight witnesses on the list, thirty-four for the prosecution and twenty-four for the defense, but it was not clear how many would actually be called. What *was* clear to everyone was how the prosecutor intended to make the case against John Snowden.

The two sisters who lived across the street would place him at the scene of the crime. The Baltimore detectives would describe his actions and the conflicting statements he had made during interrogation. Valentine Brandon would testify to his wife's condition when he left for work and when he returned home, and Snowden's ostensible connection to Lottie Brandon would be brought out by testimony by his partner Edna Wallace that she had done her laundry. The dollar bill he spent at Martin's bar would somehow be linked to the bill Valentine Brandon had left with his wife. The scars on Snowden's face would also be cited as evidence of the crime, as would the fact that Wallace had contradicted him by denying causing them, and that he had not reported for work on the day of the murder. And then there was the dark-pigmented skin found under Lottie's fingernails.[4]

The only thing that was not entirely clear was to what prosecutor Green would attribute the cause of death. He had placed the defense

**21.** Judge Frank Duncan. Collection of William R. Ennis Jr.

at a decided disadvantage when he decided the previous October to take the case to the grand jury without an inquest. Without an objective assessment of the cause of death, which an inquest would have provided, he was free to use his own experts to argue for the scenario most damaging to the defendant. As the *Baltimore Sun* put it, "The defense, at sea so far, because of the fact that no inquest was held, has been forced to feel its way and take up the testimony offered by the prosecution just as it has been presented."[5]

Green laid out his arguments in a dramatic opening statement. He also declared:

The crime as we expect to show you, gentlemen of the jury, was a most heinous and diabolical one in its conception and its perpetration, was devoid of all decency and without the slightest recognition of the laws of man or God.

We expect to show you, gentlemen of the jury, by a concatenation of events and chain of facts that will leave no doubt in your mind that the perpetrator of this horrible crime was the prisoner at the bar, John Snowden, now being tried before you.

We expect to show you that he grabbed that woman from the rear, choked her into insensibility, threw her upon that bed and then ravished her, and that then with the feeling that a dead woman tells no tales, hit her in the head and left her there for dead.

If we show you these things, gentlemen of the jury, if we show you these facts and those circumstances we shall unhesitatingly ask at your hands, in the name of the peace and good order of society, in the name of morality and decency, and proper respect for the public administration of justice, "guilty of murder in the first degree."[6]

By contrast, nobody knew what the defense's strategy was going to be, and attorney Brady, now assisted by C. Gus Grason, a Towson lawyer, in addition to Charles S. Williams of Washington, wasn't talking. He made no opening statement. Once the testimony began, however, it slowly revealed itself. Brady intended to sow doubt: by introducing other suspects and his own theory of the cause of death, and by poking holes in the testimony of the prosecution's witness wherever he could.

Valentine Brandon was the first to take the stand. Under direct examination, he recounted the events of the day of the murder and his wife's condition upon his return from work. He confirmed that he had left her with a dollar bill. Brady used his cross-examination of the witness to establish that Brandon *himself* had at one point been suspected of the crime. When the prosecution objected to his questions about Brandon's own interrogation by police, he told the court candidly that "my only reason in asking these questions is to show that the detectives were hunting for someone who committed that act, and they first suspected Brandon."[7]

Valentine was also questioned about the fact that he had had intercourse with his wife on the night before her murder, something that had come out during his interrogation. Green asked what his wife had done right after they had finished.

"Well, she didn't *tell* me what she was doing, but I *know* what she was doing," he answered.

"Did she bring you anything?"

"Yes."

"What did she bring you?"

"A small washcloth."

"For what purpose?"

"We always used a cloth after intercourse."

"For what purpose?"

"For cleansing ourselves."

"Did you use it that night?"

"Yes, sir."

"Did she use it?"

"Yes, sir."

Brady objected to this question, prompting the judge to question the witness directly. "Did you *see* her use it?"

"I didn't see her use it, no."

Brady then asked that the question and answer be stricken from the record, and Judge Duncan complied.[8]

The exchange was vitally important in light of fact that semen had been found on Lottie May's body. In probing about post-coital cleansing—a remarkably candid discussion for 1918, and one that surely made many in the audience squeamish—the prosecution was trying to establish that it could not have been her husband's semen, which had been wiped away the night before. The defense had the opposite goal: as long as there was doubt as to its source, it could not be used to accuse his client of attempted rape. Although the judge struck part of the interchange from the record, he permitted most of it, despite the fact that Snowden had not been charged with rape by the grand jury.

Brady also used the testimony of Miriam King, put up by the prosecution to confirm that she had spoken with Lottie Brandon on the morning of her death, to establish that there had been other suspects. On cross-examination, he asked whether she had known before her interrogation that her husband had been suspected of the murder. He also tried, without much success, to get into the record alleged statements by Brandon to her that Lottie had had a former admirer

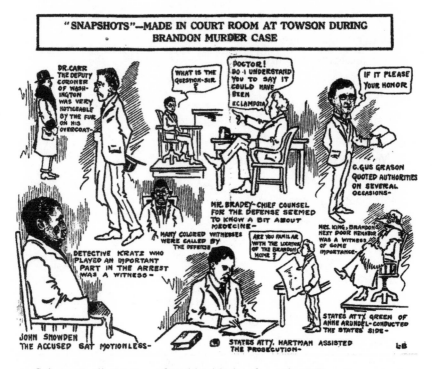

**22.** Schematic illustration of trial highlights from the *Jeffersonian*, a semi-weekly newspaper published in Towson. *Jeffersonian*, February 2, 1918.

for whom the police had searched. For the most part, the prosecution's objections to these questions were sustained and they were expunged from the record.[9]

The next day, Thursday, January 24, another component of Brady's strategy became clear. After Ida Burch and Grace Myers were put up, like Miriam King, to confirm that they had conversed with Lottie May after her husband had left for work, the prosecution called the doctors who had performed the autopsies to report on their findings.

Brady used his cross-examination to debut his argument that Lottie Brandon hadn't been murdered at all but had fallen in her kitchen, perhaps due to eclampsia, that is, seizures stemming from a disorder of her pregnancy. Had she succumbed to eclampsia, she might have fallen and struck her head on the ice box door before dragging herself to her bed, he argued, or else hit it on a chair or the bedpost. She would then have died of her head wound. The scratches, he theorized, might have been there earlier, or might have been self-inflicted by a woman grabbing at her *own* throat to get air, as eclampsia can cause edema of the lungs and she could have been having trouble breathing.

The prosecution's doctors did their best to dismiss this farfetched possibility. Dr. Joseph C. Joyce testified that in his opinion, she had been attacked from behind, strangled and then bludgeoned to death with a blunt instrument. The scratches were fresh; no scabs had formed on them, and the skin on them appeared to have been drawn backward, as if by someone positioned behind her. There had been no indication of eclampsia. And Dr. Walton Hopkins weighed in that she had surely received the final blow while on the bed, because it would have caused instantaneous death. He added that the presence of semen on her body showed that an attempt at sexual assault or rape had been made on her.[10]

Again Brady demanded that the remark about rape be stricken from the record; it was inflammatory and not contained in the indictment. Judge Duncan agreed, but he permitted extensive testimony about the semen and whether it could have been left over from intercourse with her husband the night before. Hopkins asserted that under such conditions, the heat of her body would have dried it up by the time she was found, and that any attempt at intercourse that could account for what was found on her body would have to have occurred shortly before—or after—death. But the doctors were forced to admit that they lacked concrete evidence to prove rape, which would have required penetration.

Brady also sought to exclude the report of the Washington autopsy. Doing so was crucial to his strategy, since it contained strong evidence that Lottie Brandon had been killed by an African American. Taken together with the fact that Snowden had had visible scratches on his face when he was arrested that he had not adequately explained, it would be extremely damaging—perhaps fatal—to his case.

Brady's best bet for getting the autopsy results thrown out was to focus on the possibility that the body had been tampered with, or at least, had changed materially, during its chain of custody. And a long, convoluted chain it had been. After the Annapolis autopsy had been completed, the body had been handed over to a local undertaker, then to Valentine Brandon, who Brady pointedly reminded the jury had been a suspect in the case. He had then taken it to Washington, where it had been turned over to the care of a *second* undertaker, who brought it to his establishment where it was fingerprinted by the local police and touched up. Then it was carried to the Brandon home for the funeral, buried in a grave for three days, exhumed, brought *back* to the funeral home and finally transported to a hospital for the second postmortem. Under such circumstances, Brady asserted, it would have been quite easy for the corpse to have changed materially.

Brady insisted the judge rule the results of the second autopsy inadmissible, but he refused. He simply ordered that the two undertakers who had tended to the body be heard before he would permit the physicians to testify as to its results. The likelihood that anyone had tampered with the corpse would be a matter for the jury to decide. With this, the doctors were dismissed, subject to recall.[11]

Before the day was out, C. Gus Grason of the defense team clashed several times with prosecutor Green. A great-grandson of a mid-nineteenth-century governor of Maryland and son of the former state's attorney for Baltimore County, Grason was known as a formidable lawyer with an acid tongue. During a heated and very personal exchange, he demanded to know why Green had insisted on the change in venue for the trial which had removed it from Annapolis and landed it in Towson.[12]

"Why *did* you remove this case from the county where the crime was committed?" Grason demanded.

Green got defensive. He leaned in toward Grason, his face flushed, and responded, "There is nothing I would like better than to tell why I removed the case from Annapolis." But he was interrupted by the judge and not permitted to continue, as the exchange was clearly out of order.

The *Evening Capital* summed it up in its assertion that "State's Attorney Green replied in a manner which gave the impression that he believed a jury in Annapolis might have been unfit." Later, the *Baltimore Sun* reported that "political motives which will come to light later and cause a near-upheaval among the factions represented" were responsible.

But they never did come to light. No mention was made of the potential racial makeup of the jury, which seems the most likely reason he had insisted on the change.[13]

# 15

## "Could Not Have Come
## from a White Person"

The following day, Friday, January 25, Brady suffered another setback. This time it was in his effort to suppress John Snowden's statements to the Baltimore police during his interrogation, which he alleged had been coerced. Brady insisted Snowden had been accorded "rough, cruel and hellish" treatment in Baltimore, and that anything he said at the time should therefore be thrown out of court.

This was denied by Snowden's interrogators, who insisted the prisoner had never been handled severely, and Judge Duncan admitted testimony about the statements, noting that the defense was free to put Snowden on the stand to refute them if it wished.[1]

There was also a tussle that worked to Brady's advantage, however. This one was over the testimony of Edna Wallace, put on the stand by the prosecution to confirm the statement she had made during her interrogation in Baltimore that she had not scratched John Snowden's face. Brady had tried to exclude this testimony and Edna's signed statement but was overruled.

Brady needn't have bothered. To Green's dismay and obvious annoyance, Wallace disavowed the statement entirely.

"Did you *not* positively state in the presence of two witnesses that you *did not* scratch Snowden's face?" Green demanded of her.

"I did not make that statement," Edna insisted. "You asked me at the time if I made them on *Sunday*, and I told you I did not make them *on that day*. We were playing and wrestling two or three weeks before that and I may have scratched him then." Presented with her statement, she insisted that although she had indeed signed it at the time, she had not read it. "It was read to me by someone in the office. I don't know who it was," she added. "I did not mean to say I could not have made those scratches."[2]

Wallace did admit when pressed, however, that she had corresponded with Snowden while he was incarcerated and that, in one of her letters, which had clearly been intercepted and read by the authorities, she had vowed to "stick by him."[3]

The prosecution's star witnesses on Saturday were Mary Perkins and Edith Creditt, who told essentially the same story they had told to Ella Rush Murray, State's Attorney Green, and the detectives each time they had been questioned. Mary told what she had seen, how she and her sister had identified Snowden, and why she had waited so long to come forward, noting that she had been advised to keep quiet lest her story foment a race riot.

Since these two witnesses posed the biggest threat to the defense, Snowden's attorneys sought to undermine their testimony in any way possible. Grason spent a good deal of time pulling from Perkins the names of people she had told about what she had seen before she approached Ella Murray. There were many. Though some of his questions suggested she had told them a different story, she remained firm.

It was when Edith Creditt testified that Grason raised the issue of the reward that had been offered for information leading to the apprehending of Lottie May Brandon's killer. His implication was clear: it had been the reward that had motivated the sisters to come forward with a bogus accusation. But he didn't get very far with the argument other than to put the idea into the minds of the jurors. When he asserted, after the prosecution had objected to the line of questioning, that "we offer to prove that there was a reward offered and she knew it," Judge Duncan sustained the objection and Grason was not permitted to go on.[4]

The jury also heard from Leroy Sisco, the eleven-year-old Black boy who did errands for Strohmeyer's, a West Street grocer. Frightened, and in a quavering voice, he told the court he had passed the Brandon home between eleven a.m. and twelve noon on the day Lottie Brandon was murdered on his way to deliver a sack of flour.

"I saw a lady's arm start to come out the door and somebody pulled her back and shut the door," he told the court. And although this testimony did not specifically point to Snowden, it was hurtful to the defense, so Brady did his best, on cross-examination, to suggest that the young man had been coached.

"Now, Leroy, who has been talking to you since that time about this?"
"Sheriff Lee."
"Did he tell you just what you have said?"
"Yes, sir."
"Did he tell you to tell that on the stand, when you got on the stand?"
"Yes, sir," he agreed.[5]

The rest of the testimony on Saturday revolved around the care, condition, and whereabouts of Lottie May's body between her death and her second autopsy. Getting it thrown out would require the defense to show that it was unreliable, and that, in turn, would necessitate pointing out changes it had endured, or possibly endured, during its journey.

In his direct testimony, John M. Taylor, the Annapolis undertaker called to assist on the night of the murder, insisted he had been present for the entire time the body had been at his establishment except for a period in which it had been under lock and key in his vault. He described how he and an assistant had worked into the wee hours to embalm and dress the corpse, going into a good deal of graphic detail about the process—draining blood, removing gas, injecting embalming fluid, and washing and grooming the body.

It was this last process, of course, that was most interesting to the defense attorneys, who were desperate to head off, or at least discredit, the introduction of evidence of dark-pigmented skin under the fingernails they knew would be coming.

"What portions did you cleanse?" Brady asked on cross-examination.
"Cleansed the hands—hands were a little dirty—tips of her fingers and her fingernails; cleansed those. We didn't scrub the fingers like a surgeon; it would take too much time."
"Did you cleanse *all* the nails?"

"Yes. Her fingernails were a little long and I noticed the dirt in them and took these scissors like we do in ordinary cases and clean out what dirt we can get out."

"Did you cut the nails?"

"Trim them, yes, sir; always trim them and scrape inside."

"You trimmed the nails; found dirt in the nails, between the nails and the flesh?"

"Yes, dirt from the autopsy."

"You took out all that dirt?"

"I don't say I took it *all* out."

Attorney Green wasn't going to let it go at that. On redirect examination, he asked, "Did you make any effort to get down under the fingernail between the flesh and nails?"

"No, sir," Taylor answered. "Didn't make no special effort to get away down in them."[6]

Green then recalled Valentine Brandon to describe his trip back to Washington with his wife's body and how he was met by William H. Sardo, the undertaker who took it straight to his own establishment in a hearse. It had remained there from Thursday night until the following Saturday morning, when it had been brought to the Brandon home for the funeral. He affirmed that the body had not been removed from the casket at any time.[7]

A very agitated Sardo took the stand that afternoon. His job had been to change Lottie's clothing into an outfit suitable for a funeral, but he had also touched up her makeup. He was shown several photos of her corpse taken during the second autopsy that had not previously been admitted into evidence and asked if there was any difference in her appearance from the time he received the body at the train station. He asserted that there was not, and also affirmed that although he had washed her face and applied chemicals and cosmetics to obscure the wound on her forehead, he had not touched her hands, which had been placed by Taylor in a folded position such that her nails were not visible. He had seen no need for further cleaning there.

Asked about the wounds on Lottie's throat, which he had also not touched because they were obscured by a high, ruffled collar, he volunteered, "Gentlemen, I've handled a lot of such cases as this and

I can swear that those marks on that woman's face and neck were not made by the woman through any accident." Both the judge and the attorneys attempted to stop the outburst, but not before he had also asserted, "Those marks were made by a human hand, and the hand was that of a great big man at that!"

Judge Duncan ordered the remark stricken, but the damage was done. The Towson-based *Jeffersonian* thought it was the turning point in the trial.[8]

All that was left for the prosecution was to present evidence from the second autopsy if the judge allowed it. To this end, Green intended to recall Drs. Walton H. Hopkins, Anne Arundel County health officer, and William B. Carr, deputy coroner of the District of Columbia. There was some speculation that they might actually introduce Lottie May Brandon's fingernails into evidence.

After a severe snowstorm on Monday, January 28, delayed the opening of court until two p.m.—the judge's home was snowbound and the roads and trolley line were impassable—Dr. Hopkins was recalled. When he was asked by Green for a detailed description of the findings of the second autopsy, Brady objected on the grounds that there was no value in an examination of a body so far removed from its state at the time it was discovered, since changes were inevitable. But Judge Duncan ruled his testimony admissible, reasoning that the defense would have ample opportunity to cross-examine him, and that "the value of his testimony is, of course, a matter for the jury."[9]

It was a huge setback for the defense.

Asked whether the body had been tampered with between the time he first saw it in Annapolis and when he saw it several days later in Washington, Hopkins asserted that there had been no perceptible difference in its appearance. He confirmed that the wounds on Lottie May's face had been inflicted by "the pressure of fingers" and that great force had been used.[10]

Hopkins was permitted to tell how the first three fingers on Lottie's right hand and the first two on her left hand had been removed during the second autopsy, and how the dirt and "dark substance" under the nails had been examined. But he was not allowed to speak further about *what* had been found because he was inexpert in the use of a microscope. That job would be left to Dr. Carr, who was to follow him on the stand.

Attorney Brady then made another attempt to have all testimony relating to the second autopsy stricken. He asked the judge to excuse the jury, and objected this time not on the grounds that the body might have been tampered with but that the defendant had not been present, nor had he had a representative present, at the procedure. Once again, however, he was overruled.[11]

What was left to Brady, therefore, was to undermine the testimony in any way possible. He tried to make much of the fact that Hopkins had said that Mrs. Brandon's body, when he first saw it, had been on its back with her face turned left, whereas others had said it had been turned to the right. He tried to get Hopkins to allow that the wounds on her face might have been self-inflicted but got nowhere. His chief achievement was to get the physician to admit that he could not rule out the possibility that the semen found on her body had originated with her husband.

"Now doctor, I will ask you, in view of what you have said, whether you are positive Mrs. Brandon was ravaged or raped before she died?"

"No, sir; I am not positive of it," Dr. Hopkins replied.

Seizing on this, Brady moved that *all* testimony by the various doctors the jury had heard regarding assault or rape be removed from the record.

"My object in making that motion," he told the judge, "is entirely based upon the requirements of the law in establishing *corpus delecti* which must be beyond a reasonable doubt. This is *not* a question for the jury."

Here again, however, the judge disagreed. Since "it is not alleged that by reason of rape she lost her life," he said, he would overrule the objection and allow the jury to consider the testimony. This essentially guaranteed that although Snowden was not being accused of rape, the idea that he might have sexually assaulted Lottie May Brandon, and that it might have been a motive for murder, would remain present in the mind of every juror.

What remained was for Dr. Carr to present the evidence about the skin found under Lottie May Brandon's fingernails. "What I took from those nails," he declared, "indicated the same character you'd get from a member of the colored race." He insisted, the *Washington Post* reported, that it "could not have come from a white person." He added that he had also found a number of short hairs clipped at an angle, like the beard of a man who had recently shaved.[12]

Carr did not produce any fingernails; there was no need. His testimony was sufficient, and when it was finished, the prosecution rested its case. Green had done an effective job with the evidence he had. Although it was circumstantial, it was compelling, and it would be extremely difficult for Snowden's attorneys to counter it.

As the *Sun* put it, "When the trial started last Wednesday, the opinion of the majority of those who have followed the developments of the murder was that John Snowden was not guilty. Since that time, however, as point after point was scored by the prosecution, general opinion has undergone a change." By the time the defense rested, there was general consensus that "the negro would be convicted by the jury."[13]

# 16

## "It Was Ten Minutes after Eleven When I Got Up"

Attorney Brady had declined to offer an opening statement at the outset of the trial, so it was not yet clear how he planned to argue the case. But the *Evening Capital* helpfully stepped in and told its readers what it believed it would take for him to win.

The *Evening Capital* was certain Brady would continue to try to persuade the jury that Lottie May had suffered from eclampsia due to her "delicate condition," that she had strangled herself and fallen on a piece of furniture, striking a fatal blow to her head from which she had bled to death. This, in turn, would require neutralizing the testimony of Leroy Sisco, the eleven-year-old who insisted he had seen the woman struggling with someone at the front door.

Snowden's attorneys would also need to attack the credibility of Mary Perkins and Edith Creditt. Brady and his colleagues would do this, the *Evening Capital* predicted, by showing that they told differing stories about what they had seen in the days following the event.[1]

The *Baltimore Sun* had a few predictions of its own. It had gotten wind of a rumor that the defense would put up a witness to testify that several days before her death, Lottie May Brandon had visited a realtor in an effort to find a new house because "a certain well-known businessman of Annapolis was annoying her by his attentions." This, of course, would be a tactic designed to create doubt by suggesting the possibility of an unknown murderer motivated by jealousy.

As his first witness on Tuesday, January 29, attorney Brady recalled Valentine Brandon. He once again attempted to get him to admit that he had been a suspect in the case. And since prosecutor Green had made much of the fact that the dollar bill Valentine had returned to his wife after his trip to the bakery had gone missing and had implied it was the same dollar John Snowden had spent at Martin's Bar on the afternoon of the murder, he also asked Brandon whether it was true that shortly after the murder he had told a newspaper man that he *had*, in fact, located that dollar bill and that it had not been stolen at all. The prosecution objected to both questions, however, and the judge sustained the objections, so Brandon never answered them.[2]

Then Brady called Mrs. Rachel Stewart, the maternity nurse who had been attending Lottie May Brandon. He asked her about Lottie's condition during the time she had been caring for her, hoping to establish a foundation for his contention that she had suffered from eclampsia. But the prosecution objected, and the judge did not permit her to testify on the topic.

Mrs. Stewart was helpful to the defense in another way, however. She insisted that when she entered the room where Lottie May had died, she *had* seen a crumpled bill on the bureau. She did not know its denomination but was sure it was U.S. currency. This undermined the prosecution's contention that whoever had committed the murder had also taken money from the house.[3]

Next, Brady called Mrs. Ella M. Carroll, the neighbor who had been one of the first, after Valentine and the murderer, to see Lottie May Brandon dead. He needed her to blunt the effect of Mary Perkins's testimony that she had seen a chair fly by inside the window of the Brandon home, evidence of a struggle within. Mrs. Carroll asserted that heavy screens on the windows obliterated all views of the goings-on inside.[4]

After lunch, the defense put up the Rev. Ernest Sumner Williams, the Brandons' next-door neighbor. He was one of Snowden's biggest defenders and had been cooperating with the defense. It was he who had told Grace Humiston the previous August that his wife may have overheard a dispute in the Brandon home the night before the murder,

**23.** The Rev. Ernest Sumner Williams. Courtesy of Robert L. Worden.

and it seems likely he was also the unnamed preacher who had chastised Mary Perkins for implicating a fellow Black person in a murder.[5]

Reverend Williams testified that he and the Rev. William A. C. Hughes, who was in town from Washington, had sat on his front porch from ten a.m. until one p.m. on the day of the murder and had not only heard no noise from the Brandons' home; they had also seen no one enter or leave it. Reverend Hughes, who followed him on the stand, said much the same thing. Under cross-examination, however, each was forced to admit that he had left the porch for a short time during that period.[6]

On cross-examination, State's Attorney Green raised questions about Reverend Williams's objectivity by suggesting he was biased in favor of the defendant. He asked him if he had not called a prayer meeting of his congregation to raise money for Snowden's defense. But it was Brady, rather than Williams, who answered the question.

"Yes, he called a meeting," Brady told the jury. "Further, I will tell you *what* he called it for. It was to raise money to pay *me* to handle the case!"[7]

The judge ruled these remarks out of order, but Reverend Williams went on to do what he could to undermine the testimony of the sisters who lived across the street from him. He swore, for example, that a few hours after Lottie May Brandon's body was discovered, he heard Mary Perkins say that she thought it strange that Mrs. Brandon had not been seen all day. "I have heard nothing going on over there today," he quoted her as saying, "and I just wonder if that young man has killed his wife." When recalled to the stand later, Perkins denied having said anything of the kind.[8]

Reverend Williams was followed by his wife Mary, whom the defense put up to testify to having heard noises the night before the murder, as if someone in the Brandon home were being thrown against a wall. The attorneys hoped it would suggest disharmony between the spouses and cast suspicion on Valentine. But the prosecution objected to the questioning and the judge sustained the objection.[9]

Two additional witnesses were called to impeach Mary Perkins's testimony. Mary had mentioned Julia Carroll as someone with whom she had discussed what she had seen on the day of the murder, and noted that Mary Ellen Bias had been nearby as they spoke. Brady wanted the jury to hear their versions of that conversation.

Mary Bias recalled that Perkins had said that the blinds in the Brandon home had been closed and remained so all day; this suggested she could not have seen anything through the front window of the house across the street. And Julia Carroll, like Reverend Williams, insisted that Perkins had told her she had noted nothing unusual about her neighbor's house that day.

"Did Mary Perkins say to you in that conversation that she had seen no one come out of the house or about that house that day, speaking of the Brandon house?" Brady asked.

"Yes, sir; she did."[10]

The defense had also subpoenaed Ella Rush Murray as an impeachment witness. But at the last minute the attorneys declined to call her. No reason was given.[11]

The courtroom was packed the next day, Wednesday, January 30, because word had gotten out that the defense would put John Snowden himself on the stand. Many members of Baltimore's Black community, where a collection had been taken up for Snowden's defense, made the trek to Towson to hear him.

Snowden had previously appeared in court in his work clothes, but that morning his hair had been cut and was neatly brushed, and he wore a high standing collar, a big black bow tie, and creased pants. After he was sworn in, he told his life story: that he had grown up in Annapolis, attended school only briefly, and gone to work on an ice wagon as a teenager. He recounted the names of several of his employers, the most recent being Mr. Parlett, and told the jury he lived on Acton Lane.[12]

"Did you know Mr. or Mrs. Brandon before?" Brady asked him.

"No, sir."

"Did you know where they lived?"

"No, sir. I didn't. I heard these people tell me they lived on Second Street when I was in Baltimore."

"Now, I want you to try and recall to mind the day that Mrs. Brandon's body was found dead on Second Street at her home. What time did you get up that morning?"

"It was ten minutes after eleven when I got up."

"How do you recall the time?"

"Because I have a clock sitting right at the wash stand, right at the head of the bed and the clock was ten minutes fast and I judge myself from my own time, always keeping the clock ten minutes fast. It was eleven o'clock, the right time."

"After you got up, what did you do?"

"I put my clothes on, all except shoes."

"Now, after you put on your clothes, what did you do?"

"I brought my shoes in my hand and the clock downstairs and set the clock on the sink and sat down and put my shoes on. And after I got through I washed my face. While I was wiping my face, I called Edna and gave her $1.90 and I kept $1.10."

"Where did you get that money from?"

"I got three dollars from Mr. Parlett and spent fifty cents that night and was in a crap game and won fifty cents."

"What did you do then?"

"I sat down. I went in the kitchen and got a sandwich and sat down at the table and ate it. Then I went out in the yard. I come in the house again and fooled around the house a little while and then put on my coat and cap and went around to my sister's and I saw Agnes on the steps."

"Who is Agnes?"

"My sister's little girl."

"Well, what time was that about?"

"I don't know. About twenty minutes of twelve, I guess."

"Then what did you do?"

"I played around the steps and then I went up through the lot, out through Second Street."

"What lot?"

"Right there by Preacher Williams' house."

"Then where did you go?"

"I went out through Second Street. When I got up there by Preacher Williams first I saw him on the back porch, stooping over, like he was picking up something. I bowed my head to him and when I got up on Second Street there were two ladies across the street, one on her porch and one on the other."

"Then what did you do?"

"Walking down the street I heard someone call Mutts Dorsey. I stopped and looked back. I saw a wagon but did not see anybody. I kept on up the street until I got to where Mrs. Baker was and she was standing on the porch and she spoke to me and she said to me, 'Didn't you go to work this morning?' And I said no, I had overslept myself. And she said, 'You fellows work right hard down at Parlett's.' And I kept on down the street."

"Then you went where?"

"Over to Mr. Martin's bar. I went in the bar and Pink Johnson came in the back way from the railroad track and I asked him would he have a drink and he said yes, and he said what time is it and I said five minutes of twelve."

"How long did you stay in the bar there?"

"I stayed in there until about one o'clock or half past one before I went home."

"When you went home, what did you do?"

"I asked Edna if she was going to eat with me and she said go ahead and eat and she was upstairs and I ate myself and went upstairs."

"Then what did you do?"

"Then I pulled my shoes off and laid across the bed and looked at books."

"How long did you stay there?"

"I stayed home all evening."[13]

# 17

## "The Man Shoved a Gun against My Head"

After recess, Brady turned to Snowden's interrogation. The attorney wanted any statements he had made to the Baltimore detectives after his arrest excluded, lest they differ from his testimony or that of others and be used to brand him a liar. The best way to accomplish this was to demonstrate that the declarations had been coerced. So Brady focused on Snowden's interactions with State's Attorney Green on the day of his arrest and with the Baltimore detectives afterward.

"Those gentlemen came and got me, and carried me back to a building," the defendant recalled. "They took me down in the basement and gave me my breakfast. Then they carried me to an office where three men were. I was there with those three men all that day."

"Tell us what those men did," Brady urged. "Describe, as near as you can, what was said and done to you during the time you were there."

"They carried me into the next room and sat me close to the table. The arms of the chair went under the table. They had me against the table, and they kept a-talking and a-talking to me, and I talked and talked to them. By and by they pulled the chair back and I fell on my knees and the man shoved a gun against my head and the man back of me hit me on the top of the head. And then they would put me in the chair again, put me up to the table and do the same thing again."

"They did that all the evening," he continued. "They made me take off my pants and sweater, my top shirt and my undershirt. Then one of the men went out and came back with a half a pint of whiskey. He sat it on the table and told me to take a drink. I asked him for a glass to drink out of, and he said I didn't need any, to drink out of the bottle. I drank a little bit, and he told me to drink some more, and I did. Then he carried it back and put it on a shelf."

"Then they commenced talking to me again in about five minutes. Then the man brought the whiskey back. . . . Then he said you take it and drink it, and laid the gun on the table. I looked at the table, I looked at them, and then I grabbed the whiskey and drank it."

"How long did they put you through that, Snowden?"

"All day."

"What time did you leave that building?"

"That evening."

"The next morning what did you do?"

"They came back the next morning and got me, this gentleman here."

"Where did they carry you?"

"Back up to the same place."

"What did they do that day?"

"They sat me at the table and commenced talking to me and hitting me on the head like they had done before. They did the same things to me as the first time, except the whiskey."

"Do you remember what they did to you?"

"They sat me at the table and talked to me. While I was talking, they would pull the chair away from the table, and I would fall down, they would poke the gun back of my head and hit me over the head. They said they were going to shoot, and I was afraid of all three of them. They would put me back in the chair, and I would say: 'Please don't shoot me, I haven't done anything.'"

"How long did that go on?"

"Part of that day. Not all day. Then they carried me back to a little cell inside the building. In there I waited until that evening."

State's Attorney Green conducted the cross-examination. He tried to refute any suggestion that the defendant had been treated inappropriately or denied his rights. Since he, himself, had been one of Snowden's interrogators in Annapolis immediately after his arrest, he asked questions in the first person.

"John, when I saw you in the courthouse, didn't I ask you if you would tell me where you were? Didn't I tell you that you didn't have to tell me if you didn't want to, but if you wanted to, I would like you to tell me?"

"No, sir."

"Wasn't that before I asked you any questions?"

"You told me to tell you where I was on Wednesday, and I told you at home."

"You knew you didn't have to tell me that, didn't you?"

"Yes, sir."

"You knew what you were saying, didn't you?"

"Yes, sir."

"You knew that I was state's attorney, didn't you?"

"Yes, sir."

"There wasn't any concealment about anything of that kind, was there?"

"No, sir."

He then endeavored to trip Snowden up, pointing out inconsistencies between his testimony and that of others, and between statements he allegedly made after his arrest and his current testimony. He asked many questions in the form of "Didn't you tell me that . . . ?" and in so doing kept Snowden very much on the defensive.[1]

Defense counsel Gus Grason had one witness up his sleeve he hoped would corroborate Snowden's assertion of mistreatment during his interrogation. In a dramatic move, he called George Hartman, the Baltimore County state's attorney who was assisting in the prosecution of the case, to the stand. Hartman had been present at Baltimore police headquarters during part of Snowden's examination in Marshal Carter's office, and Grason wished to quiz him on what he had seen and heard there.

"Didn't you say to people in the courthouse at Towson that you were there at Police Headquarters in Baltimore City, when the detectives that have been mentioned, Marshal Carter and Deputy Marshal House, were questioning Snowden? You stated you were there about fifteen minutes; and that you were so disgusted at the conduct of the Marshal, Deputy Marshal and detectives in the way in which they handled and questioned the accused that you left?"

Green objected to the question on narrow grounds: because the incident in question had taken place on August 17, and Snowden had only alleged that he had been subjected to the "third degree" on August 14 and 15. The judge agreed, sustaining the objection and ruling the testimony inadmissible.[2]

He also did not admit testimony from Annapolis physician Dr. Louis B. Henkel, which Brady wanted to support the alternative theory that Lottie May Brandon might have died of eclampsia. Henkel had treated at least thirty-five or forty women for the disease in his fifteen years in practice. But as soon as Brady broached the topic, prosecutor Green was ready with an objection.

"I want to ask him about the autopsy and whether or not from all the evidence brought out here bearing on the death of Mrs. Brandon she died of convulsions due to eclampsia," Brady explained to the judge.[3]

"We don't think the doctor, from his testimony, is an autopsy expert," Green retorted, and a furious debate ensued. The defense argued that it was entitled to introduce an alternate theory of the cause of death. But the judge agreed with the prosecution and found the physician, despite his experience, unqualified. It was just one of a long spate of rulings against the defense on the part of Judge Duncan. In general, Snowden's team had taken a drubbing at his hands; he appears to have ruled against them far more frequently than he did in their favor. Each time he did so, the defense attorneys would ask for an "exception," which flagged it as a point they might take up on appeal if the jury found Snowden guilty.

Green knew his case would be weakened if the statements Snowden made during his interrogation were thrown out, so he was as intent on keeping them in as Brady was in getting them excluded. Since Snowden had implicated Deputy Marshal Samuel W. House, Marshal Robert G. Carter, and Sergeant Maurice E. Pease—his three principal interrogators—in his mistreatment, Green put all three up as rebuttal witnesses the next day to deny that the defendant had been abused.

House was first. The *Evening Capital* recalled later that he had a reputation in Baltimore "of being able to do more with negro cases than any man on the force because of his belief that except in rare cases kindness would elicit more from colored persons than fear and manhandling." Had Snowden's been one of those "rare cases"?

Green asked that the defendant's testimony about causing him to fall to his knees, having a gun put to his head and forced to drink whiskey be read back. Then he asked House if any of it was true. Grason objected to House's testimony on procedural grounds, asserting that Green should have put him up while making his case, and that he was not an appropriate rebuttal witness. Here again, the judge ruled against him.[4]

"Did *anyone* in your presence put a pistol to his head and threaten to shoot him?" Green asked his witness.

"They did not."

"Did anyone else, in your presence, or you at that time hit him over the head?"

"They did not."

"Did you, or anyone else, in your presence, bring a bottle of whiskey into that room?"

"No, sir."

"Did you, or anyone else, in your presence, invite Snowden to take a drink of whiskey?"

"I did not."

"Did you, or anyone else, in your presence, pull the chair from under him and cause him to fall to the floor?"

"No, sir."[5]

The questioning continued in the same vein, with House denying Snowden's allegations, one by one. And there was more of the same when Marshal Carter, a thirty-five-year veteran of the force, and Sergeant Pease took their turns. Brady objected to their appearance but was overruled each time, and he was not notably successful in his cross-examination of them. Snowden may have lied, of course, but if he had told the truth, the "blue wall of silence" was not about to permit itself to be breached.

The upshot was that Snowden's statements during his interrogation would remain part of the official court record and thus evidence the jury was free to consider.

# 18

## "The Homes of White Women Must Be Protected"

The *Baltimore Afro-American* thought Snowden had acquitted himself well on the witness stand. "That the prisoner, in giving his testimony in a straightforward manner, made a profound impression upon those present, is generally admitted," the paper wrote, "and the opinion is widespread that the State's case, based solely on circumstantial evidence of the flimsiest kind, has received a severe jolt." It went on to report that the way he answered the questions gave many confidence in his innocence, and it took the fact that Snowden had never confessed to the crime, in spite of being abused by the authorities, as a strong indication of the same.

The paper also thought Reverend Williams had done Snowden's case some good; it took issue with a description it claimed had appeared in another newspaper that his testimony had been "insolent" and found it, on the contrary, clear and forthright. "At no point did he become nettled in his replies, notwithstanding various attempts by State's Attorney Green to confuse him," it asserted.

In reporting that the state had not convincingly proven guilt, however, the paper was perhaps taking too optimistic a view. The state's evidence was circumstantial, but it was anything but flimsy. And Snowden's testimony had been contradicted not only by the prosecution's witnesses but even by some of those put up by the defense. Brady and Grason had succeeded in poking some holes in the state's case, but were there enough of them to matter?[1]

As the trial came to a close—it had run for nine days, with one evening session—the *Washington Times* reported that Judge Duncan, State's Attorney Hartman, and even defense counsel Brady had all received anonymous letters about the case. They were postmarked, variously, in Baltimore, Annapolis, and Washington. Most insisted Snowden was not guilty, and some even suggested individuals they thought ought to be called to testify. Some of the charges in the letters were nothing short of libelous, the paper reported, and most were "finding their way to the trash basket."[2]

The closing statements of the prosecution and the defense do not survive except in snippets quoted in the press and later court documents. Green's remarks, described as "one of the most powerful addresses ever made to a Towson jury," are almost completely lost except for two comments. One, in which he maintained that Snowden had committed "a crime prompted by unbridled passion," and a second in which he asserted that Snowden had pulled down Lottie May Brandon's stocking, where she carried her money, and had taken a dollar bill from it.[3]

Baltimore County state's attorney Hartman, however, who did the rest of the summation for the state, did not shrink from racist tropes. He asserted, in the words of the *Baltimore Sun*, that "the negro who ravishes a white woman deserves the extreme legal penalty and nothing short of it."[4]

Hartman—the very man who had assured Green before the trial began that Snowden would be accorded "fair and impartial treatment"—demanded a verdict of murder in the first degree without any qualifications "because in this state the homes of white women must be protected," according to the *Evening Star*. The statement set off a round of applause among white women in the courtroom. Although Judge Duncan banged his gavel at this and insisted on order, his purpose was apparently to silence the spectators, not to admonish the attorney.[5]

When his turn came, Grason told the jury John Snowden had been victimized. He said he had been made a scapegoat by the police, who had arrested him to disguise their inability to solve the crime. He argued vigorously that the state's contention that Mrs. Brandon had been "criminally assaulted" had not been proven and, as best he could, detailed inconsistencies in the testimony of the prosecution's witnesses. Citing the total lack of direct evidence, he asked for a verdict of not guilty.[6]

At 8:25 p.m., when the summations were over, Judge Duncan charged the jury. He gave them five options for their verdict, an outgrowth of a change in state law in 1916 that had given juries in capital cases the power to decide whether or not to impose the death penalty. This had previously been left to the discretion of the judge. In his instructions, he made clear that the jury might choose to find the defendant guilty of murder in the first degree; guilty of murder in the first degree *without* capital punishment; guilty of murder in the second degree; guilty of manslaughter; or not guilty. The prosecution asked for the first option; the defense, of course, sought the last.

The jury was out for only twenty-two minutes. It was reported later that ten of the twelve jurors had immediately favored a verdict of murder in the first degree *with* the death penalty, the remaining two wishing to discuss the matter further. But by the time the first ballot was taken, those two had joined the others.[7]

When Judge Duncan was informed that the jurors had reached a decision, he admonished the crowd in advance. "This is a grave case," he asserted. "I wish to warn every person present against any utterance or demonstration approving or disapproving the verdict. Anyone who makes a sound or causes disorder will be apprehended immediately by officers and detectives now scattered about this room." There had been rumors of a possible riot, and the *Washington Post* seemed to think his remarks were directed more toward the Blacks in the courtroom than the whites.[8]

As the *Washington Times* reported it, Snowden was ordered by the court clerk to stand and raise his right hand as the verdict was read.

"Guilty," the Foreman stated.

"Is that the *complete* statement of the verdict?" Judge Duncan demanded. "Will the Foreman answer?"

Granville Simpson, the foreman, then read from the indictment. "We, the jury, find the defendant guilty of murder in the first degree, with the death penalty."[9]

By most accounts, Snowden took it stoically. Nor was there any extreme reaction from spectators when the verdict was read, and all filed out of the courtroom in orderly fashion. Mary Perkins and Edith Creditt were kept in seclusion under heavy guard, lest someone attempt revenge on them.[10]

Before court was adjourned, attorney Grason moved to defer sentencing, a motion immediately granted by the judge. The defense had three days in which to petition for a new trial, something everyone expected it would do.

Snowden made no statement as he was escorted back to his cell in the courthouse by half a dozen deputies and later taken back to Towson Jail. There, the *Sun* reported, he broke down completely, and the *Evening Capital* pronounced him on the verge of collapse. By the next morning, however, he had regained his composure; he rose early and ate a hearty breakfast.[11]

That morning, February 1, attorneys Brady and Grason went before Judge Duncan and moved formally that he vacate the judgment and order a new trial. Such motions typically argue that a judge has made one or more significant legal errors or that there was insufficient evidence to support the jury verdict, or both, and this was no exception.

Their first objection dated to the empaneling of the jury. After only two jurors had been selected, but within earshot of others yet to be chosen, the judge had instructed the jury as to the law of circumstantial evidence but had not made clear that the jury was free to disregard his comments, since they were *advisory* rather than *binding*. This was an anomaly in Maryland law that was deemed a violation of the rights of the defendant and would be declared unconstitutional in 1980, but it was very much in force in 1918. An additional objection centered on alleged errors in rulings on questions of evidence in the case, and true to form, the defense also argued that the evidence was insufficient to establish guilt beyond a reasonable doubt.

Another objection was the judge's failure to intervene when State's Attorney Green, in his closing arguments, told the jury that Snowden had pulled down Mrs. Brandon's stocking and retrieved a one-dollar bill from it. There had been no evidence introduced at trial to support this contention.

Finally, the petitioners claimed the existence of newly discovered evidence but did not specify what it was. The judge made no immediate ruling but set February 13 as the date he would hear evidence on the motion and, if it failed, sentence the defendant.[12]

On that date, the new evidence referred to in the motion was presented to the judge by attorney Brady. It consisted primarily of a lengthy affidavit from none other than Ella Rush Murray, the woman who had brought the two sisters to the authorities to accuse John Snowden and who, for some time since, had come to believe Snowden innocent of the charges against him. Mrs. Murray, who had warned the prosecution that she would be a hostile witness if called, had been on the defense's witness list, but she had never been put on the stand. This suggests that Brady might have anticipated a guilty verdict and held her testimony in reserve to use to support a motion for a new trial.

The purpose of her statement was to recollect the events of the day she brought the sisters to State's Attorney Green in a way that cast doubt on the version of the story to which they had testified. Among the items she recalled:

On Mary Perkins's statement that she had seen a chair fly by the window in the Brandon house: "I asked Mary if she could see in the windows of the Brandons' house and she said no, because Mrs. Brandon always closed the windows and pulled down the shades every morning, and they were that way that morning."

On the identification of John Snowden: "I asked Mary how she knew the man who came out of the Brandon house was Snowden if she had never seen him before and if Edith had only seen the side of his face. Mary said one Monday morning, the 13th, that she and Edith went down to Parlett's Store to identify the man, and that they waited there until Snowden came along, and that Mary then identified him to Edith, and that Edith said he was Snowden."

On how many people Mary had told about what she had seen: "I asked Mary how many other people she had told, and she replied, 'only two or three friends,' and that they had all advised her to keep quiet about it."[13]

There was nothing earth-shattering about these recollections, however, and they appear to differ from the sisters' testimony only in relatively minor details, though the part about whether events in the Brandon home had been visible through the windows was significant.

And although the defense argued that they could produce additional witnesses to prove that Lottie May Brandon's death had been due to convulsions stemming from her pregnancy—a contention that had already been litigated at trial—none of it moved Judge Duncan. After hearing the defense's arguments, he immediately overruled their motion for a new trial and proceeded to sentence the defendant.

He stated that in his view, the jury had been absolutely justified in its verdict. Without going into any detail, he acknowledged that there had been "bad management" on the part of "some persons out of the State" working on the case—likely a reference to Mrs. Humiston—but added that when the *real* detectives got on the job, the truth had come out. He said he had made a careful study of the testimony and the evidence and had concluded in light of it that "there was but one verdict" that the jury could have reached. He also noted that if there had been any doubt in their minds, the jurors would not have delivered the judgment that they did: guilty *with* the death penalty.

Asked if he had anything to say before sentence was pronounced, the defendant declared "Yes, sir! I am not guilty!"

Then the judge addressed him directly. "It is the judgment of the Court that you, John Snowden, be delivered by the Warden of the Baltimore County Jail to the sheriff of Anne Arundel County, and there be safely kept in the jail of Anne Arundel County until such time as the Governor of Maryland shall appoint when you shall be taken thence by the sheriff of Anne Arundel County and hanged by the neck until you are dead. And may God have mercy on your soul."[14]

As the sentence was read to him, John Snowden wept copiously.

Attorneys Brady, Grason, and Williams announced that they would now petition the court of appeals for a new trial, and that if it were granted, they would request removal of the case to another court.

As he was escorted out of the courtroom, Snowden shouted "not guilty" several times. Then, under guard, he was immediately returned by automobile to Annapolis to await action by Governor Harrington.[15]

He had calmed down considerably by the time he arrived. As he was readmitted to Anne Arundel County Jail, where he had spent many months waiting for his trial, he remarked to Sheriff Joseph H. Bellis, "Well, boss, they done fetched me back here for you to hang."[16]

# 19

## "Defending Snowden Is Defending the Black People of Maryland"

Apart from straight reporting about the sentence meted out to John Snowden, the white newspapers were strangely reticent about it. The local Towson paper, the *Jeffersonian*, commended the jury, and the people of Baltimore County generally, for their "intelligence and sense of fair play." But the topic did not merit comment on the editorial pages of the *Evening Capital*, the *Baltimore Sun*, or any of the Washington newspapers that had earlier made a meal of Lottie May Brandon's murder.[1]

This was not true of the Black press, which was indignant at the verdict. The *Baltimore Afro-American* put it this way: "There is a general impression in Annapolis and elsewhere that Snowden is innocent, especially in view of the fact that the grinding third degree to which he was subjected failed to force from him a confession of guilt. There is also a feeling that Snowden is being made the scapegoat in the case and that the murder was committed by some person or persons much more closely connected with the Brandon woman. The attorneys for the convicted man have also declared to have discovered new evidence that will materially affect the case."[2]

The Rev. William A. C. Hughes, who had testified at the trial, blamed the blatantly racist appeal of the prosecutors for the verdict. In a letter to the *Washington Bee*, a DC-based African American weekly, he asserted that "few who heard the proceedings in this trial believed any jury could find Snowden guilty, but when the State had finished its awful appeal to the prejudices of these men, and had reminded them that even then some 'nigger' might be in their homes to commit violence, these men, who were a few minutes before perceptibly moved by the appeals of the defense, slowly and noticeably set themselves to do just what was done, and John Snowden was found guilty. Who believed Snowden guilty except that jury? Very few people of either race."[3]

Jennie H. Ross, who had covered part of the trial for the *Afro-American*, agreed, and she found the idea of hanging Snowden indefensible. In a letter to the editor of that publication, she raised several questions: "Why did not the husband of the dead woman have to give account of *his* actions, as well as others? Why was it that the prosecution objected to all points made by the defense and objections were sustained? Why was it the Police Department were so lightly questioned and allowed so much play? Was it because the defense had not prepared its case or witnesses, or was it favoritism to the State? Was it politics or prejudice?"[4]

The announcement of the decision to appeal the case raised the issue of money. Anne Arundel County had already expended more than $2,000 on the Towson trial, and that didn't count witness fees or any of the expenses incurred during the investigation of the murder, which were expected to bring the total bill to approximately $3,500.[5]

As far as the defense was concerned, Annapolitans had raised $223.81 to defray Snowden's legal fees for the trial, and now more would be needed. Meetings were held at the Asbury United Methodist Church on February 12 and March 6 to raise funds for an appeal. In Baltimore, Allen A.M.E. Church was the site of a February 19 meeting convened by the Rev. C. H. Stepteau at which about $400 more was collected. The overall goal was $1,500, and plans were to make additional appeals at other Black churches in the city.[6]

Another meeting on February 25 at Sharp Street Memorial United Methodist Church—Baltimore's first African American congregation—was followed by a joint strategy session between ad hoc committees in Baltimore and Annapolis. Ministers from churches in both communities turned out in force. An unnamed "public-spirited citizen"—later revealed to be George W. Brown, a prominent, Baltimore-based, African American steamboat captain and resort owner—had offered a loan of $500 to secure the services of attorney Brady in carrying the case to a higher court.[7]

24. An advertisement in the *Baltimore Afro-American* invited supporters of John Snowden to a meeting to raise money for his appeal. *Baltimore Afro-American*, February 16, 1918.

On March 2 Brady and Grason filed formal notice of an appeal. The very fact of the appeal amounted to an automatic stay of execution for Snowden. Judge Duncan obligingly signed an order granting them thirty days to review the records of the case and prepare a bill of exceptions, essentially a catalog of his rulings during the trial to which they had objected. The procedure was for the defense to submit its list, for the prosecution to weigh in on each item, and then for the judge to sign his name to each exception with which he agreed. Only those items with which the judge concurred could be sent to the court of appeals for review.[8]

The *Evening Capital* reported that the move was a popular one in Annapolis, where, in light of the "frankly divergent viewpoints" as to Snowden's guilt or innocence, "it is felt that to have the highest court in Maryland pass upon the case will go a long way toward allaying the feeling engendered."[9]

When Snowden returned to Calvert Street Jail, he joined two other accused murderers there. Jerome Slaughter, a white man, was charged with the shooting death of saloon keeper Joe Gezjewski in Curtis Bay the previous November; Thomas Pindall, who was Black, stood accused of dispatching Frank Brewer, his half-brother, with an axe on Christmas day. In early April, the trio was joined by Archie Isaacs, another Black man charged with a murder that bore similarities to that of Lottie May Brandon.

Isaacs, a track walker for the Pennsylvania Railroad, was accused of beating to death thirty-two-year-old Dora Ebert of Patuxent with a blunt instrument in a desolate spot along the tracks near Odenton. His face had been badly scratched and some detritus that might have been skin had been found under her fingernails. And like Snowden before him, he accused another Black man—in his case, two Black men—of the crime. The cast of characters involved in apprehending, questioning, and prosecuting him, including the doctors brought in to perform the autopsy, was much the same as the team that had investigated the Brandon case a year earlier.

Sheriff Bellis, a former alderman and state senator who had only recently been named to his position, directed the jailer to take pains to keep Isaacs and Snowden apart. "It is thought Snowden's experience gained during his long incarceration might suggest to him the coaching of Isaacs in a manner that would interfere with officials who are trying to solve the murder under investigation," Washington's *Evening Star* noted. In the meantime, local residents began demanding "speedy execution not only for Isaacs, but for Snowden," the *Baltimore Sun* warned.[10]

Also in the county jail was John Henry Evans, a Black man charged with the rape of Mary Henson, a thirteen-year-old Black girl. In early May he, too, was sentenced to death by hanging for his crime. This was very unusual, the *Evening Capital* pointed out, as the death penalty was rarely imposed in cases of Black-on-Black crime, apart from murder.[11]

Shortly before the April 2 deadline for filing the bill of exceptions, Snowden's attorneys asked for, and were granted, an extension by the judge. For reasons not made clear at the time, several more extensions were granted, delaying the deadline until the fall.[12]

In late April, Anne Arundel County provided the army with its third group of white draftees—sixty-nine men, fourteen of whom were from Annapolis. They were called to war by the local draft board, still under the supervision of State's Attorney Nicholas H. Green. The list included the name of a former resident of the city who remained on its draft rolls: Valentine N. Brandon. He and his cohorts were ordered to report for duty on April 30, and with no band to serenade them, they left on a special train for Camp Meade. Valentine was bound for France, where, he had said several months before, he might be able to get his mind off of Lottie May's grisly and untimely death.[13]

Four months later, on the first anniversary of her death, the *Evening Capital* printed a memorial to her that he sent from the battlefields of France and had his father hand-deliver to the newspaper. It quoted a popular verse:

It is sweet to know we will meet again
Where parting is no more
And that the one I loved so dearly
Has only gone before.[14]

In the meantime, the days passed slowly for John Snowden. He was visited frequently by the Rev. James A. Briscoe, pastor of the Mt. Moriah A.M.E. Church, who served as his spiritual advisor, and spent time reading the Bible, praying, and singing. But eventually Reverend Briscoe was prevented from coming to see him because Sheriff Bellis believed his visits might be encouraging the prisoner not to confess. Briscoe's wife, Fannie, a passionate believer in Snowden's innocence, who had been elected to chair the Annapolis Committee for Snowden's Defense and who was actively involved in raising funds for his appeal, was allowed to see him, but others were barred.[15]

When July came around, Snowden was treated to a dress rehearsal for what his end might look like if he lost his appeal. Governor Harrington had declined to offer clemency to Archie Isaacs, who had confessed to murder and been convicted but later recanted, and in mid-June set July 12 as the date for his hanging. On that date, after a hearty breakfast, and as a trio of Black vocalists sang gospel hymns, Isaacs was marched to the gallows, which had been erected in the prison yard. The prisoner chanted right along with them to the end. Both John Snowden and John Henry Evans had a clear view of the spectacle from their cell windows, but both chose not to watch. They wrapped themselves in their blankets and buried their faces in their pillows until it was over.

The *Evening Star* noted that the usual practice at Calvert Street Jail was to erect an entirely new gallows and provide a new rope and a new suit of clothes for a prisoner each time there was an execution. But because this was wartime and austerity was the watchword of the day, Isaacs went to his death in the clothing he had worn when he committed the crime and was hanged on an old rope. Only the gallows were new, and they were to remain standing to accommodate others under sentence of death who exhausted their legal remedies. Lest that fact be lost on John Snowden, the *Afro-American* reported later, Sheriff Bellis had shaken his fist in Snowden's face after Isaacs was executed and told him he would be the next to hang—and from the very same scaffold.[16]

Governor Harrington, unconflicted about the Isaacs case, was more concerned about what to do about John Henry Evans, who had, after all, not committed murder, although the crime against a child of which he had been convicted was certainly heinous. In August he asked Lieutenant Joseph F. Dougherty, who had investigated the Brandon murder, to investigate the character of the girl Evans had raped. Dougherty didn't take long. He submitted his report within two weeks, immediately after which time the governor signed Evans's death warrant.[17]

Also in August, attorney Brady announced that the delay in producing and certifying the bill of exceptions in the Snowden case had been due not to the defense's need for more time but to the illness of Judge Frank I. Duncan. This was important because if the defense had been responsible for missing a deadline, the appeal would be thrown out of court. According to the official transcript of the trial, the bill of exceptions was signed by Judge Duncan on September 24.[18]

It was a race against time, however, to see whether it could be printed and forwarded to the court of appeals in time for that body to consider it during its October session. Printing was the responsibility of the appellant, not the state, which meant that money had to be raised, and raised quickly.

When the preliminary docket of the court of appeals was published and Snowden's case did not appear on it, all eyes turned to the Annapolis Committee for Snowden's Defense, which needed to come up with $875 to get the job done. The *Baltimore Afro-American* ran an alarming headline that threatened, "Unless Money Is Raised by People of Maryland in Short Time, Snowden Will Hang." It predicted that if funds were not immediately forthcoming, the appeal would be thrown out and Snowden would be executed.[19]

The alarm had been sounded, and Black people in Annapolis, Baltimore, and Washington stepped up.

The committee had already raised $860 for the Towson trial. Three hundred dollars had been sent from Baltimore via the Rev. C. H. Stepteau, who chaired the local committee; $100 had come from Washington, where the lead had been taken by Dr. M. W. Clair, pastor of the Asbury United Methodist Church, and the remainder had been raised locally in Annapolis by Mrs. Fannie Briscoe and a supporting cast of other women. Mrs. Briscoe proudly told the *Afro-American* that *all* of that money had gone to defray attorneys' fees, with not a penny diverted for travel expenses, carfare, or anything else.

But holding a mass meeting, which was the usual way to raise funds, was a dicey proposition because Annapolis, like other cities, was undergoing a wave of the great influenza pandemic and public gatherings were dangerous and discouraged. So the *Afro-American* itself agreed to receive money on behalf of the committee and print a list of subscribers. "Defending Snowden," it declared, "is defending the Black people of Maryland."[20]

By the middle of the month the necessary funds had been collected. The paper reported that ten Baltimore businessmen and ministers had met in the newspaper's offices and decided to borrow $500 and bring it to Mrs. Briscoe. They were willing to accept personal responsibility for its repayment, though they expected it to be taken care of later through a public subscription. Taken together with $242 previously collected by the organization in Annapolis, it was provided to Snowden's attorneys and, although the total fell short of the goal, it provided sufficient reassurance to the printer to go ahead and produce the bill of exceptions and the transcript of the Towson trial. Shortly afterward, another $175 was sent from Baltimore.[21]

The document reached the appellate court just in time, and the case was assigned number 95 on its docket, which meant the court would consider the case but likely not until December at the earliest.[22]

In early November, Mrs. Briscoe gave the *Afro-American* an accounting of the moneys raised by the Committee for Snowden's Defense, noting proudly that the administration of funds had been accomplished entirely by women. About $650 had come from individuals, churches, and societies in Annapolis; $475 had been raised by Reverend Stepteau's committee in Baltimore; and another $100 had come from Washington. Taken together with the $500 loan and some miscellaneous contributions received through the offices of the *Afro-American*, the total came to nearly $1,800.

Of that amount, $320 had been paid out in lawyers' fees, $85 had been expended for expert testimony, and $36 had gone to travel expenses for witnesses. Most of the rest was paid to the clerk of the court at Towson for obtaining the trial transcript and for printing costs.

Mrs. Briscoe made a special effort to call out the generosity of attorney Brady in her report. "It will be observed that the chief attorney has received no compensation whatever except what was agreed on for the first trial when it was expected the case would be disposed of in Anne Arundel County. Attorney Brady had been very considerate and kind in meeting demands for the Committee when money was not in hand."

About Reverend Stepteau's effort, however, she was less kind, noting that while the Annapolis committee had not spent a single cent on itself, the Baltimoreans had used $75 of the funds collected for Snowden for their own expenses. The *Afro-American* piled on in an editorial, observing that "it is regrettable that there was not charity enough in the hearts of Dr. Stepteau's Citizens' Committee and sympathy enough for Snowden as well as respect for the donors of the funds to see to it that all the money raised was passed on intact to the proper persons."[23]

Entreaties for funds for John Snowden's appeal came in many forms. Preachers asked for contributions from their pulpits and newspapers ran advertisements. But perhaps the most moving appeal came from a self-employed, thirty-one-year-old carpenter in Baltimore named John M. Turpin, who published a plaintive verse in the *Afro-American* urging fellow Blacks to rally behind the prisoner:

You who love your sons and daughters
Negro dwellers in this state,
Could you stand and see them slaughtered,
Victims of a cruel fate,

Well, we know the weight of hatred,
Draged [*sic*] our brother to his doom,
And would send a guiltless creature,
Disgraced thus, down to his tomb.

Let us rally to our brother
Give our money, give our time,
Thus to rescue this our fellow
Who stands guiltless of this crime.
We will fight an unjust verdict
With our money, might and brain,
And from Maryland's history wash
Away this awful bloody stain.[24]

As the appellate court worked its way through the cases on its docket, it looked as if the body would not get to case ninety-five until Christmastime. But at the request of acting attorney general Ogle Marbury, the high-profile case was allowed to jump the queue, and December 3 was designated as the day the court would hear arguments.

# 20

## "We Have Found No Reversible Error"

The court of appeals did not get to the case of *John Snowden v. State of Maryland* on December 3, 1918; it took two days beyond that before it convened in Annapolis to consider it. But before the court could hear substantive arguments, it had to deal with a procedural issue. Because the record had not been transmitted to the appellate court within the time required by law, the prosecution sought dismissal on a technicality.

Judgment had been rendered on February 13 and the order for an appeal had been filed on March 2. But the appellate court had not received the transcript until just over seven months later because Judge Duncan had not signed off on the bill of exceptions—a requirement for an appeal—until September 23. His illness had kept him from presiding in Towson from July 5 until September 16. Because this was no fault of the appellant in the case, that is, John Snowden, or of his counsel, the court dismissed the motion.[1]

The exceptions the defense had taken to various rulings by Judge Duncan on testimony and evidence formed the basis for the appeal. During the Towson trial, the defense attorneys had taken a grand total of sixty-six exceptions to his various decisions, but attorney Brady chose to raise only twenty of them in the petition to the appellate court. The court considered almost all of them anyway; of the sixty-six, the judge had declined to sign off on just three, and only those were not reviewed.[2]

Because Snowden had already been incarcerated for more than a year, a speedy verdict was expected. If the appellate court struck down any consequential rulings of Judge Duncan, a new trial would be ordered.

But if it sustained the verdict, it would then be left to Governor Harrington either to offer clemency or to sign Snowden's death warrant and choose a date for his execution.[3]

The case was heard by Chief Justice Andrew Hunter Boyd and seven associate justices. The state was represented by acting attorney general Ogle Marbury, filling in while his boss, Albert Ritchie, took a leave of absence to serve as general counsel to the War Industries Board, and by State's Attorney Nicholas H. Green. A. Theodore Brady and C. Gus Grason appeared for Snowden.

*Snowden v. State of Maryland* was the first case considered by the Court on December 5 and arguments were complete by lunchtime. The oral arguments do not survive in toto, but excerpts quoted in the press suggest that Brady's strongest one concerned the question of rape. Because rape had not been and could not be proven, Snowden had never been charged with it, and Brady insisted that because the topic was highly prejudicial to his case, *all* discussion of it should have been stricken from the record.

"The object and purpose of the State in introducing such testimony was, no doubt, to establish a motive," Brady told the justices. "We feel that a motive should be established by substantial facts and proven beyond a reasonable doubt, but to say that a woman was raped because a mucus secretion was found on her person and no other evidence to support it would be most dangerous, and an opinion of the kind . . . should not have been allowed to go to the jury."[4]

Brady and Grason also argued that Mary Perkins, one of the chief witnesses against Snowden, had had interested motives in accusing him. He pointed out that she had said nothing about what she had allegedly seen until five days after the murder, and she had come forward only after a $500 reward was offered. Judge Duncan had not permitted that subject to be explored at trial.[5]

Only the *Baltimore Afro-American* reported in any detail about State's Attorney Green's arguments, which it was sure had engendered "extreme dissatisfaction" in nearly all quarters. The paper quoted Green as contending that Snowden would have been hanged long before were it not for "certain interests in Annapolis and Baltimore" who allegedly

**25.** The Maryland Court of Appeals in Annapolis, ca. 1905. Library of Congress (LC-DIG-det-4a12575).

"kept the case alive and raised a good bit of money making capital out of it." In other words, politics.

Green had placed the Rev. Ernest Sumner Williams squarely in his crosshairs. He accused the preacher of inciting other Black witnesses not to cooperate with the prosecution and of threatening those who did "with a coat of tar and feathers." The *Afro-American* asserted that Green had insisted Reverend Williams had been the cause of the departure of the "chief colored witnesses against Snowden"—by which he surely meant Williams's neighbors, Mary Perkins and Edith Creditt—from Annapolis.[6]

On December 13, the court of appeals completed its docket and adjourned for the holidays. It was announced that it would reconvene in mid-January 1919 and would render its judgments on January 14 and 15.

The decision on *Snowden v. State* was not actually handed down until eleven a.m. on January 16, and it was a complete and total victory for the prosecution. In its ruling, delivered by Associate Justice N. Charles Burke, the court first clarified that its role was not to relitigate the case but simply to determine whether Judge Duncan had made errors of sufficient gravity to warrant a reversal of the judgment of the lower court.

"This Court has no power to pass upon the guilt or innocence of the appellant," the decision read. "He elected to be tried by a jury. They were the exclusive judges of the weight and sufficiency of the evidence to establish the guilt of the accused, and we have no power to disturb their finding unless we find that the Court during the course of the trial committed some reversible or injurious error either in the admission or rejection of testimony."[7]

The ruling went on to summarize the facts of the case that had been proven without contradiction, and then to take up the various exceptions raised by the defense one by one and to comment on each. Among them:

> The defense had objected to the introduction of photographs of the corpse unless it could be proven when they were taken, since it was possible someone had tampered with the body. The Court ruled that "as these photographs were merely representations of injuries which had been fully described by the witness, and not denied to exist, their introduction in evidence could not be held to have injured the accused."

> The defense had not been permitted to do all it could to assault the credibility of Mary Perkins and Edith Creditt, but "the jury, who saw all the witnesses and heard all their testimony, evidently believed they told the truth." That was enough for the appellate court.

> The defense had put a lot of effort into excluding testimony by Drs. Carr and Hopkins concerning the second autopsy, since it presented evidence extremely damning to its case. But the Court quoted Dr. Hopkins' assertion that "the various wounds that I mentioned that I found in the autopsy in Annapolis were still present," and did not find anything about admitting it harmful to the defendant.

> The defense had asked that all references to rape be stricken from the record, since rape had not been charged or proven. The Court ruled that the discussion of semen on the body

had been introduced for the purpose of describing its condition, and it found Judge Duncan justified in permitting it. "Whether it showed, in connection with all the other facts and circumstances in evidence, that a rape had been committed upon Mrs. Brandon," it concluded, "was a question to be determined by the jury."

The prosecution had objected to Valentine Brandon being asked whether he had told a newspaper man after the fact that he had found the dollar bill Snowden was alleged to have taken from Lottie May. The judge had sustained the objection. The appellate court found this proper, as "the question was too general and indefinite."

Rachel E. Stewart, the maternity nurse, had not been permitted to answer a question concerning her experience with eclamptic patients. The Court found that "there was no offer to prove that Mrs. Brandon had died of eclampsia." Finding nothing in the case to support such a suggestion, it ruled that excluding the question had been proper.

Mary Williams, wife of the Rev. Ernest Williams, had not been permitted to testify to having heard noises from the Brandon home the night before the murder. The defense had hoped to use her testimony to cast suspicion on Valentine Brandon, who, they asserted, had been exonerated too quickly by the police. The Court ruled that because five other witnesses had testified to seeing Mrs. Brandon alive the following morning, and "there being no evidence to connect any one, except Snowden, with the crime, or to justify a suspicion that any particular person, other than he, had committed it," the testimony was "clearly inadmissible and properly refused."

As far as Snowden's contention that he had been abused during his interrogation, Brady had sought exclusion of the testimony of Marshal Robert G. Carter and Deputy Marshal Samuel House of the Baltimore Police on the grounds that their testimony was not proper, as it was not a rebuttal. Here the Court quoted a legal text that asserted that "it is not always easy to draw the line between what is rebutting evidence and what is evidence properly adducible in chief," and that allowing it had been within the discretion of the lower court, and reviewable by the appellate court only if it had been "manifestly wrong and substantially injurious."

The appellate court noted in conclusion, "We have given the case our most careful and earnest consideration, and we have found no reversible error committed by the trial court in any of its rulings, and the judgment will, therefore, be affirmed." It sided with the defense on almost nothing, and where there was any gray area, ruled for the prosecution.[8]

Much of the reasoning cited by the appellate court in plowing in so completely behind Judge Duncan seems wrongheaded a century later, as it is easy to see several of its rulings as questionable if not shocking. Whether the justices were motivated by *racial* prejudice is not clear or provable. For better or worse, however, they set the stage for a complete shutout in favor of the state.

It remained for the denial of the appeal to be transmitted to the circuit court in Towson, from which it would be forwarded to the office of the governor. That would be the trigger for action on Governor Harrington's part—either to set a date for execution or to offer clemency.

But things didn't look good for the prisoner. The *Evening Capital* reported ominously that "those close to Governor Harrington say he is convinced of the guilt of Snowden and will not hesitate to set a date for the execution."[9]

# PART 3    1919

# 21

## "I Forgive Their False Oaths"

The task of informing John Snowden of the decision of the court of appeals fell to Sheriff Joseph H. Bellis, who attempted to use it as a lever to coax a confession out of the prisoner, as others had endeavored to do in the past. Told to prepare to meet his God, Snowden was, of course, distraught, and he wept openly. But he remained adamant that he knew nothing about the murder of Lottie May Brandon.

"If this jail were to open and God himself come down," he told the sheriff, "He would tell you the same thing."[1]

Attorney Brady told the *Afro-American* that he felt he had done everything possible to save Snowden's life. Despite Brady's earlier association with the effort to disenfranchise Annapolis's Black voters, no one ever suggested that he had not given Snowden's defense his all. He said the next step would be for interested parties to bring the case to the Governor. And that is exactly what supporters of Snowden had in mind.[2]

At that point, what the prisoner needed most was not money; it was a public outcry. Within a week of the appellate court's decision, Governor Harrington began to receive written and oral requests from local Blacks for clemency for Snowden. The first lobbying effort was spearheaded by the Rev. Simon P. W. Drew, the forty-six-year-old pastor of Washington DC's Cosmopolitan Baptist Church. An evangelist, Drew was president of several national religious organizations. He told the *Washington Herald* he could secure the signatures of six hundred thousand Black people around the country to urge clemency. And he visited Governor Harrington to tell him the same thing.[3]

Harrington also agreed to receive a delegation of seven Black community leaders in Baltimore on the morning of Saturday, January 24. Led by Dr. James Robert Lincoln Diggs, a civil rights activist and president of the Maryland Association for Social Service, and including the Rev. P. C. Neal of the First Baptist Church and the Rev. Frank Williams of the Perkins Square Baptist Church, the group appeared at the governor's office in the Union Trust Building. Diggs argued for clemency for Snowden, pointing out that an all-white jury was hardly a "jury of his peers" and stressing the fact that the testimony that convicted him was entirely circumstantial.

Harrington didn't pull any punches with them. He told the delegates that he had known Mary Perkins personally; she had worked for a time in the executive mansion and he believed her a reliable witness. He corrected Diggs, asserting that the evidence against John Snowden had been "indirect" rather than "circumstantial," even though the two terms mean essentially the same thing. He also recalled that he had personally tried fourteen murder cases while in private practice and insisted that none had been as cut and dried as the Snowden case.

Unless he could be convinced by new evidence, he said, he planned to let the death penalty stand. And as he rose to his feet, he declared to those assembled that commuting Snowden's sentence would be "the greatest injustice to your race," adding, "The man is guilty of a foul crime, and for me to interfere with his execution would be simply to prepare the way for a reign of lynch law."[4]

What he seems to have implied is that if *he* did not arrange for Snowden's death, white mobs might do the job instead.

By all accounts, Harrington took his responsibilities toward the case quite seriously. He spent much of the week on it. He read the trial transcript at least three times, and on Sunday, January 25, visited Second Street, a short walk from the governor's mansion, for a firsthand look at the scene of the crime. He not only stopped at no. 29, where the Brandons had lived, but also stood at the window of no. 30 from which the two sisters reported seeing Snowden leave the Brandon home. And he retraced the route from Acton Lane to Martin's Bar that Snowden said he had taken on the day of the murder.[5]

**26.** Governor Emerson Columbus Harrington. Collection of the Maryland State Archives (MSA SC 5161-1-22).

Finally, on January 29, the papers were delivered from the Towson court, and Governor Harrington signed John Snowden's death warrant. Snowden would hang a month thence, on February 28, from the same gallows on which Archie Isaacs and, more recently, John H. Evans had met their fate. The warrant was then sent for signature to Secretary of State Thomas W. Simmons, after which it would be delivered to Sheriff Bellis and read to the prisoner.

By February 1, however, Bellis still had not received the document, and he told the *Evening Capital* why. Secretary of State Simmons, an opponent of capital punishment, had refused to affix his signature to the death warrant. The paper speculated that if Governor Harrington were determined to see Snowden hanged, he would have to appoint a new secretary of state. Something, though, changed Simmons's mind; perhaps it was the fact that his job was at stake. Within a few days he signed the document.[6]

Signing the death warrant did not end the issue for Governor Harrington. He was still besieged with petitions for clemency. He attended a February 12 meeting with a larger group of Black lawyers, ministers, government employees, and other influentials at the John Wesley Methodist Church in Baltimore, where he heard several more pleas on Snowden's behalf. But here, too, he was clear that he had gone over the case very carefully and was firm in his decision.[7]

After Snowden was informed of the date for his execution, he was placed in the death cell on the third floor, where he took ill. He was seized with a spell of vomiting, and by some accounts suffered a nervous breakdown. Once he recovered in a day or two, his appetite returned and he was once again eating three meals a day. When he asked some friends who had visited him in jail for a cake, however, the request was vetoed by the Sheriff Bellis; condemned men were given whatever they wanted to eat, but everything had to be provided by the jailers.[8]

Snowden was now receiving daily visits from the Rev. Benjamin S. Holt, a local Black preacher who had taken over the mantle of spiritual advisor from Reverend Briscoe. He was also meeting regularly with a woman named Georgianna Brice Boston, known as Georgia, a deeply religious member of Mt. Moriah A.M.E. Church. Mrs. Boston had worked, variously, as a domestic, a janitor, a midwife, and a seamstress. With an unwavering belief in the power of prayer, she came to the jailhouse regularly to pray with the prisoners. Buoyed by her visits, Snowden became more cheerful, and spent much of his time singing.[9]

Like many death row prisoners, he found religion. As a child, he had been taken to Sunday school by his mother, but he had strayed from the church as an adult. More recently, he had occasionally allowed Edna Wallace to drag him to Baptist services, but he had not been a true believer. All of that changed after he was sentenced. "I have been brought to the foot of the cross and washed in the blood of Jesus, and now his true light shines into my soul," he told Georgia Boston. He said later that he had prayed more during the previous two months than he had in his entire life.[10]

In mid-February he dictated a lengthy statement to Boston in which he restated his innocence. But he also had surprisingly kind words for his accusers. "I want to see Mary Perkins and her sister," he said. "I want to show them the scaffold that they have been the cause of me being hung, on February 28. Then I want to shake their hands and tell

**27.** Georgianna Brice Boston, one of John Snowden's spiritual advisors. Courtesy of Deborah J. Moore.

them I forgive their false oaths and advise them to get right with God so as to meet me in heaven."[11]

He also expressed a wish to meet Governor Harrington, not to plead for a reprieve but rather to thank him for his interest in his case. He was never granted an audience, but others were. On February 20 word came that the governor would receive a visit from a delegation of local businessmen headed by attorney Brady, and a clemency petition from some forty to fifty prominent men of the city. He told the press he was receiving communications from every part of the state, and many letters to the editor appeared in local newspapers. There is little doubt that Harrington was feeling a good deal of heat: not enough to make him reconsider his position, but the pressure was such that he felt a growing need to explain his decision to the general public. He told the press he would shortly publish a summary of the evidence that had persuaded him to decline to intervene.[12]

As the governor now seemed immovable, some who believed in Snowden's innocence were hatching a new scheme to save him. It was still possible for the Supreme Court of the United States to review his case. To that end, George Luther Pendleton, a Black criminal lawyer of Baltimore who had made the daily trek to Towson to watch the trial, sprang into action. On February 19, he appeared in Annapolis and asked to see Snowden. He had with him the necessary documents to seek writs of certiorari—whereby the Supreme Court could, on its own initiative, review the case—and of habeas corpus. But they required the prisoner's signature before he could proceed.[13]

Fifty-three-year-old Pendleton, a Virginia native, had graduated from the Hampton Normal and Agricultural Institute (later Hampton University) and gone on to study law at Howard University in Washington. He had settled in Annapolis, where he began his law practice, and had relocated to Baltimore in 1908.[14]

Pendleton had not been retained by Snowden; the lawyer said he was representing the Monumental Lodge of Elks of Baltimore, and he arrived with three of his lodge brothers. His appearance was a surprise to Sheriff Bellis and to State's Attorney Green, who did not permit him to meet with the prisoner. In fact, after he stated his business, he was told by Bellis that Snowden had already cost the state enough money without dragging it through additional legal proceedings.

**28.** Attorney George Luther Pendleton. Courtesy of the Maryland Center for History and Culture (Item ID #PP240.005).

On reflection, however—and probably after realizing what weak ground he was on—Green relented and Bellis accepted the documents and had them read to Snowden by a white attorney named Jerry L. Smith, who was described in the press as the "sheriff's advisor." He appears to have been the same Jerry L. Smith who had attempted to have Snowden freed on a writ of habeas corpus shortly after his arrest in 1917.

Smith read the documents to Snowden, who agreed to sign them after consulting with Reverend Holt, and he did so in a shaky hand. They were then handed to attorney Pendleton, who was waiting outside the jailhouse.[15]

Help for Snowden was also forthcoming from one other familiar source. Ella Rush Murray, who had come to believe in Snowden's innocence, was determined to do all she could to free him. At her invitation—and presumably at her expense—she had brought New York attorney and detective Grace Humiston back to Annapolis. Mrs. Humiston, who had never been convinced of Snowden's guilt, was now asked to assist in a last-minute effort to save his life.[16]

The "woman Sherlock Holmes" arrived in Annapolis on February 21 and plunged right back into the case. She met with Sheriff Bellis and called on Reverend Briscoe. She also spoke with the governor's secretary. Declaring that she had uncovered new evidence in the case that would prove Snowden innocent, she told the press she was determined to lay it all before for the governor.

She would soon have her opportunity. Harrington announced that he would meet with any and all persons who had the least doubt concerning Snowden's guilt, and he invited all comers to an open meeting at his office in the State House at eleven a.m. on Monday, February 24.[17]

Humiston told the press she would have a statement for them that morning.

# 22

## "This Is No Case for Mercy"

Having already sat through at least five meetings with petitioners seeking clemency for John Snowden, Governor Harrington was more interested in using the Monday meeting to defend his decision than he was in hearing the same old arguments on the prisoner's behalf. Snowden was scheduled to die that Friday, and Harrington meant to ensure that he did.

That, however, did not stop between four and five hundred people— male and female, Black and white—from crowding into his conference room to meet with him. The chamber was packed to capacity.

"They were persons from all walks of life," the *Afro-American* reported giddily, "from the highest to the lowest. There were the wealthy like Mrs. Spencer Murray elegantly gowned, midshipmen, cadets, soldiers and sailors. The businessmen of Annapolis, led by Mr. James Munroe, owner of large real estate holdings and president of the local trust company were there, and then finally the townspeople and farmers. All of these were white."

"Sprinkled among them," the paper added, "was a minority of fifty colored folks. These, too, came from all walks of life, but not a one of them had a word to say. It seemed as if they had turned their cause over to the other race, and were standing back to see how well their friends would lambast the Governor."[1]

The white Annapolitans in the room did a pretty good job of that. Attorney Brady spoke first. He argued that reasonable doubt existed in the case, and that the ends of justice would still be accomplished if Snowden were permitted to live out his days in prison. Brady presented a petition signed by dozens of prominent Annapolitans and asserted it was the nearly unanimous desire of the town that Harrington commute Snowden's sentence. "I wouldn't ask this to be done if I did not believe him to be innocent," he added.

A white Baltimore man named William M. R. Campbell then attempted to speak, but he was shut down immediately by the governor, who recognized him as the writer of a controversial letter to the *Baltimore Sun* in which he had charged that Snowden was being hanged to shield someone else, and because he was a "nigger."

"Because he was handy, because he is Black, Snowden must die," Campbell had written, "a victim of race prejudice, of blind insensate hate! Poor, helpless, rude, low-born, untaught, bewildered and alone—nothing short of a miracle can save him now. With all the emphasis at my command, I hereby proclaim his trial a mockery, a farce, a flagrant travesty of justice. . . . No white man would have been convicted on such fragmentary evidence, upon arguments so unsustained, upon testimony so weak, fantastic and remote."[2]

Pointing an accusing finger in Campbell's direction, an agitated Harrington exclaimed, "I'm glad I found you out! I don't want to hear from you, and I *won't*. For God's sake, shut up! Don't come here asking about facts in this case when you don't know anything about the facts. You should be turned over to the detectives and prosecuted for writing that article." A detective then escorted Campbell out of the room and all the way to the depot, where he was placed aboard a Baltimore-bound train and told not to return.[3]

The biggest shock of the day, however, was another clemency petition that bore only eleven signatures but was by far the most important plea the governor received. It was presented to him by R. E. Lee Bosley, and was signed by Bosley himself and ten other members of the jury that had voted to convict John Snowden, including the foreman. It read: "The undersigned, members of the jury that tried John Snowden for the murder of Mrs. Brandon at Annapolis, realizing the possibility of mistake in human affairs, and after further considering the matter, feel that justice would be done if the sentence in Snowden's case was commuted to life imprisonment, and we hereby petition the Governor to commute his sentence to life imprisonment."[4]

The jury, of course, had had the option at trial of declaring Snowden guilty of murder in the first degree *without* capital punishment and had not taken it. Questioned by Harrington about this apparent change of heart, Bosley asserted that he still thought Snowden guilty of murder and acknowledged that he knew of no new facts in the case that suggested otherwise. But, he said, in view of "so much talk" about the case, he and the other signatories believed it was possible human judgment had been in error, and that commuting Snowden's sentence to life in prison would be a more prudent course.[5]

James Munroe then addressed the governor. "Whoever is guilty should hang," he said, "but let's not hang the wrong man in our haste to get the right one." He proceeded to read from a lengthy petition signed by nearly sixty white citizens, male and female, that laid out several reasons why the execution should not proceed, explaining that the lack of signatures of Blacks was because of his desire "to show that the best white people of Annapolis" wanted a commutation of the sentence. But if the governor could not see his way clear to grant this, they requested, in the alternative, a ninety-day reprieve to afford Snowden's supporters the time to secure new evidence.[6]

He made much of the fact that eleven of the twelve jurors had changed their minds. "This, we respectfully submit to your Excellency, is equivalent to their having found a verdict in the first instance, as provided by statute, of guilty of murder in the first degree without capital punishment." But he gave no reason why they had not done so in the first place other than to suggest that "there must be in their minds serious doubt as to the correctness of their verdict."

Finally, the governor addressed the crowd. He was actually ill that day and felt feverish, but that didn't stop him from going on for an hour and a quarter.

He recounted at length the evidence marshaled against Snowden, making clear his mastery of the facts of the case. He asserted that Snowden had had access to able counsel and had received a fair trial "absolutely lacking throughout any feeling of racial hostility against the accused."

He said he believed implicitly the two sisters who had testified against Snowden. And he saw no motive on their part for perjury. He couldn't imagine why they would accuse a member of their own race if he had not been guilty, especially after having been warned that to do so might cause a race riot.

"I happen to know those colored women and they have a most excellent reputation. They are not after any reward and have not asked for any. They have been made to suffer for standing squarely up for right and justice and they are entitled to praise, not censure."

He suggested that the only testimony in Snowden's favor was that of Reverend Williams. In dismissing it, however, he was careful to steer clear of directly accusing the preacher of perjury. "I do not doubt that Rev. Williams and Rev. Hughes were on the porch at some time in the morning, but I think it is very evident that they were not there between 11:30 and 12 o'clock," he said.

Governor Harrington believed Snowden's motive for entering Lottie May Brandon's home had been robbery, and that her stockings had been removed in search of cash. But "coming into contact with the white woman's flesh aroused the beast in him," he imagined, "and he committed the greater crimes, murder and rape."

He took the allegation of rape almost as an article of faith. "Dr. Joyce, Dr. Welch and Dr. Hopkins all testified that in their opinion Mrs. Brandon, beyond any doubt, had been murdered and she had been raped or an attempt at rape had been made upon her," he asserted, although this was not strictly accurate.

"I am opposed to capital punishment, but I will never start the exercise of my prerogative in a case of this character," he said. "I refused recently to commute to life imprisonment a colored man guilty of rape upon a colored girl," he said in a reference to the John H. Evans case, "and I shall certainly *not* commute the sentence of a negro who has committed, in my opinion, both murder and rape upon a *white* woman, and now seeks by falsely claiming his innocence to save himself from the gallows."

"I am a friend of the colored race," he insisted, "but I believe the greatest harm I could do to their race is to commute Snowden's sentence. The best citizens of his race *want* Snowden to pay the penalty, if guilty," he added, without citing any evidence for this claim, which was almost certainly untrue.

"The fair name of the State must be vindicated. The virtue of our women, white or Black, must be protected. Willful, deliberate, cold-blooded and ravishing murderers must pay the full penalty of the law. This is no case for mercy. This is a case, if there ever was one, where the law should be vindicated."

"I will not interfere," he said in conclusion. "The full power of the State will stand behind the sheriff of Anne Arundel County and the execution of the sentence of the court."[7]

"No governor of the state ever witnessed such a demonstration of white people in behalf of a colored man convicted of murder," the *Afro-American* declared later, noting that the disapproval of the audience was palpable and not lost on the governor. After he had finished, attorney Brady rose and asked if he might present a petition prepared by Grace Humiston and Ella Rush Murray for a ninety-day stay of execution to enable the collection of new evidence. But Harrington, who had spent two-and-a-half hours with Humiston the day before, had had his fill of her. Agitated after his long, passionate monologue, he rose and made his way to his private office.

It took some time before the guests realized he wasn't coming back. Once it was all over, one of his friends was overheard to remark, "If I were Governor, I would not have gone through this for ten thousand dollars."[8]

On its editorial page, the *Evening Capital* admired "the wonderful spirit of brotherhood" that had caused so many people to turn up at the meeting, opining that "no one can question the honesty of the motives of most of those who are taking a prominent part in the effort to save John Snowden from the gallows." But it lamented the gathering's atmosphere, in which the governor, sensing hostility, had become defensive and in which dispassionate judgment, the paper believed, had been in short supply and had given way to emotion.[9]

After Harrington left, Humiston and Murray distributed copies of their petition, which purported to set out new evidence that called the guilty verdict into question, and offered to provide the governor with documentation to support each item. Among them were these assertions:

Lottie May Brandon had told her nurse that she had "received the attentions" of a man other than her husband. She had made a similar remark to a real estate man to whom she had allegedly gone for the purpose of renting another apartment.

Late in the afternoon on the day before she was murdered, Lottie May appeared distressed and worried to a neighbor. Shortly thereafter, her husband said something to her in an angry tone of voice and she left the house abruptly and took a walk down the street.

On the night before her death, two people heard loud noises coming from the kitchen of her home. Similar sounds were heard the next morning.

When Mrs. Brandon's nurse arrived at the scene of the murder on the afternoon of August 8, the house was in order; there had been no evidence of any struggle other than the marks upon her body. Lottie's rings were on her fingers, suggesting that robbery had not been a motive for the murder.

It had been common talk among the neighbors and friends of the Brandons that their marriage was not a happy one. A young man who had called at the Brandon home at 10 a.m. days before the murder was prepared to testify that a man in shirt sleeves other than Valentine Brandon had opened the front door when he rang.

Valentine had appeared distracted on the morning of the murder. He failed to greet a friend on his way to work. After he boarded the ferry to work, he suddenly disembarked and paced up and down the wharf, suggesting something important was on his mind.

The morning after the murder, Valentine had called at the insurance office to inquire about his wife's insurance.

One of Mrs. Brandon's slippers was missing, and the nurse was prepared to testify that the fatal wound could have been made with the heel of the slipper.

When he returned to the house after having summoned the doctor for his wife, Valentine did not return to the bedroom, nor did he seem anxious to learn whether she was ill or dead. In fact, the nurse would testify that he ate a large dinner in the front room while she lay dead in the bedroom.[10]

In her effort to gather and present new evidence, Humiston had made herself obnoxious, and not only to the governor. The *Evening Star* reported on her attempt to secure a statement from one of the witnesses who had testified in the case that would contradict her own testimony. She had allegedly spoken harshly to the woman and had been ordered out of her house.[11]

But more importantly, her entire effort smacked of desperation. The bits and pieces she had come up with, many of which amounted to little more than innuendo, fell far short of anything likely to persuade a fair-minded person that John Snowden was not proven guilty beyond a reasonable doubt.

# 23

## "You Can Appeal to Me until Doomsday"

On Monday, February 24, attorney Charles S. Williams, the Washington DC lawyer on Snowden's defense team, visited the prisoner to obtain his signature on yet another affidavit. He took it immediately to the U.S. District Court in Baltimore in an apparently quixotic quest to free the prisoner on a writ of habeas corpus. Williams's argument was that the case ought to have been tried in Anne Arundel County. No one thought the plea stood much of a chance of success, but it was a necessary step before the Supreme Court could be approached. As expected, Judge John C. Rose made short work of the attorney and denied the application.[1]

Since Governor Harrington had washed his hands of the case—he had finally told a group of Snowden supporters that "you can appeal to me until Doomsday for clemency and you will not get it"—this left the Supreme Court as Snowden's last hope. Williams was working with George Luther Pendleton, and within a few minutes of the district court ruling, the two attorneys, assisted by Thomas Beckett, another Washington lawyer, filed an appeal. All they needed was for the clerk of the district court to certify it so they could take it with them to Washington.

The Supreme Court was not in session, but their plan was to present it anyway to Chief Justice Edward Douglass White, the justice responsible for the circuit court that oversaw Maryland cases. If he accepted it, it would have the effect of staying Snowden's execution until the Court either acted or declined to act on it.[2]

The substance of the appeal was that Snowden's rights had been trampled because he had been tried by an all-white jury, and because, they alleged, his case had been summarily moved out of Annapolis without his agreement. They further contended that the jury did not deliver a proper verdict when it simply pronounced him "guilty" without specifying the degree of guilt, and that it had been the *judge* who had added the words "in the first degree" on his own initiative. It is worth noting that both of these latter assertions were contrary to the facts as stated in the press at the time. The *Evening Capital* had reported that after the prosecution had insisted on a change in venue, the defense had agreed to move the trial to Towson, and in the *Washington Times'* coverage of the case, it had been the jury's foreman who added the words "in the first degree" after the judge prodded him.[3]

According to the appeal, the verdict was thus the product of the court rather than the jury, which meant that no legitimate verdict had ever actually been rendered against Snowden. This, it was argued, violated his rights under the Fourteenth Amendment, which guaranteed that "no person shall be deprived of life, liberty or property without due process of law."

The appeal also cited a technicality—that the verdict had not been entered on the docket at the time of sentencing, as the law required, but rather on the following day, "out of the presence of the jury, the court and of the condemned man."

Despite the fact that Chief Justice White was a conservative Democrat who had fought for the Confederacy and had voted with the majority in the 1896 *Plessy v. Ferguson* case that had upheld the constitutionality of racial segregation laws, Pendleton told the *Afro-American* he was hopeful of success. He explained that the Supreme Court had already handed down an opinion that had deemed it illegal "for colored people to be condemned to death by juries of which no colored man was a member."[4]

That interpretation, however, was not exactly accurate. Pendleton was doubtless referring to the 1880 case of *Strauder v. West Virginia*, in which the Supreme Court had invalidated the wholesale exclusion of a particular race of people from a jury pool, asking rhetorically, "how

29. Edward Douglass White, chief justice of the Supreme Court. Library of Congress (LC-USZ62-107142).

can it be maintained that compelling a colored man to submit to a trial for his life by a jury drawn from a panel from which the State has expressly excluded every man of his race, because of color alone, however well-qualified in other respects, is not a denial to him of equal protection?"[5]

In *Strauder*, however, the Court had *not* prohibited either the prosecution or the defense from using peremptory challenges to exclude *individual* jurors on the grounds of race. That practice was not declared unconstitutional until more than a century later, in 1986. What this meant was that Snowden had a legitimate grievance under the law if the *entire* jury pool in his trial had been deliberately engineered to be white, but not if one or more Blacks had been present on the panel but not selected because of prosecutorial challenges. Which, if either, of these scenarios had occurred is unknown.[6]

That same day, Sheriff Bellis delivered Snowden the new blue serge suit that had been ordered for him—the one in which he was to be

**30.** The only known photograph of John Snowden, taken through prison bars during the week prior to his execution. His suit is the one in which he was hanged and buried. *True Detective Mysteries*, March 1930.

hanged and buried—and a pair of black shoes. He put them on as soon as they were given to him, fell to his knees, buried his head in his arms at the side of his cot, and prayed for more than two hours. He also spent several hours with Reverend Holt and a choir of gospel singers, the only visitors he was permitted.

Snowden asked that a photograph be taken of him in his suit so he might distribute prints among his friends. Reverend Holt was asked to make the arrangements, and the sheriff gave his permission, provided the photographer shoot the picture through the bars of his cell. He was unwilling to take any chances by letting the prisoner out, even for a moment.

The appearance of the suit of clothes also raised the uncomfortable question of his burial. "I don't want to be buried in Potter's Field," Snowden told Bellis. And he was equally adamant that he wished to be interred in a casket. But although money had been raised for his defense, there was none for a funeral, and his family told the sheriff they could not afford one. Bellis insisted that unless the body could be cared for properly, it would not be released to them but rather taken directly from the gallows to Potter's Field. By Thursday, however, one day before the execution was to take place, several Black men called on Bellis to inform him that money had been raised for a proper cemetery burial.[7]

There was much ballyhoo in the run-up to Friday's planned execution. Governor Harrington received several anonymous death threats, one of which reviled him for "railroading" Snowden "merely because he was a negro," and the *Evening Capital* reported on a missive from an unknown writer—"apparently a colored person" it declared without evidence—claiming Snowden's innocence. But surely the most poignant appeal came not by mail but in person, on the day before the scheduled execution, when Sheriff Bellis was accosted by a shabbily-dressed, handicapped, and blind Black man of about sixty as he emerged from the courthouse. The man had been waiting for some time for the sheriff to emerge.

"I want to go upon that scaffold tomorrow and be hung in place of John Snowden," said the gentleman, who had traveled in from Washington to offer his own life for that of Snowden. Unmoved by this apparently sincere, if naïve, display of selflessness, Bellis replied facetiously that he would "remember him when anything in his line was needed."[8]

That same day, Snowden received a letter from a guilt-ridden Ella Rush Murray. It read, in part:

**31.** Anne Arundel County sheriff Joseph H. Bellis. *Evening Capital,* August 19, 1911.

The reason I have not tried to come to see you is because I have been so busy working for you. I have worked all day until far into the night for two weeks. . . . I shall ask the sheriff for a permit to come to see you tomorrow. If I do not come it will only be because I am not allowed to do so.

I am sure you know how hard I have worked for you and Mr. Murray also. The truth will come out in the end, and all the good element know that you are innocent. Please, please forgive me if you can for the part I have played in bringing this dreadful thing upon you. It is a heartbreaking thought to me when I was only trying to do what I thought was my duty, by taking that story to the authorities.

Forgive me if you can, and I know that I shall pray God to help you, as I hope you will say a prayer for one who truly tried to save you.[9]

There were Black-owned barbershops on either side of the jail-house, and customers reported seeing Snowden peering out of his cell window at the scaffold that had already ended the lives of two Black men. With only one day to go, the sheriff's men were using sandbags to test the gallows. Snowden could see and hear the work being done to get the scaffold ready, and as one of the deputies drove nails into it to strengthen it, he called out to him, "Every time that hammer hits a nail, it drives me just that much nearer to my God."[10]

"And if you are *not* telling the truth," the deputy shot back, "it is sending you that much nearer the other place."

Speculation as to whether Snowden would make a last-minute confession was the most popular topic of conversation in town. On Thursday, A. Theodore Brady paid a final visit to his client. "I have never in my life seen a man like Snowden," the attorney told the *Washington Times*. "He appears cheerful and happy and, when we talked of the hanging Friday, he said, 'I shall certainly be glad when it is all over, Mr. Brady. I can hardly wait for Friday to come.'" Brady told him there was still time to make a statement of "nothing but the truth" if he wished, suggesting that perhaps his counsel may not have been as convinced of his innocence as he had told the governor he was. But Snowden replied only, "Oh, you know I want to tell the truth, as I always have."[11]

Getting the gallows in working order was not the only way in which the state of Maryland was preparing for Snowden's execution. Under orders from Governor Harrington, Second Maryland Regiment State Guard militiamen under the command of Adjutant General Henry M. Warfield had been summoned to Annapolis. Warfield told the press that the troops were in town purely as a precautionary measure and that no trouble was expected. But nobody was fooled. The mood in town was so somber and bitter that the governor and his team were clearly fearful the execution might foment a race riot.[12]

At nine o'clock Thursday night, when about a hundred local African Americans assembled outside the jailhouse singing hymns, they were greeted by four mounted machine guns and twenty men stationed inside the jail as well as a detachment of men with fixed bayonets on guard outside, all from the Second Maryland Regiment. The demonstration was peaceful, but it was noisy, and it so alarmed those in charge that they called for reinforcements from the Machine Gun Company, whose men arrived on motorcycles with guns at the ready.

And that wasn't all. Forty-two traffic policemen under the command of none other than Marshal Robert Carter came in from Baltimore and joined a hundred infantrymen already stationed at various points around the town. The show of force, coupled with an order for all loiterers to move on, was sufficient to persuade the gospel singers to return to their homes. After nine p.m., the city was virtually under martial law, and the streets were practically deserted.

That evening, Snowden ate a hearty supper and received a last visit from his siblings and some other relatives. And of course he met with Reverend Holt, who arrived with his band of eight choristers. They were allowed to remain for several hours. Hymns including "Nearer, My God, to Thee" and "Rock of Ages" were sung over and over until the sheriff closed up for the night at ten p.m. The deputy on death watch, whose job it was to keep an eye on the prisoner, reported that within twenty minutes of their departure, Snowden was asleep, but not before Bellis had visited him to give him one final opportunity to confess. Snowden, of course, would have none of it.[13]

Demand for passes to witness the hanging had been heavy, and the sheriff spent the day before the event distributing white slips entitling bearers to standing room in the jail yard. He honored a request by the Board of St. John's College not to issue passes to any of their students. Only men were welcome; no women were to be admitted except those in the church choir.[14]

The admission slips would be worthless if Snowden's attorneys were successful in their mission to the nation's capital, but up until late Thursday there had been no news from Washington. In fact, it had taken a few days of concerted effort for the lawyers even to secure a meeting with Chief Justice Edward Douglass White. They finally visited him at his home on Thursday and laid their case before him.

Although the newspapers gave the impression that this had been a formal filing of papers with the Supreme Court, the National Archives has no record of the appeal today. It is likely the chief justice treated the meeting simply as an informal consultation. In any event, he took no

**32.** Government House, the residence of the governor of Maryland, as it appeared ca. 1930. Collection of the Maryland State Archives (MSA SC 182-1-51).

time to mull over the case. After hearing the petitioners out, he refused on the spot to grant either a writ of certiorari or of habeas corpus.[15]

Attorney Williams immediately sent a telegram to Governor Harrington reporting on the chief justice's denial but also asking him to await the lawyers' arrival back in Annapolis, as they had something important to discuss with him. When they failed to appear by midnight, however, the governor retired for the night. Pendleton, Williams, and Beckett finally pulled up to the jailhouse in an automobile at two thirty a.m. and asked to see Sheriff Bellis.

The news they bore was that the chief justice had left the door open a crack. He had intimated that if the case were brought to the Supreme Court on a writ of *error* from the Circuit Court, that is, a request *by that court* for a review of its *own* judgment, it would be possible for the high court to consider it and take action within ten days to two weeks. This, obviously, would require a temporary stay of execution from the governor, but Bellis refused to have Harrington roused. Once they realized they could not move him, the men then dashed over to the executive mansion, which that night was well guarded by Baltimore headquarters detectives.[16]

They were turned away.

It was time to face facts. John Snowden's fate was now sealed.

# 24

## "I Could Not Leave This World with a Lie in My Mouth"

John Snowden awoke briefly at four a.m. and lit a cigarette, but after it went out he fell back asleep. Just before six a.m., the Rev. Benjamin S. Holt and the singers—five Black men and two Black women—returned. He then rose, donned his suit, ate a modest breakfast, and sang and prayed with them until Sheriff Bellis arrived at 6:45 a.m. to tell him that the time had come.

By then, those with passes to witness the execution, who had begun to line up long before sunrise, had had their documents inspected and been admitted to the building and, through it, to the jail yard. There were two hundred in total, all male and all white, mostly government officials and newspapermen. It is unclear whether Blacks were excluded or whether none relished the idea of attending. Leading the queue were Randall Haislup and Leroy Brandon, the fathers of Lottie May and Valentine Brandon, who had arrived the night before from Washington. Valentine himself, still in service overseas, was of course unable to attend.[1]

Others without tickets massed outside; that crowd included very few Blacks. Those arrayed outside the jail yard might overhear the execution, but they would not see any of it. Screens had been erected around the scaffold so no one outside of the yard could witness the event, even from a treetop or a neighboring roof.

Asked by several newspaper correspondents if he had any last words, Snowden told them he had dictated a final statement to Georgia Boston and that she would release it after his death. He declined to speak with them further. But he told one of his jailers that he was "as innocent as a newborn babe," and also exchanged a greeting with Marshal Robert Carter.[2]

"Marshal Carter, I want to say before I go that I forgive you for the way you treated me in that sweatbox in Baltimore." He was referring, of course, to the abuse he said he had suffered during his interrogation, which Carter had denied under oath had taken place.

After a short prayer from Reverend Holt, he then began the trek to his execution with stoic calm and dignity, escorted, but not assisted, by three sheriff's deputies. The procession, in which he was followed by Holt and the faithful gospel choir, passed through the corridors of the third floor of the jail, down a winding stairway and out into the jail yard where the gallows awaited. The singers chanted the hymn "I Am a Child of the King." It was an anthem singularly appropriate to the occasion, its final stanza proclaiming that:

God is my Father and Jesus my Brother,
Since I'm adopted by heavenly love;
I am an heir in the kingdom of glory,
And have a crown that is waiting above.

Snowden sang right along with them, his stentorian voice audible above all the others, and he continued to chant even as he ascended the scaffold. He fell silent only after a deputy placed the hood over his face while another strapped his legs together and slipped the noose over his head and neck. The whole process took only about a minute and a half.

All the preparations having been made, at just before seven a.m. a deputy flashed a signal to Sheriff Bellis. In previous executions, great pains appear to have been taken to mask the identity of the man who actually controlled the springing of the trap. The mechanism had been secreted inside the jailhouse and three deputies were given ropes to pull, only one of which actually initiated the action. But this time there was no secret: it was the Sheriff himself who personally pulled the lever that released the trap.

There was only a slight shudder in Snowden's 190-pound body as he dropped four feet through the hatch. Twenty-five seconds later, his neck broken, the county health officer pronounced him dead by asphyxiation.

Then he was cut down, and by seven thirty a.m. his remains had been placed in a polished oaken casket and were on their way to the home of his sister, Sedonia Isaacs.[3]

The entire event went off without a hitch. Despite reports that local gun sales to both whites and Blacks had increased over the past few days, there were no demonstrations and there was no violence. But then it was clear to all that any unrest would have been crushed immediately with overwhelming force, if not by the police, then by the militia.[4]

It was the last hanging that would ever take place in Anne Arundel County. In 1922, because of what the state legislature derided as the "curious mobs that frequent hangings taking place in the counties of this State and who attempt to make public affairs of the same," it voted to require all executions to take place indoors at the Maryland State Penitentiary in Baltimore. It didn't end hanging in the state; that would not happen until 1955, when lethal gas was mandated to replace it. But it made certain that Annapolis would never again be host to another event like the execution of John Snowden.[5]

After it was over, Georgia Boston distributed Snowden's final statement. She explained that he had dictated it and she had written it out and given it to him to sign. In prose hauntingly eloquent and quite impressive for an uneducated man, he reiterated his innocence, expressed his hope that Lottie May Brandon's true killer would one day be found, and thanked those who had supported him and even the authorities who had imprisoned him.

It read, in part:

> I have been imprisoned for one year and six months and now I am about to shake hands with time and welcome eternity, for in a few hours from now I shall step out of time into eternity to pay the penalty of a crime that I am not guilty of. I have been telling the truth ever since I was first arrested, but they tried to make me a liar. But God knows that I am telling the truth, and after I have been hanged I am asking the authorities please to continue to search for the murderer of that lady, for I am not guilty of the crime. And if Gabriel should blow the trumpet to wake the dead, she would come forth and tell you so.

Though I have suffered, if it would have proved to the world that I was innocent, I would have willingly gone through that awful degree again. I wish that I could have opened my heart to show you how pure and clean my heart is.

He went on to express his gratitude to those who had helped him, singling out attorneys Brady and Pendleton, Ella and William Murray, Sheriff Bellis, and his two spiritual advisors, Reverend Holt and Georgia Boston, and expressing the hope that they would meet again in heaven.

"I am leaving on the everlasting arm of Jesus," he concluded, "for I know Jesus died for all mankind. I could not leave this world with a lie in my mouth."[6]

An announcement was made that John Snowden's funeral would take place at two p.m. on Sunday afternoon, March 1, at Mt. Moriah A.M.E. Church, and be conducted by the Rev. James A. Briscoe, who had earlier served as Snowden's spiritual advisor. The event would be open to the public, and it was made clear that white people were welcome. There was much good feeling on the part of Snowden's Black supporters toward those whites who had taken up his mantle; this had been very unusual. "The colored people of Maryland owe a debt to white people of the State, who were fine enough and big enough to follow their consciences for the sake of justice," the *Afro-American* declared in an editorial. And the paper also ran a letter to the editor from a William B. Bannister singling out Mrs. Humiston for thanks, noting that she had done "all she was able to do" in Snowden's behalf.[7]

Long before two p.m. that Sunday, the church was packed. The crowd filled every available inch of floor space—the galleries, the first floor, and all of the aisles—with the overflow running down the building's stairways and out onto Franklin Street. It was estimated that there were a thousand people in the building and another five hundred on the street. All was orderly, although the press of humanity made it difficult to clear a path for the pallbearers to bring in the body, which was placed in front of the altar, the casket covered with four wreaths of carnations and a sheaf of wheat.

John Snowden's sister and brother sat on benches to the left of the altar; on the right were members of the Baltimore and Annapolis

**33.** The view from the dais of the sanctuary at Mt. Moriah Church, Annapolis, where John Snowden's remains were placed during his funeral. Collection of the Maryland State Archives (MSA SC 5908-1-6).

committees who had worked for his freedom. Ella Rush Murray, one of the few whites in attendance, was seated within the chancel rail. The only others the *Baltimore American* counted were three newspaper reporters, who also had been given seats up front.

Reverend Holt, tasked with delivering a eulogy, emphasized Snowden's bravery and calm in the days leading up to his execution. He had not reacted as most men to the erection of the scaffold, and had kept his composure and his faith throughout. "There was nailing on the outside, and kneeling on the inside," he quipped. And he added his own firm conviction of the truth of the prisoner's final statement.

Georgia Boston sang "Tell Mother I'll Be There," explaining that one of Snowden's last requests was that she sing that hymn at his funeral. The congregation followed with renditions of "On the Everlasting Arm of Jesus" and "I Am a Child of the King."

"I feel as bad or worse than anyone else here," Ella Murray told the assembly when it was her turn to speak. "It is only with the greatest difficulty that I can control my voice. When I first became interested in this case I was taken advantage of." She added that "we have a double responsibility, first through the fresh evidence that is coming in every day to clear Snowden's memory, and then to see to it that the man who has misused his authority in this case regrets it."

"Men of this state have the weapon. They have the vote; they have the power by which they can see that only competent officials are put into office. They can see to it that a case of this kind shall not occur again. If women had a chance to take part in the elections, this would probably not have happened," she noted, exhibiting her own suffragist convictions.

"I would have rather been John Snowden Friday morning than the one who shut himself behind locked doors with detectives to guard him," she asserted in conclusion. "My only hope is that I can meet *my* end one half as bravely, honestly and as gallantly as John Snowden met his," she declared, bringing the audience to their feet.[8]

Reverend Briscoe spoke highly critically of the two sisters who had testified against John Snowden, neither of whom was present, as both had left town. "Those women have committed an unpardonable sin and have sent a soul to eternity," he insisted. "Snowden is here because two devils had a love for fine clothes and silks and satins, and gave false testimony against him for money. Snowden wanted to see his friends and enemies in heaven, but he will not see these two women there. There is no repentance for them; they have committed an unpardonable crime."

As far as Snowden himself was concerned, the preacher chose to make his life an object lesson.

"I believe that this whole affair happened to warn young people who are living without God. If John Snowden had stuck to the advice given to him by his mother, he would probably not be here today. Snowden was no angel. He drank, he gambled and he lived with a woman to whom he was not married. Snowden's record and reputation were against him. If he had always led a clean and upright life, I doubt very much whether he would have been hanged last Friday."

Reverend Briscoe tried to make the point that in Jim Crow Maryland, walking the street while Black was a dangerous proposition.

Elsewhere in his speech, he declared that "You know that had I or you gone down Second Street on the day of the crime as Snowden did, I or you would now be in Snowden's place." But in linking Snowden's fate to his dissolute habits, he was not only contradicting himself—since as a man of the cloth, he presumably led a more godly life—he was also, in essence, blaming Snowden for his own fate.

Whether anyone in the audience bristled at this insinuation is not recorded, but the preacher's message seems uncomfortably similar to that of a racist and highly condescending editorial that ran in the *Evening Capital* on the day of Snowden's execution that more or less blamed *all* Blacks for the racial enmity that whites bore toward them. It read, in part:

> The death of John Snowden points a moral to the colored people of Annapolis which it is well they should heed. There can be no denying that there is a latent racial feeling here just as there is every place where the two races compose the community. . . . It is to the credit of both white and black that this feeling has not been allowed to gain ascendancy in this city during the last few trying days.
>
> Colored people who are honestly convinced of the innocence of Snowden or who have even the slightest feeling that their race has been persecuted must accept the judgment of the court as good citizens. They must do more. They must so conduct themselves that racial prejudice will be dismissed even if it cannot be eliminated, and thus make less likely the possibility of injustice being done to them as a race. They must seek to gain the respect of the white people by a course of conduct equal to that of the best of whites.
>
> If the colored people wish to progress, to win the esteem of white people and earn self-respect they must first learn to deport themselves in a manner to win. . . . This is said in all friendliness to the colored people of this town and with the hope that it will be of profit to them.[9]

Once it was over, an appeal was made and $80 was collected to help defray the funeral expenses. Many of those present then accompanied

Snowden's body to the Brewer Hill Cemetery, the local African American graveyard, where it was laid to rest.

The following Tuesday, March 3, the *Evening Capital* reported that the sheriff's office had received a letter from an anonymous Washington man who declared that *he* had been Lottie May Brandon's killer. It read: "I am sorry you killed Snowden today. He is not the guilty man. I am the man. I could not stand to see another man live with my heart so I put Lottie May out of the way. I hope his sins fall on my head. I am willing to answer them. He is not the man. God will bring things right someday."[10]

The letter, of course, was taken as further proof of Snowden's innocence by those who were inclined to believe in it. But as far as hard evidence was concerned, it was useless, and would have been of little help to Snowden even if it had arrived before his hanging. If indeed the writer was the murderer, he was, in fact, clearly *unwilling* to answer for his sin, because he failed to sign his name to the letter. This rendered his statement not only unproven but also unprovable.

# PART 4    2000

# 25

## "Race Is All Over This Case"

John Snowden's sad story was never forgotten by Annapolis's Black community. It was repeated for decades after his hanging by many who took it as an article of faith that he had been an innocent victim of a "legal lynching."

For African American Annapolitans, the Snowden case became a teachable example of the perils of growing up Black. To some, it was an indication that little had changed since Snowden's ordeal in 1919, and that the chances of a Black person getting a fair trial in a white-dominated society remained equally dim.

George Phelps Jr., for example, former deputy sheriff of Anne Arundel County, who was the first African American law enforcement officer there and a sometime historian, recalled in 2000 at the age of seventy-four that the story had circulated in the Annapolis Black community for as long as he could remember, and that it was widely believed that Snowden had not received a fair trial, given the racial enmity of the time.[1]

Ninety-six-year-old Eliza Mae Robinson grew up on Calvert Street and used to deliver home-cooked meals to prisoners in the jailhouse. She wasn't born until a few years after Snowden's execution, but even in 2019 she remembered being told that the Black men who patronized the barber shops in her neighborhood had seen Snowden peer out of his cell window in the days before his death.[2]

Beatrice Marshall Smith, a ninety-eight-year-old, Annapolis-born Black woman, recounted in 2019 that things were so tense in town that her family had fled to Washington DC on the day of the hanging to avoid any trouble that might occur. Her mother never forgot the Snowden case and made certain she and her siblings knew what a terrible time it had been in Annapolis.[3]

For others like sixty-eight-year-old Phillip Chambers, a Black man who was told the story at his grandfather's barber shop, it was, he recalled in 2019, an exhortation to be wary of involvement with white girls, lest one's attentions be misinterpreted or, worse, the nature of the relationship be portrayed falsely as something other than mutually consensual.[4]

Alderman Carl O. Snowden hadn't heard about the John Snowden case until he ran into Louis Snowden as an adult. But given his knowledge of Maryland's racist history, he had little difficulty believing it was a case of justice denied. He had made an entreaty to Governor William Donald Schaefer to reexamine the case that had failed, but he had a personal connection to Schaefer's successor, Parris Glendening. Why not raise the issue of posthumous justice with *him*?

Accordingly, in a mid-March 2000 letter to Glendening praising the governor's sensitivity to racial issues, he urged, "with the stroke of a pen, you can correct this injustice." He added that "the spirit of John Snowden will not rest until this is done. In many ways, neither will our spirits find serenity, either."[5]

Alderman Snowden's appeal soon became public knowledge, and Michael Morrill, the governor's spokesman, was asked by the press what the governor intended to do about it. Morris told reporters that although many people viewed the Snowden case as a symbol, "we must look at it as we do any other request for a pardon." However that statement was intended, to those familiar with Glendening's record on capital punishment it was cold comfort. The governor, formerly a University of Maryland professor and a county executive, was a progressive on most issues, but he had run on a law-and-order platform and he did not oppose the death penalty. Glendening had already been in office for five years, and he had been neither free with pardons nor neutral on the question of capital punishment.

Indeed, during his first month in office he had listed shaving years off the death penalty appeals process as one of his policy priorities. But in response to public pressure, especially from Black legislators, he

34. Alderman Carl O. Snowden, 2019. Collection of the author.

*had* made a commitment to support a study of racial disparities in the application of the death penalty in the state, as there was no denying that Blacks were grossly overrepresented on death row in comparison to their percentage of the state population.[6]

A short-term, stop-gap measure, a gubernatorial task force organized in the summer of 1996 to look into this question, did not conclude that race was a factor in sentencing, though it did brand the apparent racial disparity "a cause for concern" and assert that the system provided a "potential for prejudice." The task force recommended diversity training for judges, prosecutors, defense attorneys, jurors, and police, among other things. But these steps did not go far, nor was this effort sufficiently comprehensive to satisfy demand for an in-depth inquiry.[7]

Throughout the governor's first term, not only was there was no sign of the promised study, but Glendening refused to delay pending executions. By 2000, when he received Carl Snowden's letter, he had already declined to intervene in two high-profile cases. In 1997 he had denied clemency to condemned killer Flint Gregory Hunt, a Black man convicted of killing a white Baltimore police officer. And in 1998, as he faced a reelection bid, he rejected a similar petition from Tyrone X. Gilliam, also Black, who had been sentenced to death for the kidnapping and killing of a white woman.[8]

But debate over the future of the death penalty, and especially its discriminatory aspects, was going on nationwide. The Rev. Jesse Jackson had inserted himself into the Hunt case and had visited Maryland, giving the case a national profile, though Glendening had not met with him. The pressure from civil rights leaders and anti–death penalty activists was growing, and some lawmakers in Annapolis were seeking to impose a three-year moratorium on executions.[9]

Glendening did not support a moratorium, but finally, in early 2000, in the middle of his second and last term, he set aside $325,000 in the state budget to honor his commitment. It would pay for a two-year University of Maryland study to determine whether racial, or any other, bias existed in the imposition of the death penalty in the state.[10]

Because he did not impose a moratorium, however, he would still have to deal with clemency petitions as execution dates drew near. Seventeen men were on death row in Maryland in May of 2000, twelve of them Black. And in the short run, Glendening would be faced with a difficult decision in the case of Eugene Colvin-el, a Black man scheduled to be executed that month for the 1980 murder of an eighty-two-year-old white woman during a break-in at her daughter's Pikesville home.[11]

The Colvin-el case was particularly vexing because the evidence against him was entirely circumstantial. The police had arrested him after he fenced two watches stolen during the break-in, and they had linked him to the Pikesville property because his fingerprints were found on broken glass outside of the home. But no evidence placed him *inside* the house. His prints did not appear on the murder weapon, a knife, nor were they found anywhere in the room in which the woman was stabbed twenty-eight times.

Colvin-el had been sentenced to death by two juries in Anne Arundel County, the first one all white. Of four Black judges who reviewed the case at the state and federal levels, three had voted to vacate the death sentence on the grounds of insufficient evidence to invoke the death penalty.

"Race is all over this case," Colvin-el's attorneys asserted in their clemency petition. And they explicitly raised the issue of the University of Maryland study, which would not be concluded until late the following year. "To proceed with the execution in this particular case is simply to say the outcome of the study does not matter," they argued.[12]

In June, pressure grew on the governor to commute Colvin-el's sentence. A hundred people marched outside the state's supermax prison in Baltimore on June 3, demanding not only clemency for the prisoner but an end to the death penalty. They were supported in this by the state's three Roman Catholic bishops and three of Maryland's representatives in Congress. And on June 4, a hard-hitting editorial in the *Baltimore Sun* raised serious questions about the state's case against the man.[13]

Glendening listened. And on June 7, he commuted Colvin-el's sentence to life in prison without the possibility of parole. "I came to the conclusion that he was almost certainly guilty of this horrible crime, but 'almost certainly' is not strong enough," he said. At the same time, however, he reaffirmed his opposition to a moratorium on the death penalty, insisting that there were cases in which it was entirely appropriate punishment.

If race had been "all over" the case of Eugene Colvin-el, however, it had certainly also been all over the nearly century-old case now working its way to Glendening's desk. And once Alderman Snowden's plea was reported in the newspapers, others filed in behind him. Two chapters of the local NAACP and the United Black Clergy of Anne Arundel County lent their voices in support of a pardon for John Snowden, as did George Phelps Jr., the Black historian and member of the state's Executive Clemency Board who had heard the story since childhood.

Perhaps the most compelling advocate for clemency, however, was forty-four-year-old Hazel Geneva Snowden, known as "Missy," a daughter of John Snowden's now-deceased brother Louis. She had read about the effort and immediately gotten involved.

Annapolis-born Hazel had, of course, never known her uncle, but she recalled her father telling her siblings and her of his ordeal when she

35. Maryland governor Parris Glendening. Wikipedia.

was a child. She remembered a photo of him her father had kept in his bedroom, together with a newspaper clipping about his hanging. And like her father before her, she was entirely convinced of his innocence.

"Despite the severe beatings and torture (which included putting a gun to his head and squeezing his genital area)," she wrote the Governor, "my uncle, John Snowden, went to the gallows without confessing to the heinous crime. The incident has been documented and investigated, and the only evidence against my father's brother was purely circumstantial," she added.[14]

In the meantime, the *Baltimore Sun* weighed in with an editorial in support of a pardon, and the growing coalition pushing for it scheduled a rally for June 10, 2000, on what would have been Snowden's 110th birthday. They hoped the event would pressure the governor to move on the pardon request by that date. A memorial committee had been formed and a thousand invitations sent out to a dedication ceremony for a special marker to be erected in Snowden's memory at Brewer

> I have been imprisoned and now I am about to shake hands with time and welcome eternity, for in a few hours from now, I shall step out of time into eternity to pay the penalty of a crime I am not guilty of. God knows that I am telling the truth, and after I have been hanged, I am asking the authorities to please continue to search for the murderer. Though I have suffered, if it would have proved to the world that I was innocent, I would have willingly gone through that awful degree again. I have offered up a prayer for you all. I want to thank everybody that have spent their time and money to help me. Through their song and prayer my soul was made alive and I am leaving on the everlasting Arm of Jesus. I could not leave this world with a lie in my mouth.
>
> *Excerpt from the last statement of*
> *John Snowden*
> *February 27, 1919*

**JOHN SNOWDEN MEMORIAL COMMITTEE**
Carl O. Snowden, Chairman
Joy C. Bramble
Jeffrey C. Henderson
Frederick C. Howard
Roger L. Murray, Sr.
George Phelps, Jr.
Hazel Geneva Snowden
Janice Hayes-Williams

Reverend Victor O. Johnson
Asbury United Methodist Church

Reverend Mamie A. Williams
Annapolis District Superintendent

Bishop Felton Edwin May
Presiding Bishop
Baltimore-Washington Conference of
The United Methodist Church

June 10, 2000

*A Luta Continual*

**36.** The John Snowden Memorial Plaque in Brewer Hill Cemetery, including an excerpt from his last statement and a list of members of the memorial committee. Courtesy of Robert L. Worden.

Hill Cemetery. An inscription on an earlier headstone over what was believed to be his grave had worn away with time. The new, three-foot-high bronze and granite monument would contain an excerpt from his final statement.[15]

The rally, which the Asbury United Methodist Church helped organize, took place just three days after the Colvin-el commutation, and for anyone who was paying attention, the two cases bore marked similarities. In both, Black men were convicted of the murder of white women by all-white juries. Neither could be linked to a murder weapon or placed in the room where the killing occurred. Both men had been sentenced to die based entirely on circumstantial evidence.

Neither the coincidence in time, nor the parallels between the two cases, was lost on Leroy Phillips Jr., who was invited to address the dedication of the memorial. Phillips had coauthored a book about the 1906 lynching of Ed Johnson, a Black man, in his home town of Chattanooga, Tennessee, before the Supreme Court could hear his appeal of his conviction for rape. That February, fully ninety-four years after his death, Johnson's conviction had been overturned on the grounds that he had not received a fair trial.

"The truth is, that in the first half of this century and last century, African-Americans were *not* granted justice in this country," Phillips told the crowd of several hundred people who showed up at the cemetery that day despite the oppressive heat. He went on to suggest that if Governor Glendening could not be certain enough of the evidence of Colvin-el's guilt to permit him to be executed, then he surely could not be certain of the evidence marshaled against John Snowden.[16]

The organizers were disappointed that there was no sign of a pardon in time for the event, but as a practical matter, Governor Glendening had not yet received a recommendation from the Maryland Parole Commission, which was still investigating the case. "The hunt for hard, objective evidence is elusive, but it continues," Len Sipes, the commission spokesperson, told the *Baltimore Afro-American*.[17]

But not all the voices the governor heard favored a pardon for John Snowden. A day or so after the rally, he received a letter from Judy Kulawiak of Millersville, Maryland, who wondered "how can we go back and rewrite history after so many years and with no new evidence?"

For Judy Kulawiak, the Snowden case was no abstraction; it was personal. She was a great-niece of Lottie Mae Brandon.[18]

# PART 5   2001–3

# 26

## "There's Great Jubilation in the Community"

The Snowden case took its time working its way through the system. By the end of the year 2000 there was still no decision. And now Governor Glendening faced the prospect of having to decide whether to offer clemency to as many as four other living death row inmates who had exhausted their circuit court appeals and were petitioning the Supreme Court to hear their cases. Three of the four were Black. Depending on when and how the high court dealt with the cases, there was a strong possibility some or all of them would reach his desk, and reach it before the University of Maryland study was complete.

"The timing doesn't enter into it," Michael Morrill, the governor's spokesperson told the press. "Politics isn't a factor." But to many minds, it *had* to be. The prospect of permitting a rash of executions to occur, only to have a study conclude after the fact that race was a factor in the way the system handled such cases, cannot have been appetizing for a Democratic governor—even one who would not be running for reelection due to term limits.[1]

Nor did it look as if the state assembly would bail him out. As the new year dawned, the legislature was set to consider a proposal to abolish the death penalty. A moratorium bill had died in committee the previous year, and although anti–capital punishment activists were hopeful, it did not appear as if there were enough votes for a ban. Mindful of the possible fate of the four men waiting on death row, legislators introduced two identical bills, one in each chamber, calling for a two-year moratorium until the University of Maryland study had been completed and its results analyzed.[2]

As it turned out, however, the pessimists were right. Due to a filibuster, the clock ran out and the bill failed in the general assembly in mid-April, just as the legislature adjourned for the year.[3]

The setback prompted fresh calls for the governor to seize the initiative and declare a moratorium himself. Religious leaders including the Catholic archbishop of Baltimore urged him to use his executive power to do so. But public opinion was mixed, with a slight plurality of voters opposed. And still Glendening resisted, vowing to consider on a case-by-case basis those petitions that crossed his desk.[4]

By the end of May 2001, the governor had received the paperwork on the Snowden case from the parole commission and had had a chance to review it. Although the actual file is inexplicably missing from the Maryland State Archives today, Carl Snowden, who was contacted at the time by Patricia K. Cushwa, then head of the parole commission, recalls her detailing the scope and breadth of their review of the case, which included engaging a researcher to review archival records and contemporary news accounts. Based on these, the commission formulated a recommendation that it passed on to the governor's office for possible action.[5]

Alderman Snowden remembers being told that the commission had focused on three factors in reaching its decision. First, the anonymous letter received by the sheriff's office several days after John Snowden's hanging; second, the fact that eleven of the twelve jurors had petitioned the then-governor for clemency; and third, the fact that given the racial climate of the time, it was probable Snowden had not received a fair trial.[6]

On May 30 the governor's office issued a public notice of Glendening's impending decision on the case, as was required by law.[7] It was followed the next day with a news release that bore the following statement:

> The search for justice has no statute of limitations. In Maryland, we pride ourselves on building an inclusive society based on a fair and balanced system of justice that protects the rights of all.

When faced with a possible miscarriage of justice—even one from the distant past—our values compel us to take a second look.

The case of John Snowden deserved just such a look. The exceptional set of circumstances surrounding this case has led me to grant Mr. Snowden a posthumous pardon. While it is impossible at this late date to establish with certainty his guilt or innocence, there is substantial doubt that justice was served by his hanging. There were enough troubling questions raised at the time that the State should not have imposed the death penalty without further investigation. Not only did two key trial witnesses recant their testimony, but 11 of the 12 jurors wrote letters asking the Governor to commute the sentence.

The refusal of a stay of execution denied the victim's family and the Snowden family the assurance that justice had been served. Based on the facts reviewed, I agree with the Maryland Parole Commission that, while it is too late to prove the innocence or guilt of Mr. Snowden, we can conclude that the hanging may well have been a miscarriage of justice. For this reason I have granted the pardon.[8]

Pardons end or preempt punishment; they may be granted to both the guilty *and* the blameless. Despite the fact that they are taken by most people to signal a determination of innocence, they are, in fact, silent on the question of guilt. Glendening believed that a declaration of innocence nearly a century after the fact was impossible. Had Snowden been alive, the governor might well have opted simply to commute his sentence, which would have left his conviction in place but reduced its consequences. The fact that he was dead left him with no options other than to decline to act, as his predecessors had, or to issue a pardon. This undoubtedly is why he went out of his way, in the statement, to make clear that he was *not* opining on Snowden's culpability for the crime.[9]

There were several problematic issues with his statement, however.

Glendening was absolutely right to cite the clemency petition of eleven of the twelve jurors; this was one of the strongest reasons Governor Harrington ought to have commuted Snowden's sentence

PARRIS N. GLENDENING
GOVERNOR

ANNAPOLIS OFFICE
STATE HOUSE
100 STATE CIRCLE
ANNAPOLIS, MARYLAND 21401
(410) 974-3901
(TOLL FREE) 1-800-811-8336

WASHINGTON OFFICE
SUITE 311
444 NORTH CAPITOL STREET, N.W.
WASHINGTON, D.C. 20001
(202) 624-1430

TDD (410) 333-3098

STATE OF MARYLAND

FULL PARDON

BE IT KNOWN, that, WHEREAS, John Snowden, Grantee, was convicted of Murder in the Circuit Court for Baltimore County on January 31, 1918, and hanged on February 28, 1919;

NOW, THEREFORE, I, PARRIS N. GLENDENING, GOVERNOR OF THE STATE OF MARYLAND, having thought proper the extension of clemency, under the authority vested in me by law do hereby grant unto John Snowden, a FULL PARDON, absolving him from the guilt of his criminal offenses and exempting him from any pains and penalties imposed upon him therefore by law.

GIVEN UNDER MY HAND AND THE GREAT SEAL OF MARYLAND, in the City of Annapolis, on this 31st day of May, 2001.

Parris N. Glendening
Governor

ATTEST:

John T. Willis
Secretary of State

37. The official pardon of John Snowden, issued May 31, 2001. Collection of the Maryland State Archives (MSA SC 5389).

eighty-two years earlier. But Glendening also criticized the state for having imposed the death penalty "without further investigation," so it is reasonable to ask what further investigation he had in mind.

Commissioner Cushwa, who had recommended clemency, explained to the press that "no investigation was ever authorized to reexamine the claims of the key witnesses or to consider the reasons for the appeal for clemency from the jurors." She was saying, in effect, that Governor Harrington should have halted the process on the strength of the "new evidence" Grace Humiston brought to him or the clemency petition from the jurors and launched a further investigation.[10]

But the detectives and the prosecution had done a very thorough job of preparing the case against Snowden, and the supposed "new evidence" presented just before the hanging was extremely vague and thin. It does not appear, with twenty-twenty hindsight, as if deploying more manpower would either have unearthed additional exculpatory evidence or exonerated the defendant.

Put another way, even if, as Grace Humiston had asserted, all had *not* been well between Lottie May and Valentine Brandon, even if they had had a loud argument the night before her death, and even if she had "received the attentions" of another man, it didn't prove anything. Valentine still had an airtight alibi, no paramour had ever been identified, and Snowden had still been seen outside the Brandon home on the morning of the murder and been unable to explain the scratches on his face. Nor did an anonymous letter after the fact ostensibly confessing to the crime qualify as evidence; it would never have been admitted at trial. What Humiston had come up with, much of which was essentially innuendo, would have been unlikely to change the verdict or warrant a new trial.

Then there was the suggestion that two key trial witnesses had recanted their testimony. There is no contemporary evidence in the documents that remain of any recanting of testimony after the trial on the part of the sisters, Mary Perkins and Edith Creditt, assuming this accusation refers to them. Recanting, in fact, is an issue that seems to have been raised only when the case was revived in the 1990s. It is not clear where this allegation originated; there is no mention of it in the press at the time of the trial or in its immediate aftermath, and the Maryland State Archives cannot locate the dossier on the case that Governor Glendening received from the parole commission.

It might have been based on the attempts by the defense during the trial to show that the sisters had changed their story between the time they first came forward and the time they took the witness stand. Rereading the newspaper coverage of their interrogation at the time of Snowden's arrest and comparing it to the transcript of their testimony at trial, however, reveals the story to have been substantially the same each time the women told it. And the jury had heard contrary testimony from several of the people to whom the sisters had spoken and, presumably, had factored it into its verdict.

The other accusation intended to impeach the credibility of the sisters was that they did not come forward until it was common knowledge that a $500 reward would be paid for information leading to the conviction of the killer. This was true, and the judge certainly ought to have allowed the defense to explore it further, although apart from their timing, there was never any indication that they were motivated by the reward, and—if Governor Harrington is to be believed—they never actually claimed the money.

Furthermore, even if a potential bounty *had* motivated them to accuse a man they knew to be innocent, why pick John Snowden, against whom they apparently bore no grudge? Why pick a Black man at all? It's very clear that they made life far worse for themselves within the Black community by doing so; one of them took ill from all of the pressure, and they both left town afterward. Accusing another African American brought them only misery, censure, and, eventually, exile.

A point the governor *might* have raised about the testimony of the two sisters is that modern research suggests that eyewitness testimony, while powerful and convincing, can be extremely unreliable. Social scientists have known since the 1960s that even very confident eyewitnesses are often quite wrong, something that DNA evidence, which revolutionized forensic science when it was first employed in the 1980s, has confirmed over and over again. It is abundantly clear that their participation in the Snowden case was extremely stressful for Edith Creditt and Mary Perkins, and stress, far from promoting the formation of accurate memories, often actually inhibits it. It's entirely possible that the 1919 jury gave their testimony far more evidentiary weight than it deserved.[11]

There were other issues the governor did not raise in his assessment that surely support the notion that race had played a role in Snowden's treatment and his conviction.

One was the relocation of the trial from Annapolis. No one seems to have brought it up as an issue except in a brief exchange at the Towson trial and in the unsuccessful appeal to the Supreme Court.

Yet it seems obvious in hindsight that race played an important role there. State's Attorney Green was coy about his reasons for suddenly requesting a change in venue after eleven jurors had been empaneled; he never revealed them. But there is no explanation more likely than that he was shopping for an all-white jury.

If the supplementary panel of jurors hastily recruited in Annapolis overnight after the initial pool had been exhausted had included at least one Black person, it's more than reasonable to assume that the prosecutor, who at that point had used up all of his peremptory challenges and could not have kept a Black man off of the jury, chose to roll the dice a second time. That would not have been against the law at the time, but it would have been motivated by racial prejudice. And if there had been no Blacks at all in the group as a result of a deliberate effort on the part of the sheriff to exclude them, which seems more likely, it would not only have been a product of racial bias; it would have been unconstitutional.

In the year 2001, however, *either* possibility would have been unconstitutional.

Another issue was Snowden's treatment during his interrogation. Although the police denied it, Snowden insisted that during the course of his various examinations, he had been repeatedly threatened, knocked down, forced to his knees, pummeled, struck over the head, made to drink whiskey to get him drunk, and had a loaded revolver pointed at him, all in an effort to break him. Apart from that, his cousin, Mrs. Elizabeth Tyler, later recalled that he told her his interrogation had been "hellish" and that "they wrang his genitals" in the process.[12]

Since the prosecution had used statements he allegedly made during interrogation to discredit his court testimony, the admission of these statements was surely prejudicial to his case, and if he had been treated as he described, they ought never to have been allowed into evidence. Furthermore, it was surely a case of abuse by law enforcement. Given the times, this was almost certainly due to his race, but even if it was not, it was monstrously cruel and unquestionably unconstitutional if it occurred as he reported.

During the trial itself, the judge made frequent rulings against the defense, some of which seem unfair or prejudicial a century later. His refusal to permit the defense to explore possible interested motives on the part of Mary Perkins and Edith Creditt, who had come forward only after a reward was offered, is a case in point. On several occasions, Judge Duncan permitted the jury to make judgments on testimony that one might reasonably argue should never have been admitted.

And although there is no specific evidence that Judge Duncan's rulings were driven by racial animus on his part, he did permit State's Attorney George Hartman to get away with some deeply prejudicial comments in his summation. Hartman's observation, quoted in the *Baltimore Sun*, that "the negro who ravishes a white woman deserves the extreme legal penalty and nothing short of it" is a particularly egregious example, because it reeked of prejudice, because Snowden had not been accused of rape, and because Hartman was asking the jury to send a message rather than to focus on the facts of the case.[13]

Nor was Hartman the only official who betrayed racial bias. Additional evidence of it can be found in statements by Governor Harrington in the run-up to Snowden's execution. It is abundantly clear that the man who had boasted that Snowden's trial had been "absolutely lacking throughout any feeling of racial hostility against the accused" bore a good measure of it himself. When he declared that because "I had refused recently to commute to life imprisonment a colored man guilty of rape upon a colored girl," he could hardly do so for "a negro who has committed, in my opinion, both murder and rape upon a white woman," it's hard to imagine that he was motivated by anything other than racial enmity. If he was simply comparing a rape and a murder, why dwell on the races of the victims? Why even mention them?

"I am a friend of the colored race," Harrington had insisted at the time, but John Snowden, for one, would have been far better off without such a friend.[14]

Finally, if Glendening needed any more persuading, he might have looked to John Snowden's refusal, from the day he was first accused to the end of his life, to offer anything in the nature of a confession. In and of itself this isn't proof of anything, of course; but his steadfast protestations of innocence, in spite of probable brutal treatment by the police, might count for something. Given Snowden's death row conversion, it's reasonable to suggest that a guilty man with faith in

God who was about to meet his maker would want to wipe his slate clean before submitting himself to eternal judgment.

Glendening's act was not Maryland's first posthumous pardon; in 1994, Governor Schaefer had pardoned Jerome S. Cardin, who had been convicted of stealing from a bank he owned, based on "his lifetime of philanthropic service, time served in prison and payment of $10 million in restitution."[15] Cardin had died the year before. But the Snowden pardon was the first example of clemency in the state granted, in part at least, based on *race*. It fell far short of an exoneration of John Snowden; Glendening had taken issue only with Snowden's execution, not his conviction. But a pardon was a pardon, and that didn't stop those who had sought it from celebrating.

"I feel like my uncle's soul is rejoicing and my father's soul is rejoicing," Hazel Snowden told the *Baltimore Sun*. When she got the news, she went to her uncle's grave to pray.[16]

Alderman Carl O. Snowden praised the governor, telling the *Capital* that Glendening was sensitive to the intolerance that had characterized Maryland's history and to the current national climate conducive to reopening racially charged cases. "This is a tremendous victory," he told the press. "It's been a long time coming. There's great jubilation in the community."[17]

But for Judy Kulawiak, it was no time for jubilation. She was deeply troubled by the governor's decision and she told him so in no uncertain terms. In a letter written on the day the pardon was issued, she asserted that given the fact that no new evidence had been uncovered, he had no legitimate basis on which to grant it. Although Glendening had insisted that the pardon had been issued without regard to broader issues, Kulawiak thought otherwise.

"Your action is tainted with political motives," she wrote.[18]

Kulawiak had grown up with the firm belief that justice had been served in Snowden's conviction. "'Pardon,'" she complained to the press, "is a very strong word. Pardon has an interpretation of innocence." She added that "I think the correct decision is no ruling at all." Lottie Brandon's seventy-five-year-old niece, Charlotte Wotring, agreed. "We're just flabbergasted that this is happening after all these years," she told the *Washington Post*.

# Posthumous pardon hailed, criticized

By BRIAN M. SCHLETER
Staff Writer

Calling his hanging a miscarriage of justice, Gov. Parris N. Glendening yesterday issued the first posthumous pardon of its kind to an African American man executed in 1919 for killing a white, pregnant Annapolis woman.

An "exceptional set of circumstances" led the governor to pardon John Snowden. One activist called it the first time in state history clemency has been granted based in part on race.

The ice wagon worker was convicted and hanged in 1919 for killing Lottie Mae Brandon in her Annapolis home.

Mr. Glendening's decision was lauded by city civil rights leaders but criticized by descendants of the victim, who felt the governor should not have interjected in the 83-year-old crime.

"I know my uncle is rejoicing and so is my father," said Hazel G. Snowden, John Snowden's niece, who lives in Landover.

Yesterday she went to his grave to pray.

"My uncle knew he was innocent then and we know he was innocent now," she said.

The brutal murder shocked the Annapolis community in 1917 and created racial tensions so severe the governor placed the city under martial law and called the national guard to keep the peace the day Snowden was hanged.

The trial was moved to Towson, where jurors convicted Snowden based on circumstantial evidence. It included testimony from two neighbors

(See PARDON, Page A12)

AP photo / By John Gillis - The Capital

Hazel G. Snowden, left, was overjoyed by the news that her uncle has been pardoned, but Judy Kulawiak of Millersville, a descendant of Lottie Mae Brandon, says the pardon "is smelling a little political."

**38.** Interviews with Hazel G. Snowden and Judy Kulawiak. *Capital*, June 1, 2001.

Kulawiak was also critical of the Glendening administration for failing to notify any of Lottie Brandon's relatives before the decision was announced. But neither she nor Hazel Snowden was without sympathy for those on the other side of the issue. Judy told the *Capital* that she understood the African American community's need for closure in the case, adding that for her, "it wasn't about race so much as it was the legal issue of granting of a pardon where there was no evidence presented." And for her part, Hazel added that "there were two lives lost; two tragedies. I realize her family member was murdered, but my uncle was murdered as well."[19]

Apart from its meaning for those with family ties to the case, a hard-hitting editorial in the *Baltimore Sun* brought home the broader significance and relevance of the pardon to twenty-first-century Maryland:

> Every Marylander should be ashamed that it took eight decades to set the record straight on John Snowden, a black man who was hanged—after an apocryphal arrest and trial—for allegedly raping and killing a white Annapolis woman. And every Marylander should be terrified by the idea that eight decades from now, someone could be apologizing for the death-penalty injustices taking place today in our state.
>
> Everything that was wrong with Snowden's execution can be found among cases along Maryland's death row today. Witnesses who changed their stories. Flimsy physical evidence. Jurors unsure

that death was the proper punishment. A rabid community push to exact the ultimate punishment when victims are white and suspects are black.

Gov. Parris N. Glendening said John Snowden's 1919 execution was probably a horrible iniquity because of the doubt that surrounded the case. But he could have been talking about any number of the inmates awaiting execution in Maryland right now, and some who have already been killed.

The question is this: What are we willing to do to stop this state from repeating its sordid history?

The editorial also described how Snowden's pardon "adds new fodder to the debate over Maryland's death penalty." Then it went on to say:

When we consider whether Anthony Grandison—one of 13 men on death row—really got a fair trial because he was allowed to represent himself, we should think of the injustices in Snowden's case. When we ponder why only two Maryland death-row inmates were convicted of killing blacks (while African-Americans make up the overwhelming majority of murder victims in the state), we should remember the racial furor whipped up in 1917 during Snowden's trial because he was accused of killing a white woman. When we look at the wispy evidence that makes up many death penalty cases (such as Eugene Colvin-el, whom prosecutors couldn't even place in the house where he was accused of committing murder), we should recall 26-year-old John Snowden, who delivered ice for a living, and who was convicted on the basis of unreliable witnesses and evidence.

Fairness continues to elude Maryland's death machine, 82 years after the state took a man's life in an egregious error. Shame should inspire us to stop our feckless public policy of state-imposed killings before another Maryland generation goes by.[20]

On June 22 the Annapolis African American community organized a program to honor Governor Glendening for his decision to extend clemency to John Snowden and for his appointments of the first Black man and the first two women to the Anne Arundel County Circuit

Court, as well as his support for increased funding for the county's schools. A hundred and fifty people attended the event, held at Asbury United Methodist Church.

Glendening entered the hall to the tune of a gospel choir singing "Maryland, My Maryland." County Executive Janet Owens spoke, as did Carl Snowden, who recognized several government officials in the audience. A short play was presented that included actors playing the parts of John Snowden and Georgia Boston. When the governor spoke, he mentioned not only the pardon, but his plans to end racial profiling, appoint more minorities to the bench, and increase support for education.[21]

In the absence of a moratorium, however, capital cases threatened to keep coming. In early 2002, thirteen inmates remained on death row in Maryland, nine of whom were Black, and all but one of whose victims had been white. And nine of the thirteen had been prosecuted in one jurisdiction: Baltimore County. Three had exhausted their appeals and it looked very much as if the Supreme Court would dash the hopes of a fourth. As Governor Glendening began his final year in the governor's mansion, he represented the last hope for all four, three of whom were Black.[22]

The case of Wesley Eugene Baker was the first up. He had been convicted of the 1991 murder of a woman in front of her grandchildren during a robbery outside of a Catonsville mall and was scheduled to die on May 13, 2002. Death penalty opponents urged Glendening to grant a reprieve until the results of the University of Maryland study, which was still not finished, were released.

Instead of acting on the petition for clemency for Baker, however, Glendening decided to step up and address the larger issue. He finally responded to the call for a moratorium but took it only so far. He ordered a one-year halt to capital punishment in Maryland to allow the study to be completed and reviewed. In so doing, he made Maryland the second state, after Illinois, to impose a moratorium on the death penalty. His action halted the execution not only of Baker but of the other men slated for lethal injection—the state's official method of execution since 1994—in the following few months.

**39.** Governor Parris Glendening speaks at a program held in his honor at Asbury United Methodist Church on June 22, 2001. Used with permission from Baltimore Sun Media. All rights reserved.

"Very serious questions have been raised about the system, about its impartiality," Glendening declared in a statement, "particularly relative to race and especially the race of the victim." He added that "there is a logical inconsistency to say we're reviewing the fairness and justice of the death penalty process and in the meantime we're going to execute." But he insisted that he still supported the death penalty, and that the men whose executions he had put on hold had committed "vicious crimes" and probably deserved to die.[23]

In a single stroke, Glendening had also made capital punishment in Maryland someone else's problem. It was bound to be a major issue in the gubernatorial contest later that year, but he would not be a candidate, nor would he have to struggle personally with any further appeals.

By June capital punishment was already a campaign issue. Lieutenant Governor Kathleen Kennedy Townsend, who, like Glendening, supported the death penalty in certain cases, had urged him to declare the moratorium, and continued to support it as she campaigned to succeed him. By contrast, U.S. representative Robert L. Ehrlich Jr., the Republican who opposed her, vowed to end the moratorium if he were elected.[24]

The University of Maryland study, due out in September, was delayed, and in November, Ehrlich won the election with 51.6 percent of the vote. The results of the study were finally released a week after he took office when, on January 9, 2003, University of Maryland professor Raymond Paternoster summed up his findings before two committees of the Maryland state legislature.

A team of seven led by Dr. Paternoster had traveled the length and breadth of the state collecting data on some six thousand homicide cases reported in Maryland since 1978. Every first- and second-degree murder conviction since that year—which was when the U.S. Supreme Court had allowed states to reinstate capital punishment, after having invalidated it six years earlier—had been reexamined. In assembling this massive database, they also reviewed state prison and parole records.[25]

Paternoster's team discovered that the race of the victim was a defining factor in sentencing. Defendants of any race who killed white people were between two and three times more likely to get the death sentence, and in such cases, Black defendants were more likely than whites to receive it. They also discovered that the location of the crime was germane. Those accused of capital offenses in Baltimore County were twenty-three times more likely to garner a death sentence than those in Baltimore city, eighteen times more likely than those in Prince George's County, and fourteen times more likely than those in Montgomery County.[26]

Undaunted by the implications of the study, Governor Ehrlich was as good as his word, and before the month was out he lifted the moratorium. Maryland carried out two more executions during his term, one of which was that of Wesley Eugene Baker. After the governor lost his reelection bid, however, the general assembly established the Maryland Commission on Capital Punishment to provide recommendations for freeing the administration of capital punishment from bias and making it fairer. In its final report, however, the commission strongly recommended abolition of the death penalty.

On March 13, 2013, Democratic governor Martin O'Malley, who had beaten Ehrlich in 2006, signed into law a bill that repealed the death penalty for all future offenders. And at the end of that year, he commuted the sentences of the four remaining death row inmates in the state, thus ending the 365-year history of the death penalty in the state of Maryland.

# Afterword

Posthumous pardons are rarities in American history, and those sought because of alleged racial bias are fewer still. They have typically been granted when a defendant is proven, or is suspected to have been, innocent; when the legal system can be shown to have violated constitutional rights or denied a person—even a guilty one—a fair shake; when the political or legal climate has changed; when sentences are believed to have been excessive; or when an individual's laudable accomplishments are thought in some way to compensate society for the crime committed against it.

In 2011 Dr. Stephen Greenspan, then a University of Colorado professor, counted only a little over a hundred such cases in the nation's past when he attempted to catalog them all, and more than half of those were individuals convicted of sedition in Montana during World War I and pardoned in 2006, having been jailed for nothing more than criticizing the government. There have been several more since Greenspan did his research, but precious few in our history have redressed racial, ethnic, anti-immigrant, religious, gender, or sexual orientation bias.[1]

Some prominent ones on the state level that have addressed such inequities include:

> The 1979 pardon by Governor Milton Shapp—the first posthumous pardon in Pennsylvania history—of Irish-born "Blackjack" Jack Kehoe, a coal miner hanged in 1878 for the murder of a mine foreman during a bitter struggle over wages between

miners and coal barons. The atmosphere, and his trial, were tinged with ethnic animus.[2]

The 1986 pardon of Leo Frank, a Jewish man convicted in Georgia of the 1913 murder of a young Christian girl, granted because the state failed to protect him from a subsequent lynching, which, of course, robbed him of the right to continue to appeal his conviction. There was also substantial evidence that he was innocent.[3]

The 1996 decision to drop charges against J. B. Stradford, a prominent Black businessman and activist attorney indicted for inciting the 1921 Tulsa, Oklahoma, race riot, which was white-initiated and in which an estimated 150–300 people were killed. Persuaded he could not count on a fair trial in Tulsa, Stradford, who had actually been acting as a peacemaker, jumped bail. Six decades after his death, he received an "honorary executive pardon" from Governor Frank Keating.[4]

The 2000 pardon in Tennessee of Ed Johnson, the Black Chattanooga man whose case was mentioned at the dedication of John Snowden's memorial. He had been sentenced to death in 1906 for sexually assaulting a white woman despite the testimony at trial of numerous alibi witnesses. The U.S. Supreme Court had stayed his execution, but he was lynched in a public hanging before it could rule on his appeal.

The 2005 pardon of Lena Baker, a Black woman executed in Georgia in 1945 for the murder of her employer, an older white man who had kept her in virtual slavery and sexually assaulted her on multiple occasions.

The 2009 pardon in South Carolina of Thomas and Meeks Griffin, well-to-do Black brothers electrocuted in 1915 for the murder of a Confederate Army veteran. They had been falsely accused by a codefendant who had probably committed the act himself.

The 2011 pardon of John Gordon, an Irish Catholic convicted of murder on circumstantial evidence in Rhode Island in 1844 and executed. Among the anomalies at his trial was an instruction given to jurors to "give greater weight to Yankee witnesses than Irish witnesses."

The 2013 pardon of those of the "Scottsboro Boys" who had not otherwise had their convictions overturned. This was the famous case of nine Black Alabama teenagers accused of raping two white women in 1931. By any standard, the courts had grievously denied them due process of law.

The 2019 pardon of the "Groveland Four," young African American men accused of the 1949 rape of a seventeen-year-old white girl in Florida, for "egregious wrongs" perpetrated against them by the criminal justice system. One was killed by law enforcement; three were beaten to elicit confessions. The U.S. Supreme Court overturned two of their convictions, but the two men were shot while in custody. One died before he could be retried; the other was retried and convicted. The fourth served a lengthy sentence.

The 2019 pardon of Grover Thompson in Illinois twenty-three years after his death in prison. Thompson, a Black man, had been wrongfully convicted in 1981 of the murder of a seventy-two-year-old white widow to which a serial murderer and rapist later confessed. His was the first posthumous exoneration in Illinois history.[5]

The 2020 pardon of civil rights activist Bayard Rustin, a confidant of the Rev. Dr. Martin Luther King Jr., convicted in California in 1953 and jailed for fifty days for violating "lewd vagrancy" laws that targeted homosexuals.

Maryland governor Larry Hogan's groundbreaking 2021 blanket pardon of thirty-four Black lynching victims accused of various crimes between 1854 and 1933 who were denied due process and equal protection of the law. One recipient was identified only as "Frederick," his surname having been lost to history.[6]

On the federal level, there was also the 1999 pardon by President Bill Clinton of Lieutenant Henry O. Flipper, the first African American to graduate from West Point, who was court-martialed and dishonorably discharged from the Army in 1882 for alleged financial improprieties. Many thought it had been a set-up to force him out of the service.[7]

Flipper had tried to clear his name while he lived; after his death in 1940, his relatives had taken up his cause. In 1976 they had asked the Army Board for Correction of Military Records to review Flipper's court-martial and dismissal. The board found his conviction and punishment to have been "unduly harsh and unjust" and at its recommendation, his dismissal was reclassified as an honorable discharge. But the board lacked the power to overturn his court-martial conviction.

Presidential action could accomplish this, but Flipper's relatives were stymied by a Department of Justice policy that flatly prohibits consideration of posthumous pardons. Getting President Clinton to issue what would be the first such presidential pardon in history was thus an uphill battle. To accomplish it, they retained the law firm of Arnold and Porter, whose attorneys drafted a lengthy memo not only setting out the reasons Flipper deserved a pardon but also the flaws in the Justice Department's arguments opposing one.

At the time, the department's longstanding hostility to posthumous cases was based on four very early court cases—one from as far back as 1833–and one opinion of a Civil War–era attorney general. The principal argument was that the president was not empowered to issue such pardons because a pardon had to be *accepted* by a grantee to be valid, an impossibility in the case of a deceased petitioner. A secondary concern was the administrative burden that a potential flood of applications following any change in the policy would place on the small coterie of lawyers and paralegals who made up the Office of the Pardon Attorney.

The Arnold and Porter team filed a clemency application with the Department of the Army in late 1997, arguing that Flipper's was a special case to which the arguments that supported the Justice Department's policy were not germane. The firm also cited later authorities— including a 1974 Supreme Court decision that derided the requirement of consent as a "legal fiction"—to demonstrate that there is, in fact, *no* legal requirement that a pardon must be accepted to be effectuated. They argued further that the Flipper petition was unique and would therefore not set any broad precedent if it were granted.[8]

By the spring of 1998, the Army was on board, and it forwarded the file to the Office of the Pardon Attorney. By this time the White House had received letters of support from several members of Congress, and perhaps as a result, the Justice Department did not dismiss the matter out of hand, as it had previous posthumous cases.

But that didn't mean it relished the idea. Roger C. Adams, the pardon attorney, prepared a lengthy memorandum on the probable negative effects of favorable action on the Flipper request, focusing primarily on the feared additional administrative hardship. The office already received an average of two hundred petitions for pardons and four hundred for clemency annually, he wrote, and a rash of posthumous requests, which by their nature often require extensive historical research, would overburden the staff, which lacked the necessary research skills. Adams suggested a work-around whereby the president might issue a proclamation in lieu of a pardon.[9]

Within a week, however, Assistant Attorney General Eric H. Holder Jr. informed the White House that the Justice Department *would* support the Flipper application. And on February 19, 1999—118 years after his conviction—Lieutenant Henry O. Flipper received the first posthumous presidential pardon in American history.[10]

Today the Department of Justice no longer asserts any substantive legal arguments against posthumous pardons, but it is no less hostile to applications for them. According to the department's website:

> It is the general policy of the Department of Justice not to accept for processing applications for posthumous pardons for federal convictions. The policy against processing posthumous pardon petitions is grounded in the belief that the time of the officials involved in the clemency process is better spent on the pardon and commutation requests of living persons. Many posthumous pardon requests would likely be based on a claim of manifest injustice, and given that decades have passed since the commission of the offense and the historical record would have to be scoured objectively and comprehensively to investigate such claims, it is the Department's position that the limited resources available to process applications for Presidential pardon are best dedicated to applications submitted by living persons who can truly benefit from a grant of clemency.[11]

This argument, which continues to suggest that a wave of applications would be forthcoming and would impose an unbearable administrative burden, was anticipated in the Flipper application. The attorneys who drafted the application pointed to the paucity of posthumous state-level cases as an indication that the burden would likely be a light one. They asserted that states that had granted such pardons averaged only one or two cases each in their entire history.

"The infrequent number of posthumous pardon requests at the state level—where the bulk of the criminal cases in our nation are handled—suggests that petitions to the President for posthumous pardons will be very rare, indeed," they maintained in their brief. And even if there were a slight increase in the number of such requests, they argued, "administrative inconvenience is an insufficient justification to warrant imposing a blanket rule prohibiting posthumous pardons."[12]

No reasonable person would argue that pardons for living persons should not enjoy pride of place over those for the deceased, but it is wrongheaded for the federal government to refuse *categorically* to investigate posthumous cases. Society as a whole benefits when historic wrongs are righted, a process that may carry tremendous symbolic importance.

Nor has the government been consistent in applying the Justice Department's policy. Apart from the Flipper case, witness President Donald Trump's 2020 pardon of iconic suffragette Susan B. Anthony, convicted in 1872 of voting at a time when it was illegal for women to do so. Or his 2018 pardon of heavyweight boxing champion Jack Johnson, convicted in 1913 of violating the Mann Act, which forbade the transport of a woman across state lines for "immoral purposes" and which, by all accounts, was enforced unevenly to the detriment of African Americans. Presidents George W. Bush and Barack Obama had both declined to pardon him, as the Justice Department did not recommend doing so. But Trump was lobbied by actor Sylvester Stallone, and he issued the Johnson pardon with little or no input from the Department of Justice. Four of the six posthumous presidential pardons that have ever been issued were granted by him, all apparently bypassing the department.[13]

The Constitution places the power of the pardon squarely with the president. As a practical matter, the Justice Department has traditionally served presidents as the gatekeeper for all clemency applications; federal regulations require that the attorney general make a recommendation that the president is free to accept or reject. The actual reviews are undertaken by the Office of the Pardon Attorney, ensuring that standardized criteria are used in evaluating applications and presumably imposing a measure of fairness on the process.

It should go without saying that there is nothing remotely just about a system in which the ostensible gatekeeper has declared the gates closed but in which those with White House connections may do an end run around it. Such a system is patently unfair in that it denies petitioners equal access, a travesty that is doubly acute when one considers the allegations of racially motivated injustice that infect cases similar to those cited above. Fortunately, most states do not have such policies, and governors who have chosen to act on deserving posthumous cases are to be applauded. Presidents should do the same where action is warranted, and neither be hamstrung by, nor hide behind, arbitrary Justice Department policies. With the stroke of a pen, a president can instruct the department to change its rules. All it takes is the will to do so.

The national conversation about making amends for our racist past has recently centered on removal of monuments to the Confederacy and renaming institutions that bear the names of slaveholders. It has also included a more nuanced discussion of reparations—and not just for slavery but for peonage, convict leasing, sharecropping, and redlining, among other abuses—than in the past. But the conversation should not stop with the wrongs perpetrated by the executive and legislative branches of government. The third leg of the stool—the judiciary— must not be overlooked.[14]

Where the judicial system has failed a group of citizens and where there is potential benefit in reexamining its sins, a strong argument exists for taking a second look and for making amends where appropriate. Considering posthumous cases for presidential pardons, however, would surely require a larger appropriation for the Department of Justice, which has consistently maintained that resources for such an effort are lacking.

The Office of the Pardon Attorney's seven lawyers, assisted by a small coterie of paralegals and clerical staff, had their hands more than full in fiscal year 2020 with a backlog of nearly 2,500 petitions for pardons and nearly 12,000 more for clemency.[15] Adding posthumous cases to their dockets would increase this already unmanageable burden and would, at minimum, necessitate hiring additional staff with specialized historical research skills. But Congress should certainly provide the necessary funds; any additional appropriation required would be lost in the rounding in the Justice Department's annual $28 billion budget.

The names of several notable individuals who may deserve posthumous pardons have been put forward in recent years. Some are alleged to have been treated unfairly because of race. Among them:

Marcus Garvey, the prominent Black nationalist known for his role in the "Back to Africa" movement and the founding of the Universal Negro Improvement Association. Targeted by F.B.I. director J. Edgar Hoover for his advocacy of civil rights, he was convicted of mail fraud in 1923 and ultimately deported to his native Jamaica.[16]

John Anthony Copeland Jr., who participated in the 1859 raid at Harper's Ferry alongside abolitionist John Brown and tried to lead a rebellion to end slavery. He was hanged by the state of Virginia for his freedom-fighting efforts.

Leaders of major slave revolts or suspected conspiracies, including Gabriel Prosser (1800), Charles Deslondes (1811), Denmark Vesey (1822), and Nat Turner (1831).[17]

The "Oberlin rescuers," Charles Langston and Simeon Bushnell, one Black, one white, convicted in 1859 in federal court for violating the Fugitive Slave Act by rescuing John Price, an escaped slave, from slave hunters.

Geronimo, the Native American warrior who fought white incursion on Apache land. After he surrendered, he spent the rest of his life at hard labor as a prisoner of the U.S. Army. He was incarcerated for far longer than his surrender agreement called for, and was frequently trotted out as a tourist attraction and a "living museum piece."[18]

A systematic investigation of *all* potentially racially tainted cases in the history of the country would, indeed, surely be an unmanageable task. The list would simply be too long. But the tragic extent of America's racially unjust past must not be an excuse to avoid revisiting it, at the very least in cases in which evidence of bias survives and there is a constituency for a second look. Here some modern form of adjudication is not only desirable; it is imperative, and on both the state and federal levels.

Congress routinely addresses historic acts it determines to be unjust, repealing and replacing them. The courts do the same, as the Supreme Court did in its 2018 repudiation of its appalling 1944 decision in the case of *Korematsu v. United States* that had upheld the forcible internment of Japanese Americans during World War II. Should the executive branch do any less? Taking a second look at problematic cases sends a powerful message that we the people are committed to addressing our imperfections and past transgressions, to vindicating those who have suffered, and to ensuring that future defendants are treated fairly. A country that declines to reexamine its past is a country prone to repeat its mistakes.

John Snowden's pardon did not garner the national attention accorded the effort in Charlottesville to dethrone Robert E. Lee, or the toppling of many similar monuments that followed the 2020 death of George Floyd under the knee of a Minneapolis policeman. But to many it was no less important an event, if only because it demonstrated an enduring commitment to racial justice, which, although it may at times be backward looking, is first and foremost about the living.

If Governor Glendening was right in asserting that "the search for justice has no statute of limitations," then where the judicial system has ill served a definable group of citizens, and where there is something to be gained by reexamining its sins, the nation has an obligation to make things right. Even cases of those long dead may be very much alive in the present and continue to affect us; these should be given a fair hearing. As long as the government and the American people remain open to learning from their past errors and making amends for the wounds of the past, justice delayed need not, ultimately, be justice denied.

# Epilogue

Hazel Geneva Snowden, daughter of Louis Snowden, played an important role in the effort to secure a posthumous pardon for her uncle John. She remembered from her childhood the photograph of him that her father kept on his bedroom mirror and recalled how bitterly he had resented his brother's execution. Ms. Snowden never doubted her uncle's innocence. "I would look into his face," she recalled, "and I knew it was the face of an innocent man."[1]

When she first heard from Carl Snowden—who was no relation to her but whom she had known since she was twelve years old—that he was pressing for a pardon for her uncle, she was all in. She attended meetings, wrote letters, phoned the parole board, participated in the memorial committee, and contributed a good deal of the money for the memorial they erected on her uncle's grave. She is certain her letter to Governor Parris Glendening was one of the reasons he agreed to ask the parole board to delve into her uncle's case and ultimately issued the long-sought pardon.

The day the pardon was finally secured was one of the happiest and proudest of her life. "I could feel his peace," Ms. Snowden told the newspapers, speaking of the uncle she had never met. And that evening, she visited his grave at the Brewer Hill Cemetery to pray for his soul and to weep for him.[2]

Every year since that time, on or near John Snowden's birthday, Hazel has held a cookout in her uncle's honor. Friends, relatives, and others who helped secure the pardon are invited to celebrate his life. It is a happy occasion but one with its somber moments. Someone is asked to read aloud the text of the pardon, and someone else recites the soaring rhetoric of John Snowden's last statement.

Anyone who dismisses the value of posthumous pardons simply because they do nothing for the defendant would do well to attend one of Hazel Snowden's barbecues. They are eloquent testimony to the significance such acts may have for people who are very much alive today.[3]

# Acknowledgments

This nonlawyer received invaluable help in understanding the finer points of John Snowden's journey through the legal system from a "dream team" of well-respected attorneys. My heartfelt thanks goes to Joshua N. Friedman, Richard H. Gordin, Steven A. Herman, Deborah Leff, Michael A. Millemann, Paul M. Sandler, and Glenn P. Sugameli, all of whom reviewed the manuscript, and to Marsha A. Cohan, Natalie G. Lichtenstein, and Deborah S. Strauss. All patiently fielded my endless questions about legal procedure and strategy.

I'd also like to thank others who provided feedback on the book, including Margery Elfin, Luisa F. Foley, Lawrence Gotfried, Rita Gotfried, Stephen Mink, Richard L. Peterman, Wilbur Richardson Jr., Will Schwarz, Jamal Simmons, Richard Thaler, Robert L. Worden, and Suzanne A. Zunzer.

Several individuals who were personally involved in the campaign for a posthumous pardon for John Snowden graciously shared their stories and offered other assistance. I'd like especially to single out Carl O. Snowden, Hazel G. Snowden, and Janice Hayes-Williams, the latter of whom also assisted me in my research, as well as the late Judith J. Kulawiak. I'd also like to thank Phillip T. Chambers, Eliza Mae Robinson, and Beatrice Marshall Smith for sharing memories.

Books like this depend heavily on the kindness and expertise of archivists. My thanks to Jennifer Hafner Abbott, Emily Oland Squires, Megan Craynon, and especially Christopher E. Haley of the Maryland State Archives; Rebecca Sharp of the National Archives and Records Administration; Leslie Eames of the Maryland Center for History and

Culture; and Savannah Wood of the Afro-American Newspapers for help in locating records and images. I'd also like to thank James Ball, Linda Brown, Bob Jackson, Deborah J. Moore, Kay Ennis, and Susan Riedy for helping me acquire some of the illustrations used in the book.

Others who have pointed me in useful directions or provided materials, support, and encouragement along the way include Jeffrey Crouch, Stephen Greenspan, Caroline Griffith, Steven H. Johnson, Melanie Kirkpatrick, Margaret Love, Martha Nace-Johnson, Madelyn Ross, Karen H. Rothenberg, and Stephen H. Sachs.

And finally, my appreciation to my literary agent, Peter W. Bernstein, and to Thomas Swanson, Sara Springsteen, Taylor Rothgeb, Rosemary Sekora, Anna Weir, and their colleagues at Potomac Books and the University of Nebraska Press for their continued support and confidence in me, and to copyeditor Amy Pattullo for her meticulous review of the manuscript.

# Chronology

**1916**

October 16    Valentine N. Brandon and Lottie May Haislup, both of Washington DC, are married in Baltimore, Maryland.

**1917**

January 1    Brandon begins work as a stenographer at Annapolis's Naval Engineering Experiment Station, located on an island in the Severn River.

August 8    Returning from work, Brandon discovers his partially clad, pregnant wife dead in their home. Annapolis authorities suspect foul play and call in detectives from Baltimore for help in solving the crime.

August 9    An autopsy determines that Mrs. Brandon had been struck on the head and strangled. Police interview neighbors and grill Valentine Brandon, who has an airtight alibi and is released.

August 10    The *Washington Times* retains Grace Humiston, a well-known New York detective, to solve the crime and offers a $500 reward for information leading to the conviction of Mrs. Brandon's killer.

August 11    District of Columbia police are enlisted in the search for suspects.

Lottie May Brandon is buried in Washington.

| August 12 | Baltimore detectives work with Mrs. Humiston and focus on several suspects, including a neighbor, a peddler, a possible former lover, and a jealous woman, but none appears guilty. |
|---|---|
| August 13 | Ella Rush Murray is approached by two daughters of her African American laundress who claim to have seen a Black man emerge from the Brandon home on the morning of the murder. She escorts them to the authorities to tell their story. They identify the man as John Snowden, an ice man, who is questioned, arrested, and spirited off to Baltimore for safety. |
| August 14 | Snowden is photographed and fingerprinted and subjected to intensive grilling, possibly involving torture. He steadfastly maintains his innocence. Police continue searching for evidence. |
|  | Lottie May Brandon's remains are exhumed for a second autopsy, which points to an African American assailant. |
| August 15 | Interrogation of John Snowden continues. He refuses to confess, but his account of his actions on the day of the murder does not square with those of other witnesses. He tells reporters he had not known Mrs. Brandon and had never been in her house. |
| August 16 | All of the evidence marshaled against Snowden is circumstantial, but two attorneys fail in an attempt to obtain his release on a writ of habeas corpus. |
| August 21 | Detectives conclude that Snowden is the murderer they have been seeking. They end their investigation and turn the case over to State's Attorney Nicholas H. Green. |
| October 2 | Snowden is secretly transferred to Anne Arundel County Jail in Annapolis. |
| October 18 | Annapolis grand jury indicts John Snowden for first- and second-degree murder. |

| October 29 | Fifth Judicial Circuit Court begins the voir dire process for the trial of John Snowden. |
|---|---|
| October 30 | After eleven jurors have been empaneled and the prosecution runs out of peremptory challenges, State's Attorney Green suddenly insists, without explanation, on a change in venue. The trial is moved to Towson. |

### 1918

| January 23 | John Snowden's murder trial begins in the Baltimore County Circuit Court at Towson. |
|---|---|
| January 31 | After deliberating for just twenty-two minutes, the jury finds Snowden guilty of murder. Only when prompted by the judge does the foreman specify that the verdict is first degree murder with the death penalty. |
| February 1 | Attorneys for Snowden petition the judge to vacate the judgment and order a new trial. |
| February 13 | The judge denies the motion and sentences Snowden to be hanged. |
| March 2 | Snowden's attorneys petition for an appeal. They secure several extensions in the ensuing months for filing a bill of exceptions. |
| September 24 | Judge signs bill of exceptions, which is printed and forwarded to the court of appeals in Annapolis. |
| December 5 | Court of appeals hears arguments in the case of *John Snowden v. State of Maryland*. |

### 1919

| January 16 | Court of appeals sustains the verdict against Snowden. |
|---|---|
| January 24 | Maryland governor Emerson C. Harrington, who is petitioned for gubernatorial clemency, receives a delegation of Black preachers and others who wish to plead for Snowden's life. He is disinclined to interfere. |
| January 29 | Governor Harrington signs John Snowden's death warrant, specifying February 28 as the date for his execution. |

| February 21 | Attorney and detective Grace Humiston returns to Annapolis at the behest of Ella Rush Murray to plead Snowden's case based on new evidence. |
| --- | --- |
| February 24 | At a final meeting with white and Black Snowden supporters, Harrington announces that it is no case for mercy and that he refuses to intervene. |
| | Attorneys for Snowden acquire his signature on papers to enable them to petition the U.S. Supreme Court for his release. |
| February 27 | As preparations for the execution begin, Snowden's attorneys meet with U.S. Supreme Court chief justice Edward Douglass White, who declines to intervene. |
| February 28 | John Snowden is hanged in the Calvert Street Jail yard in Annapolis. |
| March 1 | After a standing-room-only funeral service at Mt. Moriah A.M.E. Church in Annapolis, Snowden is interred at Brewer Hill Cemetery. |

**1990**

Annapolis alderman Carl Snowden asks Maryland governor William Donald Schaefer to reexamine the Snowden case. The governor agrees but does nothing.

**2000**

| March | Carl Snowden, now special assistant to the Anne Arundel county executive, petitions Governor Parris N. Glendening for clemency for John Snowden. Prodded by other John Snowden supporters, Glendening agrees to look into the case. |
| --- | --- |
| | In the meantime, his administration commissions a University of Maryland study to examine potential racial bias in the imposition of the death penalty in the state. |

| June 7 | Glendening commutes the sentence of Eugene Colvin-el, a Black man convicted of murder, whose case bears a certain similarity to the Snowden case. |

**2001**

| May 31 | Declaring that "the search for justice has no statute of limitations," Glendening grants a full pardon to John Snowden. |
| June 22 | The Annapolis African American community honors Governor Glendening, in part for granting the Snowden pardon. |

**2002**

| May 9 | Governor Glendening orders a one-year moratorium on the institution of the death penalty in Maryland. |

**2003**

| January 7 | University of Maryland researchers conclude that sentencing in capital cases is uneven in the state. They determine that the race of the victim is a defining factor, that Black defendants are more likely than whites to receive the death penalty, and that the location of the crime is germane. |
| January 15 | Glendening's successor, Maryland governor Robert L. Ehrlich, lifts the moratorium on the death penalty in the state. |

**2013**

| March 13 | Maryland governor Martin O'Malley signs bill repealing the death penalty and commutes the sentences of the four inmates remaining on death row. |

# Notes

## Preface

1. "SPLC Launches Digital Initiative to Promote Honest Discussion of Confederate History," Southern Poverty Law Center, accessed June 12, 2019, https://www.splcenter.org/news/2019/04/09/splc-launches-digital-initiative-promote-honest-discussion-confederate-history; "Roger Taney Statue Removed from Maryland State House Grounds Overnight," *Baltimore Sun*, August 18, 2017; "List of Monuments and Memorials Removed during the George Floyd Protests," Wikipedia, https://en.wikipedia.org/wiki/List_of_monuments_and_memorials_removed_during_the_George_Floyd_protests#United_States.

## Prologue

1. "Activist Snowden, 22, Relies on Compromise," *Baltimore Sun*, April 21, 1976; Carl Snowden Biography, History Makers, accessed February 17, 2020, https://www.thehistorymakers.org/biography/carl-snowden-42.
2. "Carl Snowden Wins Respect for Social Activism," *Baltimore Sun*, October 30, 1977.
3. Jennifer Clough, "Hanging: Was John Snowden Guilty? Question Refuses to Fade," *Evening Capital*, August 11, 1980.
4. Carl Snowden, interview with the author, May 9, 2019.
5. "Henry Davis Strung Up and Riddled with Lead," *Macon Telegraph*, December 22, 1906.
6. "Panel Develops 'Fair' Death Penalty Plan," *Capital*, January 13, 1993; "Senate Panel Opens Hearings on Death Penalty," *Capital*, March 16, 1993.
7. "Three Pursue Posthumous Pardon," *Baltimore Sun*, March 14, 2000.
8. Carl Snowden, interview with the author; "The Honorable Carl Snowden Recalls Securing the Posthumous Pardon of John Snowden," History Makers, accessed June 26, 2019, https://www.thehistorymakers.org/biography/honorable-carl-snowden-42.

### 1. "A Love Match, Pure and Simple"

1. Much of the description of the Brandons' life in Washington and Annapolis comes from the testimony of Valentine Brandon, Archives of Maryland, Court of Appeals (Records and Briefs), John Snowden, October term 1918, case no. 95, vol. 1, 26–46, https://msa.maryland.gov/megafile/msa/speccol/sc3500/sc3520 /013600/013632/html. Additional sources include "Marks on Throat to Be Focus of Study," *Washington Times*, August 9, 1917; "Both Murdered Woman and Her Husband Lived in District Formerly," *Washington Times*, August 9, 1917; "Diagram of Annapolis' Shocking Crime and Picture of Lottie May Brandon of Washington, the Victim," *Washington Times*, August 9, 1917; "Finds His Wife Slain," *Washington Post*, August 9, 1917; "Murdered Wife Was Washington Woman," *Baltimore Sun*, August 9, 1917; "Young Woman Soon to Become Mother Slain: Mystery in Crime," *Evening Capital*, August 9, 1917; "Brandon Murder Case Still Clothed in Deepest Mystery," *Evening Capital*, August 10, 1917; "Suspicion Attaches to Washington Man Who Disliked Husband," *Washington Times*, August 10, 1917; "Clue in Annapolis Murder Mystery Leads to Capital," *Evening Star*, August 10, 1917; and "Fought with Slayer," *Washington Post*, August 10, 1917.
2. "Mystery Cloaks Killing of Wife," *Evening Star*, August 9, 1917.
3. R. J. Haislup, "Girl's Father Thanks the Times for Efforts," *Washington Times*, August 10, 1917.

### 2. "Aren't You Going to Come and Kiss Me?"

1. "Marks on Throat to Be Focus of Study," *Washington Times*, August 9, 1917.
2. "Marks on Throat."
3. "Crime Detectives of Rare Ability Seek Assassin," *Washington Times*, August 14, 1917.
4. "Crime Detectives of Rare Ability."
5. Clinton McCabe, *History of the Baltimore City Police Department, 1774–1907* (Baltimore: Board of Police Commissioners, 1907), 117–18, 124–25, 128–29; "Baltimore Detectives Who Are Working on the Brandon Murder Mystery," *Washington Times*, August 12, 1916; Joseph F. Dougherty and K. S. Daiger, "Behind Drawn Blinds," *True Detective Mysteries*, March 1930; "Crime Detectives of Rare Ability."
6. "Mystery Cloaks Killing of Wife," *Evening Star*, August 9, 1917; "Young Woman Soon to Become Mother Slain: Mystery in Crime," *Evening Capital*, August 9, 1917.
7. Testimony of Dr. Joseph C. Joyce, Archives of Maryland, Court of Appeals (Records and Briefs), John Snowden, October term 1918, case no. 95, vol. 1, 70–98, https://msa.maryland.gov/megafile/msa/speccol/sc3500/sc3520/013600 /013632/html.

### 3. "Altogether Separate and Different Lives"

1. U.S. Department of Commerce, Bureau of the Census, *Fourteenth Census of the United States Taken in the Year 1920: General Report and Analytical Tables* (Washington DC: Government Printing Office, 1922), 2:77.
2. Philip L. Brown, *The Other Annapolis, 1900–1950* (Annapolis: Annapolis Publishing, 1994), 33.
3. Brown, *Other Annapolis*, 11–15.
4. "Colored Folk Put Out of Sunday's Tabernacle," *Evening Capital*, March 6, 1916; "The Rev. Williams," *Evening Capital*, March 6, 1916.
5. "Colored Voters Indignant at Jim-Crow Feature," *Evening Capital*, October 22, 1915.
6. "School Fund Inequities," *Evening Capital*, January 4, 1904; Brown, *Other Annapolis*, 53–55; Jane W. McWilliams, *Annapolis, City on the Severn: A History* (Baltimore: Johns Hopkins University Press, 2011), 198–200.
7. "Negroes Boycott White Man," *Baltimore Sun*, March 19, 1904; "Mr. Kerbin to Negroes," *Baltimore Sun*, October 25, 1907.
8. David S. Bogen, "Precursors of Rosa Parks: Maryland Transportation Cases between the Civil War and the Beginning of World War I," *Maryland Law Review* 63, no. 4 (2004): 744–46.
9. McWilliams, *Annapolis, City on the Severn*, 247–49.
10. Brown, *Other Annapolis*, 11.
11. Hannah Jopling, *Life in a Black Community: Striving for Equal Citizenship in Annapolis, Maryland, 1902–1952* (Lanham MD: Lexington Books, 2015), 83.
12. "Terrible Outrage upon a Young Lady," *Aegis and Intelligencer* (Bel Air MD), June 11, 1875; "The Annapolis Lynching Affair," *Daily Critic* (Washington DC), June 15, 1875.
13. "The Lynching of Geo. Briscoe," *Evening Capital*, November 29, 1884; "Lynching a Notorious Robber," *Evening Capital*, November 28, 1884.
14. "Negro Identified," *Baltimore Sun*, September 8, 1898; "Lynched by a Maryland Mob," *Pawtucket Times*, October 5, 1898.
15. "Prisoner's Life Was in Peril," *Baltimore American*, January 18, 1903; "Boyd Held for Killing Kerns," *Baltimore American*, January 16, 1903.
16. "The Suspect Is Arrested," *Evening Capital*, December 17, 1906; "Accused Negro Confesses," *Evening Capital*, December 19, 1906; "Annapolis Mob Had No Mercy," *Baltimore American*, December 22, 1906; "Henry Davis Strung Up and Riddled with Lead," *Macon Telegraph*, December 22, 1906.

### 4. "All Annapolis Is Shocked"

1. "Sheriff Offers $500 for Brandon Slayer," *Baltimore Sun*, August 10, 1917; "A Tragedy Near Home," *Evening Capital*, August 9, 1917.

2. "Tragedy Near Home."

3. "Home Guard Urged by Woman Editor to Protect Wives," *Washington Times*, August 10, 1917.

4. "Mystery Cloaks Killing of Wife," *Evening Star*, August 9, 1917; "Marks on Throat to Be Focus of Study," *Washington Times*, August 9, 1917.

5. "City Police Dread Psychic Effects of Annapolis Crime," *Washington Times*, August 9, 1917.

6. "Suspicion Attaches to Washington Man Who Disliked Husband," *Washington Times*, August 10, 1917.

7. "Brute Killed My Wife, Says 'Val' Brandon," *Washington Times*, August 10, 1917.

8. "Brandon Murder Case Still Clothed in Deepest Mystery," *Evening Capital*, August 10, 1917.

9. "Suspicion Attaches to Washington Man."

10. "Haislup Appeals to District Police," *Evening Star*, August 10, 1917.

11. "Brandon Was Model Husband, Says Haislup," *Washington Times*, August 11, 1917.

12. "Capital Detective Engaged by Times to Solve Mystery," *Washington Times*, August 10, 1917; "Mrs. Humiston Coming to Washington," *Washington Times*, August 10, 1917; "Criminologist Says Degenerate Did Foul Crime," *Washington Times*, August 10, 1917.

13. "Girl's Father Thanks Times for Efforts," *Washington Times*, August 10, 1917; "Authorities Join in Commending Times for Reward Offer," *Washington Times*, August 10, 1917; "Clue in Annapolis Murder Mystery Leads to Capital," *Evening Star*, August 10, 1917.

14. "Arrest in Capital Is Made to Solve Annapolis Murder," *Evening Star*, August 11, 1917.

15. "Detectives Working on Clue of Negro in Brandon Murder," *Evening Capital*, August 11, 1917.

16. "Suspicion Attaches to Washington Man"; "Clue in Annapolis Murder Mystery."

17. "Clue in Annapolis Murder Mystery."

### 5. "Not the Faintest Clue"

1. "Two Negroes Sought in Hunt for Slayer of Mrs. Brandon," *Baltimore Sun*, August 11, 1917.

2. "Colored Man Is Arrested by Police of Washington for Annapolis Authorities," *Evening Star*, August 11, 1917; "Police Free Third Man Suspected of Crime," *Washington Times*, August 11, 1917; "Two Negroes Sought"; "Police Seek Clue in Murder Case," *Washington Herald*, August 12, 1917.

3. "Brother-in-Law of Brandon Has Alibi: Released," *Washington Times*, August 11, 1917.

4. "Mrs. Brandon's Sister Gives Police New Lead," *Baltimore Sun*, August 11, 1917; "Brandon Neighbor Looked to for Clue," *Washington Times*, August 12, 1917.

5. "Arrest in Capital Is Made to Solve Annapolis Murder," *Evening Star*, August 11, 1917.

6. "Judge Green, of Annapolis, Dies in Florida," *Washington Post*, April 10, 1935; "N. H. Green Is the Man," *Evening Capital*, January 21, 1905.

7. Telegram from Randall J. Haislup to Governor Emerson C. Harrington, August 11, 1917, Archives of Maryland, Governor (Subject File), Brandon Murder, folder no. 45 (MSA S1046, 2-30-1-4).

8. "Valentine Brandon Goes Back to Annapolis to Aid Work on Murder Mystery," *Evening Star*, August 12, 1917; "Brandon Appeals to Mayor," *Baltimore Sun*, August 12, 1917.

9. Telegram from Valentine N. Brandon to Governor Emerson C. Harrington, August 11, 1917, Archives of Maryland, Governor (Subject File), Brandon Murder, folder no. 45 (MSA S1046, 2-30-1-4).

10. "Brandon Believes Police Are Doing All in Their Power," *Washington Times*, August 12, 1917.

11. "No Solution in Sight in Brandon Mystery: Police Still at Sea," *Washington Times*, August 11, 1917; "Police Free Third Man"; "Still Shrouded in Mystery," *Evening Capital*, August 11, 1917.

12. "Was Brandon Girl's Former Lover Involved?" *Washington Times*, August 11, 1917.

13. "Boy Husband in Collapse as He Starts to Grave," *Washington Times*, August 11, 1917; "Mrs. Brandon's Funeral Attracts a Large Crowd," *Evening Star*, August 11, 1917.

### 6. "The Woman Sherlock Holmes"

1. "Capital Detective Engaged by Times to Solve Mystery," *Washington Times*, August 10, 1917.

2. "Criminal Knew Brandon House, Says Detective," *Washington Times*, August 11, 1917.

3. "Criminologist Says Degenerate Did Foul Crime," *Washington Times*, August 10, 1917.

4. Brad Ricca, *Mrs. Sherlock Holmes* (New York: St. Martin's Press, 2017).

5. "Missing Schoolgirl Who Is Believed to Have Been Kidnapped," *New York World*, February 15, 1917; "Body of Missing High School Girl Found in Cellar," *Daily Capital Journal*, June 16, 1917; "The Woman Sherlock Holmes Who Has Shaken New York," *Boston Herald*, October 13, 1917.

6. "Mrs. Humiston Coming to Washington," *Washington Times*, August 10, 1917; "Snowden's Stories Quickly Disproved," *Washington Times*, August 16, 1917.

7. "Bride Killed by Man Who Was Familiar with House," *Washington Times*, August 11, 1917.

### 7. "The More Delicate Hand of a Woman"

1. Church Notices, *Washington Times*, August 12, 1917; "Heaven Will Assist, Evangelist Declares," *Washington Times*, August 12, 1917; "Brandon Crime Hits Every Home, Pastor Declares," *Washington Times*, August 12, 1917; "Pastors Praise Times for $500 Murder Reward," *Washington Times*, August 12, 1917.
2. "Annapolis Eyes All Turned to Mrs. Humiston," *Washington Times*, August 14, 1917.
3. Joseph F. Dougherty and K. S. Daiger, "Behind Drawn Blinds," *True Detective Mysteries*, March 1930.
4. "Mrs. Humiston Says Brandon Crime May Have Been the Work of a Woman," *Washington Times*, August 12, 1917.
5. "Bradford Sticks to Belief Crime Was by Neighbor," *Washington Times*, August 13, 1917.
6. "Mrs. Humiston Says: Lottie Brandon's Body Should Be Disinterred and Her Wounds Carefully Examined," *Washington Times*, August 13, 1917.
7. "Brandon Neighbor Looked To for Clue," *Washington Times*, August 12, 1917; "Murder Arrest Near," *Washington Post*, August 13, 1917; "Eyes on Woman in Murder Case," *Baltimore Sun*, August 13, 1917.
8. "Neighbor Declares She Heard Outcry at about 1 O'Clock," *Washington Times*, August 13, 1917; "Dying Screams of Mrs. Brandon Heard by Four Women Neighbors," *Washington Times*, August 13, 1917.
9. "Mrs. King Not Jealous of Husband, Sister Declares," *Washington Times*, August 13, 1917.
10. "Police Free Third Man Suspected of Crime," *Washington Times*, August 11, 1917.

### 8. "His Name Is Snowden"

1. 1 Acton Place, accessed May 20, 2019, https://www.1actonplace.com; Historic Sites Survey Field Sheet, Individual Structure Survey Form, survey no. AA-360, Maryland Historical Trust, August 1983, accessed May 20, 2019, https://mht.maryland.gov/secure/medusa/PDF/AnneArundel/AA-360.pdf; Wendi Winters, "Home of the Week: Historic 18th-century Architecture Updated for 21st-Century Lifestyle," *Capital*, October 30, 2013; Elihu S. Riley, *A History of Anne Arundel County in Maryland* (Annapolis: Charles G. Feldmeyer, 1905), 141.
2. "W. M. Murray Dead: Noted Engineer, 68," *New York Times*, January 10, 1942.
3. "Mrs. William S. Murray," *New York Times*, March 28, 1943; U.S. Passport Application for Ella Rush Murray, April 25, 1913, Ancestry.com, accessed May 19, 2019; Mary Jane Brown, *Eradicating This Evil: Women in the American Anti-Lynching Movement, 1892–1940* (New York: Routledge, 2015), n.12.
4. "Police Certain of Snowden's Guilt," *Washington Times*, August 14, 1917.
5. Testimony of Mary Perkins, Archives of Maryland, Court of Appeals (Records and Briefs), John Snowden, October term 1918, case no. 95, vol. 1, 109–27, 127–

29, vol. 2, 75–77, 149, 167, 237–38; Affidavit of Ella Rust [*sic*] Murray, Archives of Maryland, Court of Appeals (Records and Briefs), John Snowden, October term 1918, case no. 95, vol. 1, 13–18, https://msa.maryland.gov/megafile/msa/speccol /sc3500/sc3520/013600/013632/html; "New Evidence Sought against Negro Driver with Marks on Face," *Washington Times*, August 14, 1917; "Police Certain of Snowden's Guilt."

6. "Negro Is Held as Annapolis Slayer," *Washington Post*, August 14, 1917.

7. "Too Much Christmas," *Evening Capital*, December 26, 1911; "Arrest Negro in Brandon Mystery," *Baltimore American*, August 14, 1917; "Snowden's Stories Quickly Disproved," *Washington Times*, August 16, 1917.

8. "Arrest Negro in Brandon Mystery"; "Negro Cringes under Grilling: Break Predicted," *Washington Times*, August 14, 1917.

9. Many sources refer to Edna Wallace as John Snowden's common-law wife, but this was not the case. At trial, the prosecutor referred to the couple as "living in consort" and noted that she had separated from her husband.

10. "Arrest Negro in Brandon Mystery."

11. Joseph F. Dougherty and K. S. Daiger, "Behind Drawn Blinds," *True Detective Mysteries*, March 1930; Testimony of John Snowden, Archives of Maryland, Court of Appeals (Records and Briefs), John Snowden, October term 1918, case no. 95, vol. 2, 120, https://msa.maryland.gov/megafile/msa/speccol/sc3500/sc3520 /013600/013632/html.

12. "New Clues Appear Following Arrest Made in Annapolis," *Evening Star*, August 14, 1917.

13. "Negro under Arrest in Murder Mystery," *Evening Capital*, August 14, 1917.

14. "Snowden Safe in Cell," *Baltimore Sun*, August 14, 1917.

15. "Negro Is Held as Annapolis Slayer."

### 9. "We Have Got This Negro Dead Right"

1. "Snowden Safe in Cell," *Baltimore Sun*, August 14, 1917.

2. "Snowden Makes Partial Confession," *Baltimore Sun*, August 14, 1917.

3. 1900 United States Federal Census Online Database, Ancestry.com, accessed August 4, 2019, https://www.ancestry.com/search/collections/1900usfedcen; 1910 United States Federal Census Online Database, Ancestry.com, accessed August 4, 2019, https://www.ancestry.com/search/collections/1910uscenindex.

4. "Snowden Makes Partial Confession."

5. "Bradford Thinks Mystery Solved by Negro Arrest," *Washington Times*, August 14, 1917.

6. "New Clues Appear Following Arrest Made in Annapolis," *Evening Star*, August 14, 1917; "New Evidence Sought against Negro Driver with Marks on Face," *Washington Times*, August 14, 1917.

7. "Mrs. Humiston Says: Although Evidence against Snowden, the Negro under Arrest, Appears to Be Damaging, There Are Other Clues Which Should Be Followed," *Washington Times*, August 14, 1917.

8. "Comb Negro District for Bottle Believed Used for Death Blow," *Washington Times*, August 14, 1917; "New Evidence Sought against Negro Driver"; "Snowden Makes Partial Confession."

9. "New Clues Appear Following Arrest"; "Negro under Arrest in Murder Mystery," *Evening Capital*, August 14, 1917.

10. "Negro Cringes under Grilling: Break Predicted," *Washington Times*, August 14, 1917; "Snowden Makes Partial Confession."

11. "Snowden Makes Partial Confession."

12. "Snowden Makes Partial Confession"; "Negro in Brandon Case Held on His Story," *Baltimore Sun*, August 15, 1917.

13. "Snowden Makes Partial Confession."

**10. "A Maze of Circumstantial Evidence"**

1. "Arrangements Are Made to Exhume Body and Hold Second Autopsy Tonight," *Evening Star*, August 14, 1917; "Brandon Obtains Permit to Exhume Body of Victim," *Washington Times*, August 14, 1917.

2. "Annapolis Mystery," *Alexandria Gazette*, August 15, 1917; "Man Is Responsible for Death of Mrs. Brandon, Second Autopsy Shows," *Evening Star*, August 15, 1917.

3. "Net Tightens around Negro Whose Face Is Scratched," *Washington Times*, August 15, 1917; "Negro Is Held as Annapolis Slayer," *Washington Post*, August 14, 1917; "Lawyers Seek Release of Negro Murder Suspect," *Daily Banner* (Cambridge MD), August 17, 1917.

4. "Mrs. Humiston Says: I Am Glad I Suggested Disinterment and So Released Innocent People from Suspicion," *Washington Times*, August 15, 1917.

5. "Father Anxious for Vengeance with Both Hands," *Washington Times*, August 15, 1917.

6. "Murder Mystery Remains Unsolved," *Evening Capital*, August 15, 1917; "Police Net around Snowden Is Tighter," *Baltimore Sun*, August 15, 1917.

7. "Net Tightens around Negro"; "Suspect Is Defiant," *Alexandria Gazette*, August 16, 1917.

8. "Net Tightens around Negro."

9. "Snowden to Be Taken before Formal Inquest at Annapolis Tonight," *Washington Times*, August 15, 1917.

10. "Snowden to Be Taken before Formal Inquest."

11. "Snowden to Be Taken before Formal Inquest"; "Check Up Murder Data," *Washington Post*, August 16, 1917.

12. "Annapolis Opinion Divided," *Baltimore Sun*, August 16, 1917.
13. "Inquiry of Murder Is Still Under Way," *Evening Capital*, August 16, 1917; "Murder Mystery Is as Deep as Ever," *Evening Capital*, August 17, 1917.
14. "Victim Is Reburied as Husband Watches," *Washington Times*, August 15, 1917; Gertrude Stevenson, "Husband Is Kept from Graveyard at Disinterment," *Washington Times*, August 15, 1917.

## 11. "I Ain't Scared"

1. "Expects Solution Soon of Brandon Mystery," *Philadelphia Inquirer*, August 16, 1917; "Makes Snowden Quail," *Baltimore Sun*, August 16, 1917.
2. "Snowden Tells Conflicting Tales," *Evening Star*, August 16, 1917.
3. "Snowden Tells Conflicting Tales."
4. "Check Up Murder Data," *Washington Post*, August 16, 1917; "Colored Clergyman Says He Saw No One Enter the Brandon Home August 8," *Evening Star*, August 20, 1917.
5. "Delay Inquest for Evidence," *Washington Herald*, August 16, 1917.
6. "Mrs. Humiston Says," *Washington Times*, August 16, 1917.
7. "Deny Snowden Story," *Washington Post*, August 17, 1917.
8. "Snowden Tells Conflicting Tales."
9. "Sure Now That Snowden Is Guilty," *Baltimore American*, August 17, 1917.
10. "Snowden's Stories Quickly Disproved," *Washington Times*, August 16, 1917.

## 12. "Guilty Men and Women"

1. "Snowden Afraid to Return Home: Will Be Charged," *Washington Times*, August 19, 1917.
2. "Brandon Inquest Delayed by Draft of Annapolis Quota," *Washington Times*, August 17, 1917.
3. "Deny Snowden Story," *Washington Post*, August 17, 1917; Testimony of Florence Baker, Archives of Maryland, Court of Appeals (Records and Briefs), John Snowden, October term 1918, case no. 95, vol. 1, 192, https://msa.maryland.gov/megafile/msa/speccol/sc3500/sc3520/013600/013632/html.
4. "Brandon Shows Father through House of Tragedy," *Washington Times*, August 18, 1917.
5. "Predict Snowden Will Not Confess," *Evening Star*, August 17, 1917.
6. "Snowden to Ask Change of Venue: Fears Mob," *Washington Times*, August 17, 1917.
7. "Brandon Shows Father through House"; "No Hope of Confession," *Washington Post*, August 18, 1917.
8. "Brandon Inquest Delayed"; "Snowden Afraid to Return Home."
9. "Snowden Afraid to Return Home."

10. "May Induce Confession," *Alexandria Gazette*, August 23, 1917; "Religion to Get Chance in Brandon Murder Case," *Evening Star*, August 23, 1917; "Minister to See Snowden," *Washington Post*, August 24, 1917.

### 13. "Fairer for the Man"

1. "Engineering Company Gets Jail Contract," *Evening Capital*, September 25, 1912; "The New County Jail," *Evening Capital*, July 13, 1912.
2. "Negro Suspect Taken to Jail at Annapolis," *Evening Star*, October 6, 1917; "Snowden, Held as Brandon Slayer, Back in Annapolis," *Washington Times*, October 6, 1917.
3. "Brandon Murder Case Cost County $1,000," *Evening Capital*, September 14, 1917.
4. "Politics Agog and Will Hold Spotlight," *Evening Capital*, August 22, 1917; "Four Names Mentioned for Vacant Judgeship," *Evening Capital*, August 20, 1917; "Moss Picked for Judge," *Baltimore Sun*, August 22, 1917.
5. "Judge Robert Moss Dies at Catonsville," *Cumberland Evening Times*, August 20, 1940; "Former Jurist Dies," *Frederick Post*, August 21, 1940.
6. In 1880 the U.S. Supreme Court had decided in *Strauder v. West Virginia* that categorically barring Blacks from jury service was a violation of the equal protection clause of the Fourteenth Amendment to the Constitution. Of the potential jurors named in the *Evening Capital*, all but five can be confirmed as white by their listings in the 1920 United States Federal Census Online Database on the Ancestry.com website. The balance of the names are ambiguous and might refer to Black or white men; Jane W. McWilliams, *Annapolis, City on the Severn: A History* (Baltimore: Johns Hopkins University Press, 2011), 384.
7. Hannah Jopling, *Life in a Black Community: Striving for Equal Citizenship in Annapolis, Maryland, 1902–1952* (Lanham MD: Lexington Books, 2015), 30.
8. "Important Cases for the Grand Jury," *Evening Capital*, October 15, 1917; "Urges Speedy Justice," *Evening Star*, October 15, 1917.
9. "Grand Jury Will Clear Up Brandon and Edelstein Tragedies," *Washington Post*, October 14, 1917; "John Snowden Up for Murder," *Baltimore American*, October 30, 1917.
10. "Snowden Case Goes to Grand Jury Tomorrow," *Evening Star*, October 14, 1917; "Trial of John Snowden Is Set for Tomorrow," *Evening Star*, October 28, 1917.
11. The description of Snowden as "short" here is odd; his height had been recorded by the police as five feet ten inches.
12. "Snowden Trial Halts for Lack of Jurors," *Evening Capital*, October 29, 1917; "Brandon Case Opened," *Baltimore Sun*, October 30, 1917.
13. Michael P. Parker, "Circling the Square: The City Park and the Changing Image of Annapolis," *Maryland Historical Magazine* 109, no. 1 (Spring 2014): 61–62.

14. "Prosecutor Wins Change of Venue in Snowden Trial," *Washington Times*, October 30, 1917; "Snowden, Held as Brandon Slayer, Back in Annapolis," *Washington Times*, October 6, 1917; "Ashbie Hawkins, Attorney for 50 Years, Dies at 78," *Baltimore Afro-American*, April 12, 1941.

15. "Brandon Murder Trial Delayed at Annapolis," *Evening Star*, October 29, 1917; "Colored Draftees Are Off for Meade," *Evening Capital*, October 29, 1917.

16. "Snowden Trial Halts for Lack of Jurors."

17. "John Snowden Up for Murder."

18. "Choose Jury to Try Negro for Death of Mrs. Brandon," *Washington Times*, October 29, 1917.

19. "John Snowden Up for Murder."

20. "Snowden's Trial Is Transferred," *Washington Post*, October 31, 1917.

21. "Trial of Snowden in Baltimore Co. Court," *Evening Capital*, October 30, 1917; "Snowden Case Goes to Towson," *Baltimore American*, October 31, 1917.

22. "Trial of Snowden in Baltimore Co. Court."

23. Michael Millemann, Rebecca Bowman-Rivas, and Elizabeth Smith, "Digging Them Out Alive," *Clinical Law Review* 25, no. 365 (Spring 1919): 422–23.

24. Strauder v. West Virginia, 100 U.S. 303 (1880).

25. "Snowden Trial Not Set," *Evening Capital*, November 2, 1917.

### 14. "Most Heinous and Diabolical"

1. "Snowden Faces Trial Tomorrow in Brandon Case," *Washington Times*, January 22, 1918; "Snowden in Balto: Ready for His Trial," *Evening Capital*, January 23, 1918; "Four Jurors Are Chosen as Snowden Trial Opens," *Washington Times*, January 23, 1918.

2. "Alleges Brutal Methods Used to Make Snowden Confess Crime," *Baltimore Afro-American*, February 2, 1918.

3. "Four Jurors Are Chosen"; "Trial of Snowden under Way Today," *Evening Capital*, January 23, 1918.

4. "Four Jurors Are Chosen."

5. "Snowden's Trial Blocked by Storm," *Baltimore Sun*, January 28, 1918.

6. Opening Statement of State's Attorney Nicholas H. Green, Archives of Maryland, Court of Appeals (Records and Briefs), John Snowden, October term 1918, case no. 95, vol. 1, 23–26, https://msa.maryland.gov/megafile/msa/speccol/sc3500/sc3520/013600/013632/html.

7. Testimony of Valentine Brandon, Archives of Maryland, 40–41.

8. Testimony of Valentine Brandon, Archives of Maryland, 44–45.

9. "Snowden on Trial in Brandon Murder," *Washington Post*, January 23, 1918.

10. "Mrs. Brandon Killed by Blow," *Baltimore Sun*, January 24, 1918.

11. Testimony of Dr. Joseph C. Joyce, Archives of Maryland, Court of Appeals (Records and Briefs), John Snowden, October term 1918, case no. 95, vol. 1, 70–98,

https://msa.maryland.gov/megafile/msa/speccol/sc3500/sc3520/013600/013632
/html; Testimony of Dr. Walton H. Hopkins, Archives of Maryland, Court of
Appeals (Records and Briefs), John Snowden, October term 1918, case no. 95,
vol. 1, 226–55, https://msa.maryland.gov/megafile/msa/speccol/sc3500/sc3520
/013600/013632/html; "Snowden to Testify in His Own Defense," *Evening
Capital*, January 25, 1918.

12. "Judge Grason Dies at 71 in Nursing Home," *Baltimore Sun*, February 19, 1953.
13. "Snowden Lawyers Ask for New Trial," *Baltimore Sun*, February 1, 1918; "Snowden
to Testify in His Own Defense."

**15. "Could Not Have Come from a White Person"**

1. Discussion between Judge Frank I. Duncan and Attorney A. Theodore Brady,
Archives of Maryland, Court of Appeals (Records and Briefs), John Snowden,
October term 1918, case no. 95, vol. 1, 297–98.
2. "Snowden Will Testify in Defense," *Washington Times*, January 25, 1918.
3. "Fear of Race Riot Protected Snowden," *Evening Capital*, January 26, 1918.
4. Testimony of Mary Perkins, Archives of Maryland, 109–30; Testimony of Edith
Creditt, Archives of Maryland, Court of Appeals (Records and Briefs), John
Snowden, October term 1918, case no. 95, vol. 1, 130–41, https://msa.maryland
.gov/megafile/msa/speccol/sc3500/sc3520/013600/013632/html.
5. Testimony of Leroy Sisco, Archives of Maryland, Court of Appeals (Records
and Briefs), John Snowden, October term 1918, case no. 95, vol. 1, 183–85, https://
msa.maryland.gov/megafile/msa/speccol/sc3500/sc3520/013600/013632/html.
6. Testimony of John M. Taylor, Archives of Maryland, Court of Appeals (Records
and Briefs), John Snowden, October term 1918, case no. 95, vol. 1, 141–60, https://
msa.maryland.gov/megafile/msa/speccol/sc3500/sc3520/013600/013632/html.
7. Testimony of Valentine Brandon, Archives of Maryland, 152–58.
8. Testimony of William H. Sardo, Archives of Maryland, Court of Appeals
(Records and Briefs), John Snowden, October term 1918, case no. 95, vol. 1,
160–70, https://msa.maryland.gov/megafile/msa/speccol/sc3500/sc3520/013600
/013632/html; "Big Man Slew Mrs. Brandon, Jury Is Told," *Washington Times*,
January 27, 1918; "Worse for Snowden," *Baltimore Sun*, January 27, 1918; "John
Snowden, Colored, Found Guilty at Towson for Brutal Murder at Annapolis,"
*Jeffersonian* (Towson MD), February 2, 1919.
9. Testimony of Dr. Walton H. Hopkins, Archives of Maryland, Court of Appeals
(Records and Briefs), John Snowden, October term 1918, case no. 95, vol. 1, 226–27,
https://msa.maryland.gov/megafile/msa/speccol/sc3500/sc3520/013600/013632
/html.
10. "Brandon on Stand: Not Allowed to Tell Story," *Washington Times*, January 29,
1918.
11. "Brandon on Stand."

12. "Dr. Carr Aids Case against Snowden," *Washington Post*, January 29, 1918.

13. "Snowden's Trial Blocked by Storm," *Baltimore Sun*, January 28, 1918.

### 16. "It Was Ten Minutes after Eleven"

1. "Snow Holds Up Court at Towson Today," *Evening Capital*, January 28, 1918.

2. "Says Woman May Have Caused Death," *Baltimore Sun*, January 29, 1918.

3. Testimony of Rachel E. Stewart, Archives of Maryland, Court of Appeals (Records and Briefs), John Snowden, October term 1918, case no. 95, vol. 2, 123–41, https://msa.maryland.gov/megafile/msa/speccol/sc3500/sc3520/013600 /013632/html; "Prosecution Ends in Brandon Murder Case," *Evening Capital*, January 29, 1918; "Brandon on Stand: Not Allowed to Tell Story," *Washington Times*, January 29, 1918; "Says Woman May Have Caused Death."

4. "Says Woman May Have Caused Death."

5. "Snowden to Be Taken before Formal Inquest at Annapolis Tonight," *Washington Times*, August 15, 1917; "Check Up Murder Data," *Washington Post*, August 16, 1917.

6. "May Quiz Prosecutor," *Washington Post*, January 30, 1918.

7. "Snowden Put on Stand by Defense to Clear Self," *Washington Times*, January 30, 1918.

8. "Snowden Put on Stand by Defense."

9. Testimony of Mary J. Williams, Archives of Maryland, Court of Appeals (Records and Briefs), John Snowden, October term 1918, case no. 95, vol. 2, 168–72, https:// msa.maryland.gov/megafile/msa/speccol/sc3500/sc3520/013600/013632/html.

10. Testimony of Mary Bias, Archives of Maryland, Court of Appeals (Records and Briefs), John Snowden, October term 1918, case no. 95, vol. 2, 64–71, https:// msa.maryland.gov/megafile/msa/speccol/sc3500/sc3520/013600/013632/html; Testimony of Julia Carroll, Archives of Maryland, Court of Appeals (Records and Briefs), John Snowden, October term 1918, case no. 95, vol. 2, 194–95, https:// msa.maryland.gov/megafile/msa/speccol/sc3500/sc3520/013600/013632/html.

11. "Brandon Murder Case Goes to Jury Tonight," *Evening Capital*, January 31, 1918.

12. "Snowden's Trial Blocked by Storm," *Baltimore Sun*, January 28, 1918.

13. Testimony of John Snowden, Archives of Maryland, Court of Appeals (Records and Briefs), John Snowden, October term 1918, case no. 95, vol. 2, 81–94, https:// msa.maryland.gov/megafile/msa/speccol/sc3500/sc3520/013600/013632/html; "Snowden Put on Stand by Defense."

### 17. "The Man Shoved a Gun against My Head"

1. Testimony of John Snowden, Archives of Maryland, 99–122.

2. Testimony of State's Attorney George Hartman, Archives of Maryland, Court of Appeals (Records and Briefs), John Snowden, October term 1918, case no. 95,

vol. 2, 190–201, https://msa.maryland.gov/megafile/msa/speccol/sc3500/sc3520
/013600/013632/html.

3. Testimony of Dr. Louis B. Henkel, Archives of Maryland, Court of Appeals
(Records and Briefs), John Snowden, October term 1918, case no. 95, vol. 2, 176–84,
https://msa.maryland.gov/megafile/msa/speccol/sc3500/sc3520/013600/013632
/html.

4. "Snowden Witness Seeks Retirement," *Evening Capital,* April 5, 1918.

5. Testimony of Deputy Marshal Samuel W. House, Archives of Maryland, Court
of Appeals (Records and Briefs), John Snowden, October term 1918, case no. 95,
vol. 2, 204–13, https://msa.maryland.gov/megafile/msa/speccol/sc3500/sc3520
/013600/013632/html.

### 18. "The Homes of White Women"

1. "Alleges Brutal Methods Used to Make Snowden Confess Crime," *Baltimore
Afro-American,* February 2, 1918.

2. "Snowden Put on Stand by Defense to Clear Self," *Washington Times,* January
30, 1918.

3. Motion for a New Trial, Archives of Maryland, Court of Appeals (Records and
Briefs), John Snowden, October term 1918, case no. 95, vol. 2, 12–13; "Sentence
to Die Deferred at Request of Lawyers," *Washington Times,* February 1, 1918.

4. "Sentence to Die Deferred"; "Snowden to Hang," *Baltimore Sun,* February 1,
1918.

5. "Snowden Found Guilty of Brandon Murder," *Evening Star,* February 1, 1918;
"Snowden to Hang."

6. "Snowden Found Guilty of Brandon Murder"; "Alleges Brutal Methods Used."

7. "Snowden Lawyers Ask for New Trial," *Baltimore Sun,* February 1, 1918; "John
Snowden, Colored, Found Guilty at Towson for Brutal Murder at Annapolis,"
*Jeffersonian* (Towson MD), February 2, 1919.

8. "Snowden to Hang"; "Snowden Found Guilty of Brandon Murder"; "Sentence
to Die Deferred"; "Find Snowden Guilty," *Washington Post,* February 1, 1918.

9. "Sentence to Die Deferred."

10. "Snowden Lawyers Ask for New Trial."

11. "Snowden Lawyers Ask for New Trial"; "Snowden Found Guilty of Brandon
Murder."

12. Motion for a New Trial, Archives of Maryland, 12–13; "New Trial Asked for John
Snowden," *Washington Times,* February 2, 1918; "To Ask New Trial for Snowden,"
*Baltimore Sun,* February 13, 1918.

13. Statement of Ella Rush Murray, February 3, 1918, Archives of Maryland, Court
of Appeals (Records and Briefs), John Snowden, October term 1918, case no. 95,
vol. 2, 14–18.

14. Docket Entries, Archives of Maryland, Court of Appeals (Records and Briefs), John Snowden, October term 1918, case no. 95, vol. 1, 3–4.

15. "Judge Duncan Imposes Death Penalty on Negro," *Evening Capital*, February 14, 1918; "Snowden Is Sentenced to Be Hanged for Crime," *Evening Star*, February 13, 1918; "Snowden Given Death Penalty in Brandon Case," *Washington Times*, February 14, 1918.

16. "Snowden Still a Stolid Prisoner: No Confession," *Evening Capital*, February 19, 1918.

## 19. "Defending Snowden"

1. "John Snowden, Colored, Found Guilty at Towson for Brutal Murder at Annapolis," *Jeffersonian* (Towson MD), February 2, 1919.

2. "Appeal for New Trial in Snowden Case Refused," *Baltimore Afro-American*, February 16, 1918.

3. "Is Snowden Guilty?" *Washington Bee*, February 16, 1918.

4. "The Brandon Case," *Baltimore Afro-American*, February 16, 1918.

5. "Snowden Trial Very Expensive," *Evening Capital*, March 20, 1918; "Snowden Trial Cost $3,500," *Baltimore Sun*, March 21, 1918.

6. "Is Snowden Guilty?"; "Protest Snowden Verdict," *Washington Herald*, February 13, 1918; "Appeal for New Trial in Snowden Case Refused," *Baltimore Afro-American*, February 16, 1918; "$400 Raised for Snowden Appeal," *Baltimore Afro-American*, February 22, 1918; "In the Social Whirl," *Washington Bee*, March 2, 1918.

7. "Brady at Work on Snowden Case," *Baltimore Afro-American*, March 1, 1918; "$875 Needed for Snowden's New Trial," *Baltimore Afro-American*, October 11, 1918.

8. "Formal Notice of Appeal Filed in Snowden Murder Case," *Baltimore Sun*, March 3, 1918; "John Snowden's Case Appealed," *Evening Capital*, March 4, 1918.

9. "John Snowden's Case Appealed."

10. "Baltimore Police in Murder Hunt," *Evening Star*, April 8, 1918; "Whites Are Aroused against Negro Isaac," *Baltimore Sun*, April 10, 1918.

11. "Evans to Hang, Assault on a Girl," *Evening Capital*, May 9, 1918.

12. "Brandon Pays a Tribute to Murdered Wife," *Evening Capital*, August 8, 1918.

13. "Anne Arundel to Send Quota," *Evening Capital*, April 26, 1918; "More Annapolis Lads Off to War," *Evening Capital*, April 30, 1918.

14. "Brandon Pays a Tribute."

15. "$875 Needed for Snowden's New Trial."

16. "Hangman's Noose Ends Isaac's Song," *Evening Star*, July 12, 1918; "Prompt Action Gives Snowden Another Chance," *Baltimore Afro-American*, October 18, 1918.

17. "To Have Detectives Work on Evans Case," *Evening Capital*, August 17, 1918; "Still Investigating the Evans Petition," *Evening Capital*, August 23, 1918; "Evans' Death Warrant Read to Him Today," *Evening Capital*, August 30, 1918.

18. Docket Entries, Archives of Maryland, 3–4; "Says Snowden Trial Exceptions Are In," *Evening Capital*, August 9, 1918.

19. "Snowden Case to Be Appealed," *Baltimore Afro-American*, October 4, 1918; "$875 Needed for Snowden's New Trial."

20. "$875 Needed for Snowden's New Trial."

21. "Prompt Action Gives Snowden Another Chance."

22. "Snowden Appeal Seems Likely to Come to Naught," *Evening Capital*, September 24, 1918; "Judges of Court of Appeals," *Evening Capital*, October 15, 1918; "Prompt Action Gives Snowden Another Chance."

23. "Nearly $2,000 Raised for the Snowden Case," *Baltimore Afro-American*, November 8, 1918; "Old Brotherhood and the New," *Baltimore Afro-American*, November 8, 1918.

24. "An Appeal for John Snowden," *Baltimore Afro-American*, November 8, 1918.

### 20. "We Have Found No Reversible Error"

1. "John Snowden vs. State of Maryland," in *Reports of Cases Argued and Adjudged in the Court of Appeals of Maryland*, edited by William H. Perkins Jr. (Baltimore: King Brothers, 1919), 133:627–28.

2. "John Snowden vs. State of Maryland," 628–29.

3. "Ask New Trial for Snowden," *Washington Herald*, December 6, 1918.

4. "Rape Charge Was Not Proven," *Baltimore Afro-American*, December 6, 1918.

5. "Green's Prejudiced Appeal in Snowden Case," *Baltimore Afro-American*, December 13, 1918.

6. "Green's Prejudiced Appeal."

7. "John Snowden vs. State of Maryland," 629.

8. "John Snowden vs. State of Maryland," 636.

9. "Snowden Must Hang; Last Hope Dashed by High Court Opinion," *Evening Capital*, January 16, 1919.

### 21. "I Forgive Their False Oaths"

1. "John Snowden Learns of Lost Hope, Weeps," *Evening Capital*, January 17, 1919.

2. "Court of Appeals Reaches Decision Thursday Morning," *Baltimore Afro-American*, January 17, 1919.

3. "600,000 Colored People to Try to Save Snowden," *Washington Herald*, January 20, 1919; "Governor Fails to Grant Reprieve," *Baltimore Afro-American*, January 31, 1919.

4. "Negroes Make Plea to Save Snowden," *Baltimore Sun*, January 25, 1919; "To Make Appeal for Snowden," *Baltimore Sun*, January 25, 1919; "Governor Fails to Grant

Reprieve"; "Governor Seals Snowden's Fate," *Democratic Advocate*, February 7, 1919.

5. "Governor Sifts Case of Snowden to Bottom," *Evening Capital*, January 28, 1919.

6. "Respite for Snowden Seems Possible Now," *Evening Capital*, February 1, 1919; "In the Valley of the Shadow," *Baltimore Afro-American,* February 7, 1919.

7. "Snowden's Last Hope for Clemency Is Gone," *Evening Capital*, February 13, 1919.

8. "Death Cell Shakes Nerve of Snowden," *Evening Capital*, January 31, 1919; "Snowden Has Breakdown," *Washington Post*, January 31, 1919; "Respite for Snowden Seems Possible Now."

9. "Snowden's Chance to Escape Death Slight," *Evening Capital*, January 21, 1919; Deborah J. Moore, email to the author, August 6, 2019.

10. "Gallows Suit Upsets Slayer," *Washington Herald*, January 26, 1919.

11. "Snowden Would Talk to Women Accusers," *Evening Capital*, February 15, 1919.

12. "Every Effort Made to Avert Hanging," *Evening Capital*, February 20, 1919.

13. "Every Effort Made to Avert Hanging."

14. "George Luther Pendleton, Distinguished Lawyer of Annapolis, MD," Black Then, accessed July 23, 2019, https://blackthen.com/george-luther-pendleton -distinguished-lawyer-annapolis-md/?utm_source=FB&utm_medium= Black+Then+FB&utm_campaign=SNAP%2Bfrom%2BBlack+Then&fbclid= IwAR3aFfadi3liPq6kBa0emw1UuefqOFG_ljbq_V0iIuIvibtYatEYWKz7mAQ.

15. "Snowden Signs Writs of Habeas Corpus and Certiorari," *Baltimore Afro-American*, February 21, 1919.

16. "Mrs. Murray Aids Snowden Appeal," *Washington Times*, February 21, 1919; "Seeking to Save Life of Convicted Slayer," *Evening Star*, February 21, 1919.

17. "Noted Woman Lawyer Would Save Snowden," *Evening Capital*, February 22, 1919.

**22. "This Is No Case for Mercy"**

1. "Governor Stands Firm," *Baltimore Afro-American*, February 28, 1919.

2. "What Campbell Would Have Said," *Baltimore Afro-American*, February 28, 1919.

3. "Denies Snowden Plea," *Baltimore Sun*, February 25, 1919; "Governor Adamant on Pleas for Snowden," *Baltimore Sun*, February 25, 1919.

4. "Governor Stands Firm."

5. "Denies Snowden Plea"; "Governor Refuses Any Clemency for Snowden," *Evening Capital*, February 24, 1919.

6. "Governor Stands Firm."

7. "'Will Not Interfere,' Says Gov. Harrington," *Evening Capital*, February 25, 1919.

8. "Governor Refuses Any Clemency for Snowden"; "Governor Stands Firm."

9. "The Snowden Case," *Evening Capital*, February 25, 1919.

10. "Offers New Evidence of Snowden Innocence," *Evening Capital*, February 25, 1919.

11. "Sentence of Death for Snowden Stands," *Evening Star*, February 25, 1919.

### 23. "You Can Appeal to Me until Doomsday"

1. "Washington Colored Lawyer in New Move for Snowden's Life," *Evening Capital*, February 24, 1919; "Offers New Evidence of Snowden Innocence," *Evening Capital*, February 25, 1919.

2. "Cards Issued for Snowden Hanging," *Washington Times*, February 27, 1919; "Supreme Court Last Hope Ray for Snowden," *Evening Capital*, February 25, 1919; "Gallows Suit Upsets Slayer," *Washington Herald*, January 26, 1919.

3. "Trial of Snowden in Baltimore Co. Court," *Evening Capital*, October 30, 1917; "Sentence to Die Deferred at Request of Lawyers," *Washington Times*, February 1, 1918.

4. "Snowden Signs Writs of Habeas Corpus and Certiorari," *Baltimore Afro-American*, February 21, 1919.

5. Batson v. Kentucky, 476 U.S. 79 (1986).

6. The author is extremely grateful to Professor Michael Millemann of the University of Maryland Law School for his interpretation of these cases.

7. "Money to Save Life: None to Bury Snowden," *Evening Capital*, February 26, 1919; "Cards Issued for Snowden Hanging."

8. "Facts to Be Accepted," *Evening Capital*, February 27, 1919; "Supreme Court Not to Interfere," *Baltimore Sun*, February 28, 1919; "Modern Damon Offers His Life for Snowden," *Evening Capital*, February 27, 1919.

9. "Mrs. Murray Writes Letter to Snowden," *Evening Capital*, February 28, 1919.

10. Eliza Mae Robinson, interviewed by Janice Hayes-Williams, July 31, 2019, unpublished transcript.

11. "Cards Issued for Snowden Hanging."

12. "Maryland Machine Gunners Ordered to Hanging," *Evening Sun* (Hanover PA), February 27, 1919.

13. "Snowden Hanged at Annapolis Jail," *Baltimore Sun*, February 28, 1919.

14. "Fashionably Dressed Women Morbid as Men," *Evening Capital*, February 28, 1919.

15. "Money to Save Life"; "Supreme Court Not to Interfere."

16. "Fight to Last to Save Life of Snowden," *Evening Capital*, February 28, 1919; "John Snowden Hanged for Brandon Murder," *Evening Star*, February 28, 1919.

### 24. "I Could Not Leave This World with a Lie"

1. "Murdered Woman's Kin View Closing Act of Retribution," *Evening Capital*, February 28, 1919.

2. "John Snowden Hanged," *Alexandria Gazette*, March 1, 1919.

3. "Arnold Martin Hanged, Executed For Murder," *Evening Capital*, January 7, 1916; "Snowden Goes to Death with a Song on His Lips," *Evening Capital*, February 28, 1919; "Snowden Pays Penalty," *Baltimore Sun*, March 1, 1919.

4. "Snowden Hanged at Annapolis Jail," *Baltimore Sun*, February 28, 1919; "Snowden Goes to Death With a Song on His Lips."

5. *Laws of the State of Maryland Made and Passed at the Session of the General Assembly Made and Held at the City of Annapolis on the Fourth Day of January, 1922 and Ending the Third Day of April, 1922* (Baltimore: King Bros. State Printers, 1922), 1027.

6. "Snowden's Statement," *Evening Capital*, February 28, 1919.

7. "In Time of Need," *Baltimore Afro-American*, February 28, 1919; "Says Governor Thirsted for Snowden's Blood," *Baltimore Afro-American*, March 7, 1919; "Snowden Funeral Sunday," *Evening Capital*, February 28, 1919.

8. "Bitter Feeling at Snowden's Funeral," *Baltimore American*, March 3, 1919.

9. "Bitter Feeling at Snowden's Funeral"; "Big Funeral Closes Last Snowden Chapter," *Evening Capital*, March 3, 1919; "Snowden a Hero, Not a Criminal," *Baltimore Afro-American*, March 7, 1919; "The Colored Citizen's Part," *Evening Capital*, February 28, 1919.

10. "Anonymous Letter Writer Says He Is the Brandon Murderer," *Evening Capital*, March 3, 1919.

### 25. "Race Is All Over This Case"

1. Matthew Mosk, "Pardon Sought to Heal a Community," *Washington Post*, March 14, 2000.

2. Eliza Mae Robinson, interviewed by Janice Hayes-Williams.

3. Beatrice Marshall Smith, interviewed by Janice Hayes-Williams, July 31, 2019, unpublished transcript.

4. Phillip T. Chambers, emails to the author, May 31, 2019, and June 1, 2019.

5. Mosk, "Pardon Sought to Heal a Community."

6. Mosk, "Pardon Sought to Heal a Community."

7. "Reforms Recommended to Reduce Race Disparity in Death Penalties," *Baltimore Sun*, December 21, 1996.

8. "Petition for Clemency for Hunt Is Rejected," *Baltimore Sun*, June 25, 1997; "Race, Justice and the Hunt Case," *Baltimore Sun*, June 9, 1996; "Lawmakers Want Execution Delayed," *Baltimore Sun*, May 22, 1996; "After Gilliam's Death, Activists Fight for Inmates," *Capital*, November 18, 1998; "Death Row Mercy Plea May Hurt Glendening," *Baltimore Sun*, October 10, 1998.

9. "Glendening: No Regrets about Execution," *Frederick News*, July 7, 1997.

10. "Jackson to Join Fight against Death Sentence," *Baltimore Sun*, May 29, 1996; "Lawmakers Want Execution Delayed," *Baltimore Sun*, May 22, 1996; "Governor Proposes Study on Fairness in Executions," *Capital*, February 9, 2000.

11. "Governor Exhorted to Halt June Execution," *Baltimore Sun*, May 10, 2000.

12. "Colvin-el Case Merits Clemency," *Baltimore Sun*, May 28, 2000; "Colvin-el's Lawyers File Petition Asking Governor to Stop Execution," *Baltimore Sun*, May 16, 2000.

13. "Marchers Rally outside State Prison to Demand Glendening Halt Execution," *Baltimore Sun*, June 4, 2000; "Capital Case Filled with Doubt," *Baltimore Sun*, June 4, 2000.

14. Letter from Hazel G. Snowden to Governor Parris Glendening, March 29, 2000. Copy provided to the author.

15. "Rally to Underscore Push for Man's Posthumous Pardon," *Baltimore Sun*, May 14, 2000; "Pardon John Snowden," *Baltimore Sun*, May 26, 2000.

16. "81 Years after Hanging, Group Pushes Pardon," *Baltimore Sun*, June 11, 2000.

17. Margot Mohsberg, "Honor at Last? Plaque Memorializes Hanged Man," *Baltimore Afro-American*, June 11, 2000.

18. Letter from Judith J. Kulawiak to Governor Parris Glendening, May 16, 2000. Copy provided to the author.

### 26. "There's Great Jubilation"

1. "Governor May Face Execution Decisions," *Baltimore Sun*, January 2, 2001.

2. "Assembly Has Its Work Cut Out for It," *Baltimore Sun*, January 7, 2001; "Time Starting to Run Out on Death Penalty Bills," *Baltimore Sun*, March 22, 2001.

3. "Death Penalty Bill Fails in Last Hour of Session," *Baltimore Sun*, April 10, 2001.

4. "Death Penalty Pleas Revived," *Baltimore Sun*, April 14, 2001.

5. Carl Snowden, interview with the author, May 9, 2019.

6. "The Honorable Carl Snowden Recalls Securing the Posthumous Pardon of John Snowden," History Makers, accessed July 14, 2019, https://www.thehistorymakers .org/biography/honorable-carl-snowden.

7. "Glendening to Rule on Pardon in 1917 Case," *Washington Post*, May 31, 2001.

8. Office of the Governor, State of Maryland, News Release, May 31, 2001, Archives of Maryland [MSA SC 3520-13632], https://msa.maryland.gov/megafile/msa /speccol/sc3500/sc3520/013600/013632/pdf/035021-0000a.pdf.

9. Brian C. Kalt, "Five Myths about Presidential Pardons," *Washington Post*, June 7, 2018.

10. "Glendening Pardons Black in 1919 Murder," *Baltimore Sun*, June 1, 2001.

11. Greg Hurley, "The Trouble with Eyewitness Identification Testimony in Criminal Cases," National Center for State Courts, accessed July 15, 2020, https:// www.ncsc.org/trends/monthly-trends-articles/2017/the-trouble-with-eyewitness -identification-testimony-in-criminal-cases; Stephen L. Chew, "Myth: Eyewitness Testimony Is the Best Kind of Evidence," Association for Psychological Science, accessed July 15, 2020, https://www.psychologicalscience.org/teaching /myth-eyewitness-testimony-is-the-best-kind-of-evidence.html.

12. "Alleges Brutal Methods Used to Make Snowden Confess Crime," *Baltimore Afro-American*, February 2, 1918; "Attorneys for Defense Try to Prove Third Degree," *Washington Times*, January 31, 1918; Jennifer Clough, "Hanging: Was John Snowden Guilty? Question Refuses to Fade," *Evening Capital*, August 11, 1980.

13. "Snowden to Hang," *Baltimore Sun*, February 1, 1918.

14. "Governor Refuses Any Clemency for Snowden," *Evening Capital*, February 24, 1919; "Governor Stands Firm," *Baltimore Afro-American*, February 28, 1919.

15. Stephen Greenspan, "Posthumous Pardons Granted in American History," Death Penalty Information Center, March 2011, accessed July 15, 2020, https://files.deathpenaltyinfo.org/legacy/documents/PosthumousPardons.pdf.

16. "Posthumous Pardon Hailed, Criticized," *Capital*, June 1, 2001; "Glendening Pardons Black in 1919 Murder," *Baltimore Sun*, June 1, 2001.

17. "Autobiography Work Leads to a Crusade," *Capital*, June 2, 2001; "Posthumous Pardon Hailed, Criticized."

18. Letter from Judith J. Kulawiak to Governor Parris Glendening, May 31, 2001. Copy provided to the author.

19. Jay Apperson and Andrea F. Siegel, "Glendening Pardons Black in 1919 Murder," *Baltimore Sun*, June 1, 2001; Matthew Mosk, "Symbol of Justice, Source of Pain," *Washington Post*, June 1, 2001; "Posthumous Pardon Hailed, Criticized."

20. "Death's Unfairness Not New in Maryland," *Baltimore Sun*, June 3, 2001.

21. "Tribute to Honor Governor Tonight," *Baltimore Sun*, June 22, 2001; "In Annapolis, Reconciled with a Pardon," *Bay Weekly* (Annapolis), June 28–July 4, 2001.

22. "A Death Sentence That Can't Pass Muster," *Baltimore Sun*, October 17, 2001.

23. "Glendening Halts Executions," *Baltimore Sun*, May 10, 2002.

24. "Ehrlich Sets Reforms for Justice System," *Baltimore Sun*, June 2, 2002; "Townsend Seeks Halt to Executions," *Cumberland Times-News*, May 4, 2002; "Death Penalty Stands Differ," *Baltimore Sun*, August 6, 2002.

25. "UM Study May Shape Future of Death Row," *Baltimore Sun*, May 11, 2002.

26. "Death Penalty Study Is Reviewed," *Baltimore Sun*, January 10, 2003.

### Afterword

1. Stephen Greenspan, "Posthumous Pardons Granted in American History," Death Penalty Information Center, March 2011, accessed July 15, 2020, https://files.deathpenaltyinfo.org/legacy/documents/PosthumousPardons.pdf.

2. "From John Kehoe's Cell," *Myth of Molly Maguires* (blog), accessed July 15, 2020, http://mythofmollymaguires.blogspot.com.

3. "Georgia Pardons Victim 70 Years after Lynching," *New York Times*, March 12, 1986.

4. "Oklahoma Clears Black in Deadly 1921 Race Riot," *New York Times*, October 26, 1996.

5. "Grover Thompson," National Registry of Exonerations, accessed June 30, 2019, https://www.law.umich.edu/special/exoneration/Pages/casedetail.aspx?caseid=5488.

6. "Maryland Governor Grants Posthumous Pardons for 34 Black Lynching Victims," *Washington Post*, May 8, 2021.

7. "First Black from West Point Gains Pardon," *New York Times*, February 20, 1999.

8. Darryl W. Jackson et al., "Bending toward Justice: The Posthumous Pardon of Lieutenant Henry Ossian Flipper," *Indiana Law Journal* 74, no. 4 (1999): 1265–70; Albert A. Alschuler, "Bill Clinton's Parting Pardon Party," *Journal of Criminal Law and Criminology* 100, no. 3 (Summer 2010): 1165.

9. Memorandum from Roger C. Adams, Pardon Attorney to Meredith Cabe, Associate Counsel to the President, July 14, 1998, in subject file Judicial and Legal Matters, Records of the White House Office of Records Management (Clinton administration), 1993–2001, William J. Clinton Library, Little Rock AR.

10. Memorandum from Deputy Attorney General Eric H. Holder Jr. to Charles F. C. Ruff, Counsel to the President, July 20, 1998, in subject file Judicial and Legal Matters, Records of the White House Office of Records Management (Clinton Administration), 1993–2001, William J. Clinton Library, Little Rock AR.

11. Policies, Office of the Pardon Attorney, United States Department of Justice, accessed June 13, 2019, https://www.justice.gov/pardon/policies.

12. Jackson et al., "Bending toward Justice," 1289–90.

13. "Susan B. Anthony Was Arrested for Voting When Women Couldn't: Now Trump Will Pardon Her," *Washington Post*, August 18, 2020; "Trump Pardons Jack Johnson, Heavyweight Boxing Champion," *New York Times*, May 24, 2018; "The Cottage Industry Behind Trump's Pardons: How the Rich and Well-Connected Got Ahead at the Expense of Others," *Washington Post*, February 5, 2001.

14. The case for reparations was famously and persuasively laid out by author Ta-Nehisi Coates in "The Case for Reparations," *Atlantic*, May 21, 2014.

15. "Clemency Statistics," Department of Justice, accessed February 1, 2021, https://www.justice.gov/pardon/clemency-statistics.

16. Shantell E. Jamison, "How the Son of Marcus Garvey Is Demanding Justice," *Ebony*, September 29, 2016.

17. "President Trump Is Looking for Suggestions for Pardons: So We Asked 7 Historians for Their Thoughts," *Time*, June 21, 2018.

18. Gilbert King, "Geronimo's Appeal to Theodore Roosevelt," *Smithsonian*, November 9, 2012, https://www.smithsonianmag.com/history/geronimos-appeal-to-theodore-roosevelt-117859516.

### Epilogue

1. Hazel Geneva Snowden, interview with the author, May 7, 2019.

2. Andrea F. Siegel, "Autobiography Work Leads to a Crusade," *Baltimore Sun*, June 2, 2001.

3. Siegel, "Autobiography Work Leads to a Crusade."

# Further Reading

Archives of Maryland

    Biographical Series: John Snowden (1890–1919), MSA SC 3520-13632.

        Biography: https://msa.maryland.gov/megafile/msa/speccol/sc3500/sc3520/013600/013632/html/13632bio.html.

        Governor's Press Office Release on Snowden Pardon: https://msa.maryland.gov/megafile/msa/speccol/sc3500/sc3520/013600/013632/pdf/035021-0000a.pdf.

        Images: https://msa.maryland.gov/megafile/msa/speccol/sc3500/sc3520/013600/013632/html/13632images.html.

        Related Collections: https://msa.maryland.gov/megafile/msa/speccol/sc3500/sc3520/013600/013632/html/13632collect.html.

        Sources (List): https://msa.maryland.gov/megafile/msa/speccol/sc3500/sc3520/013600/013632/html/13632sources.html.

        Trial Transcript, vol. 1. https://msa.maryland.gov/megafile/msa/speccol/sc3500/sc3520/013600/013632/pdf/34561.pdf.

        Trial Transcript, vol. 2. https://msa.maryland.gov/megafile/msa/speccol/sc3500/sc3520/013600/013632/pdf/34562.pdf.

        Trial Transcript Index. https://msa.maryland.gov/megafile/msa/speccol/sc3500/sc3520/013600/013632/html/index.html.

Brown, Philip L. *The Other Annapolis, 1900–1950*. Annapolis: Annapolis Publishing, 1994.

Brugger, Robert J. *Maryland: A Middle Temperament, 1634–1980*. Baltimore: Johns Hopkins University Press, 1996.

Clough, Jennifer. "Hanging: Was John Snowden Guilty? Question Refuses to Fade." *Evening Capital*, August 11, 1980.

Dougherty, Joseph F., and K. S. Daiger. "Behind Drawn Blinds." *True Detective Mysteries*, March 1930.

Greenspan, Stephen. "Posthumous Pardons Granted in American History." Death Penalty Information Center. March 2011. https://files.deathpenaltyinfo.org/legacy/documents/PosthumousPardons.pdf.

Hayes-Williams, Janice. "Our Legacy: The Last Hanging." *Capital Gazette*, February 3, 2015.

"The Honorable Carl Snowden Recalls Securing the Posthumous Pardon of John Snowden." History Makers. https://www.thehistorymakers.org/biography/honorable-carl-snowden.

Jackson, Darryl W., Jeffery H. Smith, Edward H. Sisson, and Helene T. Krasnoff. "Bending toward Justice: The Posthumous Pardon of Lieutenant Henry Ossian Flipper." *Indiana Law Journal* 74, no. 4 (1999): 1265–70.

Jopling, Hannah. *Life in a Black Community: Striving for Equal Citizenship in Annapolis, Maryland, 1902–1952*. Lanham MD: Lexington Books, 2015.

McWilliams, Jane W. *Annapolis, City on the Severn: A History*. Baltimore: Johns Hopkins University Press, 2011.

Mosk, Matthew. "Pardon Sought to Heal a Community." *Washington Post*, March 14, 2000.

Policy on Posthumous Pardon Applications. Office of the Pardon Attorney. U.S. Department of Justice. https://www.justice.gov/pardon/policies.

Ricca, Brad. *Mrs. Sherlock Holmes*. New York: St. Martin's Press, 2017.

Snowden, Hazel G. *Missy: Joy and Pain*. Annapolis: privately printed, 1999.

Snowden v. State, 133 Md. 624 (Md. 1919) Court of Appeals of Maryland, January 16, 1919. Casetext. https://casetext.com/case/snowden-v-state-30.

# Index